Daughter of the Swan

Daughter of the Swan

LOVE AND KNOWLEDGE

IN EUDORA WELTY'S FICTION

Gail L. Mortimer

The University of Georgia Press

Athens & London

© 1994 by the University of
Georgia Press
Athens, Georgia 30602
All rights reserved
Designed by Richard Hendel
Set in Galliard and Sabon
by Tseng Information Systems, Inc.
Printed and bound by Maple-Vail
Book Manufacturing Group
The paper in this book meets the guidelines
for permanence and durability of the
Committee on Production Guidelines for
Book Longevity of the Council on Library
Resources.

Printed in the United States of America
98   97   96   95   94   C   5   4   3   2   1

Library of Congress Cataloging
in Publication Data
Mortimer, Gail L. (Gail Linda), date.
Daughter of the swan : love and knowledge
in Eudora Welty's fiction / Gail L.
Mortimer.
p.   cm.
Includes bibliographical references and
index.
ISBN 0-8203-1633-4 (alk. paper)
1. Welty, Eudora, 1909–   —Criticism
and interpretation.   2. Knowledge, Theory
of, in literature.   3. Love in literature.
I. Title.
PS3545.E6Z78   1994
813'.52—dc20   93-41117

British Library Cataloging in Publication
Data available

FOR DAVID

For even daughters of the swan can share

Something of every paddler's heritage—

—W. B. Yeats,

"Among School Children"

CONTENTS

. . .

ACKNOWLEDGMENTS

I thank the many friends, family, and colleagues who have helped me in the course of thinking through and writing this book. I am particularly grateful to the Stanford Humanities Center, where I was appointed Ethel Wattis Kimball Fellow for a year of study during which several of the ideas here pursued first took shape. Ian Watt and Mort Sosna, then directing the center, provided an extraordinarily stimulating intellectual environment in which to work. It is a pleasure to thank them and Albert Gelpi, Barbara Gelpi, Diane Middlebrook, Drew Faust, John Felstiner, and the late Arturo Islas for their warm collegiality and support.

I am indebted, as well, to Sandra Gilbert and Susan Gubar, with whom I studied in a National Endowment for the Humanities Summer Seminar. The example provided by their broad knowledge and incisive thinking has contributed in a variety of ways to the scope of what I have attempted in this book. Together with other members of the seminar, Susan and Sandra have continued to offer their friendship and encouragement.

Walter Taylor and Douglas Meyers provided helpful commentary on early versions of portions of this book, and Frederick Martin shared his wide knowledge of myth and his critical acuity in numerous conversations. My students have relentlessly asked the sort of questions that help one's thinking become clearer, and their interest and enthusiasm during our discussions of Welty's fiction were a significant source of energy for my work. Peggy Whitman Prenshaw, Robert H. Brinkmeyer, Jr., David Hall, and Sandra Blystone all read penultimate versions of the book with great care, offering their wisdom, their suggestions, and their timely challenges to some of my ideas. The argument is stronger than it would have been without their diligent attention, and I am grateful to each of them. Sandra, in particular, has generously offered her time and insight throughout my writing of the book.

For various acts of kindness, encouragement, and assistance, I thank Judith Wittenberg, Madelon Sprengnether, Guy Davenport, Mark Shechner, Carolyn Porter, Carl Jackson, Diana Natalicio, Larry Johnson, Suzanne Marrs, and Patti Carr Black.

What I owe to earlier Welty scholars is for the most part reflected in my notes, but I especially acknowledge how much I have learned from the work of the late Ruth Vande Kieft and of Michael Kreyling, who both saw so much so early in the scholarly consideration of Welty's texts.

Portions of chapter 1 and chapter 5 were adapted from essays appearing earlier in the *Faulkner Journal* (1991) and *American Literature* (1990). My thanks go to both journals for permission to reprint this material.

Working with the staff at the University of Georgia Press has been a genuine pleasure. Nancy Grayson Holmes, Karen Orchard, Madelaine Cooke, and Kelly Caudle, in particular, have unfailingly offered helpful advice and devoted their skill to the intricacies of bringing this manuscript through its several production stages.

To Eudora Welty, of course, my indebtedness is obvious. Her fiction has brought unanticipated challenges and pleasures to my work as a teacher and scholar.

Listed below are abbreviations for the works cited most frequently in this study; they are used in parentheses with the relevant page number in my text. Original dates of publication are given below when I have used a more recent edition.

CS *The Bride of the Innisfallen and Other Stories.* 1955. Reprinted in *Collected Stories,* 1980.

CS *The Collected Stories of Eudora Welty.* New York: Harcourt Brace Jovanovich, Harvest, 1980.

Con *Conversations with Eudora Welty,* edited by Peggy Whitman Prenshaw. Jackson: University Press of Mississippi, 1984.

CS *A Curtain of Green and Other Stories.* 1941. Reprinted in *Collected Stories,* 1980.

DW *Delta Wedding.* 1946. New York: Harcourt Brace Jovanovich, Harvest, 1979.

ES *The Eye of the Story: Selected Essays and Reviews.* 1978. New York: Random House, Vintage, 1979.

CS *The Golden Apples.* 1949. Reprinted in *Collected Stories,* 1980.

LB *Losing Battles.* 1970. New York: Random House, Vintage, 1978.

OWB *One Writer's Beginnings.* Cambridge: Harvard University Press, 1984.

OD *The Optimist's Daughter.* New York: Random House, 1972.

PH *The Ponder Heart.* 1954. New York: Harcourt Brace Jovanovich, Harvest, 1978.

RB *The Robber Bridegroom.* 1942. New York: Harcourt Brace Jovanovich, Harvest, 1978.

ST "A Sketching Trip." *Atlantic* (June 1945): 62–70.

CS *The Wide Net and Other Stories.* 1943. Reprinted in *Collected Stories,* 1980.

Daughter of the Swan

....

All around swam the fireflies. Clouds of them,
trees of them, islands of them floating, a lower order
of brightness . . .
Welty, "Moon Lake," Collected Stories of Eudora Welty

Introduction

The Paradoxical Interplay of Love and Knowledge

Ever since Plato banned poets from his Republic because he believed them to be out of their minds, philosophers and critics and, more
recently, psychologists have speculated about the origins of artistic achievement. Although we are still far from having a definitive theory about the
etiology of creativity, a number of theorists have argued in recent decades
that the artistic impulse springs, at least in part, from a personal sense
of loss, that only a need to compensate for some deeply felt deprivation
could account for the sheer effort and investment of the self that art re-
quires. Numerous studies have traced the disappointment, trauma, and
suppression in individual artists' lives: the failure of Franz Kafka's father to
acknowledge any worthiness in his son, Virginia Woolf's abuse by family

members, the early deaths of a beloved mother and siblings in the Brontës' home, the unrequited love of William Butler Yeats (for Maud Gonne) and of William Faulkner (for Estelle Oldham). Such studies, at their best, show us how the content of artists' work may echo the psychological dilemmas posed by the particular kind of suffering an artist has known.[1] The question, however, of why some transform the inevitable human experience of suffering and loss into artistic beauty while others are led merely to neurotic preoccupation continues to be as much a mystery as ever.

Beginning from these premises, it becomes particularly interesting to consider the genius of someone like Eudora Welty, who insists that hers was a happy childhood and that, in fact, her writing is a continuation of pleasures first experienced as a youngster. She has said that she grew up in a nearly perfect environment for an aspiring writer, with parents who loved reading and encouraged it in their children. As she notes, "I learned from the age of two or three that any room in our house, at any time of day, was there to read in, or to be read to" (OWB 5). Her parents appear to have guided and indulged her imagination by turns, and the Jackson, Mississippi, of her youth was a safe and friendly place to grow up. Her father was particularly forward-looking for his time; he chose the University of Wisconsin at Madison for the completion of his daughter's education, despite its distance from Mississippi, because of his conviction that it offered the finest liberal education available. If some sense of loss does underlie Welty's achievement, its nature remains elusive, especially inasmuch as she has revealed little about her personal life, and she insists, moreover, on the happiness her work brings her.[2]

We have little reason to doubt Welty when she speaks of the ease and pleasure of her work. A few critics, however, *have* questioned the unclouded happiness of her childhood, recorded in *One Writer's Beginnings* and elsewhere, considering it (necessarily, in their view) only part of the story. Carolyn Heilbrun, for example, suggests that Welty's childhood anecdotes reflect a world too-good-to-be-true. They are, she argues, misleading to readers who might have learned more about overcoming inevitable disappointments and difficulties if Welty had shared her experiences more fully.[3] As a young woman with aspirations as a writer in the early decades of this century, Welty must have faced discouragement and delay, yet she writes that she had only good luck in her friends, agent, editors, and literary mentors.[4] She believes that her gender has never been a factor in the acceptance of her work and acknowledges no real obstacles in her early life or career.[5]

Welty's hesitation to concede that any shadows darkened her childhood or her family life is particularly provocative in view of the explicit messages found in her late novel *The Optimist's Daughter* (considered at length in chapter 5). One of the basic lessons Welty has her protagonist learn is that she must let go of her need to remember only the positive things about her parents and husband, all of whom are now lost to her. Laurel Hand's recognition and acceptance of disruptive and painful facts about her loved ones' lives is basic to Welty's message about the value of allowing memories to remain flexible and open enough to accommodate new understandings of the past, including moments of pain and fear. Students often ask how, after writing so deliberately in *The Optimist's Daughter* about the need for candor, Welty could, within a dozen years, publish *One Writer's Beginnings*, whose autobiographical essays offer scarcely a hint of discord or difficulty in her family life. The answer lies in the two genres involved. *The Optimist's Daughter* is a work of fiction, although it records a number of specific events borrowed from Welty's family history, and in her novel Welty is able to convey, through Laurel's experiences, a sense of the value and importance of reconciling the complex and difficult dimensions of one's past.

In *One Writer's Beginnings,* however, Welty explicitly discusses her family's history. Women brought up in a certain social class in the South—to be ladies—as Welty assuredly was, are taught not to talk about family problems or personal disappointments. Their obviously pleasurable participation in the tradition of storytelling so central to southern life involves specific kinds of stories, anecdotes that are amusing, playful, and suggestive of eccentricity.[6] It is from within this tradition that Welty writes of her childhood memories, a factor that may well account for the palpable charm and affection of those essays. Anyone who has heard Welty speak or give a reading is likely to recognize that these are the only kinds of realities she will acknowledge. It would be out of character for her to do anything else. Even Carolyn Heilbrun, despite her disappointment with Welty's reticence, which she believes has contributed to a false picture of the writer's life, acknowledges the intense privacy that is so deeply a part of Welty's nature: "There can be no question that to have written a truthful autobiography would have defied every one of her instincts for loyalty and privacy."[7]

Whatever one might conclude about how truthfully Welty's memory has preserved her childhood, one is fully justified in believing that the *feelings* recorded in *The Optimist's Daughter do* record a truth—perhaps an emotional occasion on which Welty herself was brought to reconcile various memories and experiences of her own analogous to those that Laurel had. Welty has often said that though she does not write about actual people, who "do not yield to, could never fit into, the demands of a story," she always writes out of "the *whole* fund of my feelings, my responses to the real experiences of my own life" when, with time and perspective, she has come to discover their "dramatic counterpart" (OWB 100). Moreover, in her essay "Words into Fiction" (ES 134–45), she says of the novelist: "all his past is in his point of view; his novel, whatever its subject, is the history itself of his life's experience in feeling" (ES 142). Thus there can be no question that she has felt the bewilderment, longing, sorrow, ecstasy— the entire range of emotions she posits for her fictive characters, including Laurel's shifting feelings as she struggles to come to terms with the loss of her loved ones.

Although Welty's childhood may for the most part have been a benign and happy one, however, she did, indeed, experience a frustration whose consequences are reflected throughout her fiction. She does not dwell on this aspect of her experience, and her allusions to it are typically oblique, but Welty does say that her childhood was "overprotected" (OWB 18). When she speaks of being allowed as a child to go beyond the usual boundaries set for her, her excitement at the opportunity to go somewhere new, learn something new, and possibly find adventure is palpable. I suggest that this dimension of her early experience—and, in particular, her family's conception of love as protection—lies at the thematic center of much of her fiction. Her stories reflect a paradox that she has nearly always known. Her parents' love for her, although clearly cherished, was enacted by them as a protectiveness that she often resisted because it held her back from the greatest passion of her life—her longing to know. Time and again, Welty's characters try to move past the boundaries set for them, to learn what lies beyond. There is a virtual "radius of safety" beyond which lies the unknown, the possibility for new knowledge, and Welty's characters are powerfully drawn toward it. The fact that love should keep one from one's deepest desire constitutes a basic motif in her fictive world.

A particularly vivid example of how Welty's desire for knowledge was experienced within the context of parental love is found early in *One Writer's*

Beginnings. Welty recounts a moment in her childhood when her mother came close to revealing a long-withheld adult mystery.

> It was when my mother came out onto the sleeping porch to tell me goodnight that her trial came. The sudden silence in the double bed meant my younger brothers had both keeled over in sleep, and I in the single bed at my end of the porch would be lying electrified, waiting for this to be the night when she'd tell me what she'd promised for so long. Just as she bent to kiss me I grabbed her and asked: "Where do babies come from?"
>
> My poor mother! But something saved her every time. Almost any night I put the baby question to her, suddenly, as if the whole outdoors exploded, Professor Holt would start to sing. The Holts lived next door. . . . His wife, usually so quiet and gentle, was his uncannily spirited accompanist at the piano. . . .
>
> "Dear, this isn't a very good time for you to hear Mother, is it?"
>
> . . . She'd told me that the mother and the father had to both *want* the baby. This couldn't be enough. I knew she was not trying to fib to me, for she never did fib, but also I could not help but know she was not really *telling* me. And more than that, I was afraid of what I was going to hear next. This was partly because she wanted to tell me in the dark. I thought *she* might be afraid. In something like childish hopelessness I thought she probably *couldn't* tell, just as she *couldn't* lie.
>
> On the night we came the closest to having it over with, she started to tell me without being asked, and I ruined it by yelling, "Mother, look at the lightning bugs!"
>
> In those days, the dark was dark. And all the dark out there was filled with the soft, near lights of lightning bugs. They were everywhere, flashing on the slow, horizontal move, on the upswings, rising and subsiding in the soundless dark. Lightning bugs signaled and answered back without a stop, from down below all the way to the top of our sycamore tree. My mother just gave me a businesslike kiss and went on back to Daddy in their room at the front of the house. Distracted by lightning bugs, I had missed my chance. The fact is she never did tell me. (OWB 15–16)

This scene is charming just as many of her childhood stories are because of the vividness and humor with which Welty recalls its details. It serves as an especially apt focus for beginning to explore her beliefs about the nature of knowledge, for the scene constitutes a paradigm for Welty's conception of the context within which the search for knowledge takes place. Implicit in her memory is a striking visual metaphor for the act of seeking knowledge. The known world from within which one searches for understanding is reflected in scenes analogous to this one: from a dark, safe place (the sleeping porch) under a dome of nighttime sky, an inquiring child looks up toward a knowledge she believes the flickering lights promise her. Apparently close to achieving her goal because her mother, *this* time, begins to speak on her own, the girl nevertheless interrupts the very event she wants to bring about by stopping to give her attention to the fireflies. Whether she interrupts unwittingly or deliberately is unclear, for the passage shows that her mother's frequent evasions have left young Eudora "afraid of what [she] was going to hear next," but the result in either case is indisputable. Distracted by the fireflies, the child discovers she has missed what she was looking for—worse, she has prevented it from happening. And, as Welty recognizes, missed opportunities to learn something rarely return.

Visually, this scene is structured in ways familiar to Welty's readers. She often imagines the known world as covered, domelike, by a sky that serves as a type of outer boundary of what is known, whose stars and moon beckon with their light toward some fuller knowledge assumed to exist outside the visible world. This spatial sense of there being a known, protected space within which we live, a domelike physical space beyond which the unknown exists, may well have been reinforced in Welty's childhood imagination by the rotunda in the state capitol in Jackson that she went by (or more often, through) on her way to school and to the Carnegie Library, itself a "rotunda lined with shelves" (ES 280–81), where she discovered the world of books (OWB 29). Both places seem deeply associated in her mind with her acquisition of knowledge. Welty's narrators and characters take note of the domes in their landscapes and seem anchored by them, as if to places familiar and safe. Her sense of the protectiveness and serenity of such shapes finds expression in recurrent imagery revealing the concavity of sky and the cool, umbrella-shaped shade beneath trees:

Above everything in the misty blue dome of the sky was the full white moon. (CS 218)

The night sky was pale as a green grape, transparent like grape flesh over each tree. (CS 359)

The sky was pure, transparent, and round like a shell over this hill. (CS 200)

Behind its iron railings, the courthouse-and-jail stood barely emerging from its black cave of trees. (CS 618)

The library rotunda that Welty came to know shed strong light down into the building and even provided a guard in the person of the librarian who inspected each female child who entered to be sure the girl had on enough petticoats so the sun would not shine through. These factors may have given the young Eudora some feeling of having to be found worthy of the experience offered there and no little sense of wonderment at what sort of truths had to be so protected from children (and children from the truths). Welty recalls not only the names of the books she "devoured" (as in her essay "A Sweet Devouring") but also those to which her mother explicitly forbade the librarian to give her access. As discussed more fully in chapter 2, adults worked together to circumscribe Welty's entry into the world of knowledge.

At the domelike periphery of the knowable world, Welty tends to depict the sky and stars as forming stable patterns of movement against which what occurs terrestrially is measured. The stars come to represent a promise of meaning in the ordered patterns they reveal to her characters. Especially when viewed in the form of constellations, they suggest that the world beyond our phenomenal world makes a kind of sense, is meaningful, and that the world we occupy in some ways mirrors that world. The light of stars reaches us, beckoning, from outside the edges of the known, from a place that for the most part remains dark to us. The image is to some degree Platonic, for it suggests both the stability of things beyond this sublunary world and the idea that the phenomena we experience approximate an order, meaning, or perfection insofar as they mirror that outer world. Welty believes, as Plato suggests in his allegory of the cave, that we see somewhat darkly in our world, confusing shadows for reality, and that we rarely glimpse truth. She believes, moreover, that we are distracted by things that are *like* stars, things that promise us a more accessible but ultimately less satisfactory kind of knowledge. The fireflies constitute an image of this promise implicit in things close at hand, and the fact that reaching for them prevents truer knowledge from taking place is reenacted throughout Welty's fiction by her characters' assuming that various sorts of immediately available data could constitute knowledge.

The seeker—in the recollection above, the child Eudora—is actually anyone made childlike by virtue of his or her relationship to the unknown.

Attending to the lightning bugs, the little girl prevents the revelation she has hoped for; like many searchers in Welty's world, she becomes distracted by immediate impressions, by looking at the "wrong" things. For Welty, reaching directly for knowledge is a sure way to miss it, and a particular, receptive frame of mind is necessary if knowledge is to come to us.[8] This elusiveness of knowledge is so central a theme of Welty's thought that it has become a basic feature of her style of revealing information to her readers. Her manner of withholding information from her readers, her characters, and even at times from her narrators constitutes an oblique form of revelation that accurately reflects her beliefs about how understanding is achieved in daily life and the attitudes that make understanding possible. Her experimentation with point of view is often a direct expression of her preoccupation with how knowledge is possible.

The scene on the sleeping porch also has a crucial human element. It emphasizes the child's relationship with her mother, an adult who has the power to give her the information she desires. This constitutes another basic motif in Welty's work, that of the inquiring self as an outsider hoping to become an insider, trying to join a group characterized by its fuller knowledge of things one wants to know. There is again a sense of a boundary, this time one outsiders must cross as their status changes and new forms of experience become possible. Moving from outside to inside, the child enters adulthood, the outsider joins a family, and the female learns aspects of male experience through events such as marriage.

The sense of what is being withheld because one *is* still an outsider is powerfully conveyed in Welty's stories. This should not come as a surprise if one recognizes the particularly strong southern habit of treating newcomers with caution. Welty's parents, Christian Webb Welty and Chestina Andrews Welty, had come "from away" at the time of their marriage, leaving Ohio and West Virginia, respectively, to begin their life together in an entirely new location, Jackson, Mississippi.[9] Although Welty herself was born and raised in Jackson, her acute social consciousness would have made her well aware of the degree to which her parents were considered newcomers in the town.

Notice, too, that the adult Welty, recalling the events on the sleeping porch, projects back onto her childhood self a vivid intuition about her mother's attitudes toward the knowledge she withholds. The passage appears to have as its subject the knowledge the child wants but cannot get, but it also chronicles Welty's sensitive understanding of the meanings behind its being held back. This understanding, too, finds its way into her fiction as she explores not only misunderstandings and pieces of misinformation but also their causes.

.   .   .

In this book I explore a number of Welty's assumptions about the nature of knowledge and the contexts in which it can take place, using as clues her explicit treatment of the subject and the premises that come through in her use of imagery and her narrative choices. Welty has said, in her characteristically modest way, that hers is "the most common type of mind, the visual" (ES 31). But one cannot begin to do justice to the richness of her work unless one recognizes how complex and evocative her imagery truly is. She works within the long tradition of poets such as Coleridge, Keats, Shelley, and Yeats, who have explored configurations of images (dome, cave, labyrinth, river) that suggest various aspects of human consciousness, as well as the relationship between the sublunary world and what might lie beyond it.[10] And although the images Welty uses have been part of our cultural heritage for so long that they embody even classical associations, Welty uses them (as the poets before her did) in idiosyncratic ways that reveal her own unique understanding. Her characters' and narrators' assumptions about the degree of knowledge possible involve specific beliefs about the nature of the perceiver, the sorts of things that can be known, the elusiveness of certainty, and the role of memory in structuring how we understand. These assumptions illuminate a variety of issues in Welty's fiction, ideas of ongoing importance to her thought as well as her evolving understanding. Hers has been a lifelong fascination with the longing to know and the ways in which life eludes, obfuscates, and partially fulfills that desire.

In chapter 1 I consider the theme of love and separateness through the lens of Nancy Chodorow's psychoanalytic object-relations theory. Chodorow considers the implications of relationship as it is experienced by those in our culture who define themselves either more autonomously or more in terms of connection with others. Although Welty and her characters do not represent either extreme in any pure sense, the questions raised by this theory are helpful in understanding how her characters' assumptions about relationship affect what they are capable of understanding. In this chapter especially, but at times elsewhere in the book, I use William Faulkner's texts as examples of one extreme position (reflected with remarkable consistency by a number of his protagonists and narrators) to show the degree to which Welty's texts, characters, and narrators differ and the implications of those differences. These two preeminent Mississippi writers reveal startlingly different perceptual assumptions about even rather similar fictive events, and an increasing alertness to these differences was one of several factors that drew me into Welty's stories and the present book. The comparisons with Faulkner illuminate the complexity of Welty's vision of how particular views of relationship have consequences for the achievement of knowledge.

Chapter 2 begins with a consideration of Welty's childhood, particularly her relationships with adults, which played such an important role in her evolving sense of what sorts of things can be known and how knowledge comes about. Her childhood reading was among the factors that led her to an early sense of the world as benign and of knowledge as systematic and orderly, impressions that were soon subverted as she came to see how often truths were kept from children by the falsity, evasion, and silences of adults. Welty's early experiences led her toward a fictive preoccupation with the motives and implications of the secrets people so often keep from one another, as well as the versions of reality they perpetuate. Although Welty's characters continue to treat the unknown as full of promise, and her texts support this vision by specific narrative features, Welty builds into her texts an awareness that people often settle for limited or delusory types of knowledge (reflected in the image of fireflies) rather than the more permanent, "truer" knowledge they believe exists beyond the reach of their senses (which they project into the image of constellations). As people grow older, their self-generated stories about their lives tend to interfere with their grasping more accurate truths. The harmony that Welty's characters assume and search for, however, is one she will ultimately deny.

Chapter 3 explores the position and nature of the perceiver, whose readiness to reach new perspectives on the world is crucial to the act of knowing. Welty believes that, optimally, one should be both an insider and an outsider in order to recognize the dynamics of what is taking place in a particular context. Through two images, the circle and the labyrinth, Welty elaborates on the existential circumstances affecting the perceiver's ability to learn. I discuss how characters' assumptions about relationship enhance or preclude new knowledge and show why Welty features children as protagonists when she wants to reveal the conflict between the received truths of adults and the openness to understanding more typical of children. The protective love mentioned earlier is here seen to constitute a particular kind of obstacle for some of her characters in their desire to understand.

In chapter 4 I discuss the ambiguous nature of what is known, especially as this conveys Welty's ideas about language and its relation to meaning, about the "fictions" people create for one another, and the general role of falsity suggested by misleading surfaces, masks, and naming. This notion accounts to an important degree for Welty's treatment of characters who feel misunderstood, cheated, or otherwise have their experience falsified by the interpretations of others. Welty has adopted an increasingly ironic vision of the functioning of language, which is evident in her focus on the implications of naming, but she is far from sanguine about the devastation its misuse can cause to individuals who fall outside the categories through which a community is willing to think of its citizens, as the tragedy of Miss Eckhart in *The Golden Apples* exemplifies. The human cost of the self-protectiveness most people adopt—through language, personae, and stories about their lives—is an ongoing concern in Welty's characterizations of individuals and communities. The illusions of harmony and benignity that people insist on in the stories they tell are made possible by the ambiguity of language, but this is an appearance that bears only a tenuous relationship to reality.

Chapter 5 returns to the theme of love as protection, showing why Welty came to see the concept as a limited one and what she has come to put in its place. Love, like a belief in harmony, comforts the self but ultimately may prevent the acquisition of truer knowledge. In her culminating vision in *The Optimist's Daughter,* Welty shows that she advocates, instead, the courage to face even the harshest realities. She uses an extensive mythological substructure for this novel to remind readers of the interplay between order and disorder, harmony and chaos, of the ancient world.[11] Through this cultural memory, Welty demonstrates how personal memories function to structure and limit what people believe about their lives, and she suggests that memories, too, may be taught to remain open to new understandings. People need not, she argues, succumb to the "versions" of reality that most of them take for granted as truth.

Because the book explores various themes, images, and issues that illuminate basic features of Welty's imagination and her assumptions about knowledge and language, I have not attempted to present her stories in any sort of chronological order. This does not imply an absence of development (of either theme or narrative technique) in Welty's fiction; other critics have demonstrated cogently the growth that has occurred in her work, particularly in the 1940s, when in some respects her talent and productivity reached their peak.[12] Her work has seemed to change quite dramatically at times as she has moved from text to text with a growing sense of experimentation and re-visioning of her subject.[13] But it is equally true that her most recent writing continues to reflect issues and images that suggest an ongoing preoccupation with the subjects of this book. Thus, with the exception of the argument that *The Optimist's Daughter* reveals a basic shift in Welty's perspective on protective love, I address matters that have remained relatively constant throughout her writing.

I have based my discussions on the aptness of specific stories for clarifying ideas that inform her work as a whole. Because a few of these stories address several issues, some of them are considered in more than one context. A few of her works have received lengthy attention, especially where interpretations required fuller discussion. Other texts are dealt with more briefly or, in a few cases, not at all; again, this has more to do with my concern with the imaginative principles underlying her vision as a whole than with any assumptions about the preeminence of one story over another within her canon. My goal is always to address the patterns of thought and perception that pervade her writing.

. . .

The title of my book borrows an image from William Butler Yeats's poem "Among School Children." Beyond the fact of Welty's longtime fascination with Yeats's poetry, her fiction reveals a number of affinities with his work and the tradition it represents.[14] Throughout her writing, images, themes, and aesthetic principles indicate how deeply Yeats's poetry has touched her. In his poem "Among School Children" in particular, Yeats's idea that insofar as we continue to seek knowledge, we are all childlike, is fully congenial with Welty's treatment of the search for knowledge. Although many of her characters are too locked into limited perceptions and unquestioned assumptions to learn much that is new, Welty's fictive children and those characters who are able to remain childlike share the curiosity, wonder, and openness that make learning possible.

The image of the swan, though rarely highlighted, haunts Welty's stories, inviting readers to consider its many possible connotations, a significant number of which recall Yeats's use of the image.[15] Birds appear as images frequently in Welty's texts, but the swan, in particular, often implies the search for knowledge. Both she and Yeats view it as a symbol for the solitary human soul, a meaning Yeats expresses directly:

> Some moralist or mythological poet
> Compares the solitary soul to a swan;
> I am satisfied with that,
> Satisfied if a troubled mirror show it,
> Before that brief gleam of its life be gone,
> An image of its state;
> The wings half spread for flight,
> The breast thrust out in pride
> Whether to play, or to ride
> Those winds that clamour of approaching night.[16]

The legendary brevity of the swan's life here expresses Yeats's persistent concern with how human dreams are cut short by an awareness of the nearness of death ("approaching night" or, later in the poem, the "winds of winter") and the realization "that we were crack-pated when we dreamed."[17] And though Welty certainly does not share Yeats's preoccupation with the imminence of death, she does explore a wide range of the other connotations associated with the swan: its ability to soar into the sky, which makes it a perfect image of human aspiration (a meaning it shares with other birds); its majesty, connoting royalty or supremacy, just as the presence and power of the gods themselves is implicit in Yeats's "Leda and the Swan," with Zeus assuming the form of a swan to reach Leda; and the special beauty of the swan at rest, especially moving to human observers because its apparent serenity and harmony with nature are states they long to achieve.

At the end of "Leda and the Swan" Yeats asks a question that Welty paraphrases in "Sir Rabbit":

> Did she put on his knowledge with his power
> Before the indifferent beak could let her drop?[18]

Yeats wonders if Leda's experience with the god has given her a glimpse or intuition of the long history to follow from this act of rape: the birth of Helen, her abduction, the Battle of Troy, the death of Agamemnon— love and death/war springing from the same seed. The idea of knowledge is prominent here. As a kind of emissary between heaven and earth, able to view what occurs from both perspectives, the bird suggests a more celestial and encompassing kind of knowledge than humans can achieve. Its apparent serenity, in contrast to the typical distress of Yeatsian personae, is an indication of this transcendent perspective. But the particular kind of knowledge Yeats posits for Leda is a knowledge of contraries, of how opposites coexist or even constitute one another. This same opposition is a recurring motif in Welty's stories. Love and hate, dark and light, good and evil, all exist in perpetual relationship with one another.[19]

In "Among School Children" Yeats writes of how the image a mother worships in holding her infant may bear little resemblance to the grown-up "shape / With sixty or more winters on its head."[20] Yeats's speaker looks at a schoolroom of children and imagines what the woman he loves ("a Ledaean body") might have been like as a child. He wonders

> . . . if she stood so at that age—
> For even daughters of the swan can share
> Something of every paddler's heritage—
> And had that colour upon cheek or hair,
> And thereupon my heart is driven wild:
> She stands before me as a living child.[21]

Yeats is imagining Maud Gonne as a child. Possibly he is thinking of all that might have been possible had he known her then, especially inasmuch as he was tormented as an adult at not being able to dissuade her from some of her revolutionary ideas and activities on behalf of Ireland. What he saw as the adult woman's intractability provides a sharp contrast with the picture of an open-minded, inquiring little girl. But if Maud Gonne is associated with Leda (in her "Ledaean body") and with the knowledge that Leda might have had of the future, she is also associated with Helen, that daughter of the swan who shares to some degree the nature of her father (his majesty, knowledge, beauty). Limited to earth though she may be—possessing "Something of every paddler's heritage"—Yeats's woman/child nevertheless carries within her something supernal, something of the swan, the divine Zeus. The poem is especially relevant to this book because it focuses on children, knowledge, and how children partake of the nature of their parents. Welty is deeply concerned with the legacies children receive from the adults in their world, with the assumptions and biases children discover they already have when they begin to learn for themselves. In a sense, recognizing and replacing these ideas, which have already been deeply assimilated, is a necessary step in the achievement of more accurate understanding.

Eudora Welty is an artist intrigued with Leda, her daughter Helen—in fact, all the daughters of Zeus—and what they represent: what the parent bequeaths to the child in the way of expectations, images, and dreams; how the child grows up to address those legacies; how the human soul struggles with its aspirations in light of its emerging knowledge. Among the myriad daughters of Zeus who share a place in Welty's artistic imagination—making themselves evident in recurrent mythic allusions—are Athena, goddess of wisdom, crafts, and birds; the nine Muses of literature, dance, and music; their mother, Mnemosyne ("memory," so basic to Welty's ideas about knowledge); and Persephone, whose story is echoed in a number of Welty's texts.[22]

Zeus's sons Apollo, Hermes, and Dionysus are also evoked in her stories. As *Brewer's Dictionary of Phrase and Fable,* one of Welty's favorite reference works, explains, "one Greek legend has it that the soul of Apollo, the god of music, passed into a swan," and this story together with the fable that the swan sings beautifully just before it dies led to "the Pythagorean fable that the souls of all good poets passed into swans."[23] Reading Brewer, Welty would have learned about the Swan of Avon (Shakespeare), and the Swans of Mantua (Virgil), Meander (Homer), Lichfield (Anna Seward), and Usk (Henry Vaughan). To the degree she has experienced William Butler Yeats as a literary forefather, she might well find the idea of being daughter of *this* particular swan/poet imaginatively appealing.

Welty's own use of the swan image is characteristically lighthearted yet subtly resonant. In *The Golden Apples*—just one of many texts in which it appears—it is first found in Katie Rainey's exclamation, "I swan!" (CS 263), which means roughly "I swear!," "I declare!," or "I'll be!" This southern expression is used when some new piece of information causes surprise, chagrin, or amazement, and it conveys the need to assimilate the new knowledge. Welty keeps the image before us through apparently inconsequential details, such as the swan made of a cream puff served at the rook party in "June Recital" (CS 328) and the parody of Yeats's "Leda and the Swan" in "Sir Rabbit," but however playfully called forth, it urges us to remember the associations with beauty and knowledge. The colloquialism "to swan about" means to move around aimlessly, to wander or meander, and this, too, echoes one of the most prominent themes in Welty's stories, that of wandering.[24] Welty ends *The Golden Apples* at a moment when Virgie Rainey appears to see herself in relation to the entire physical world and to all times, past and present. In the final words of the text, Virgie hears "through falling rain the running of the horse and bear, the stroke of the leopard, the dragon's crusty slither, and the glimmer and the trumpet of the swan" (CS 461). The swan's association with the searching soul and (through the idea of the swan song) the last work of a poet may be intended to suggest a final understanding on Virgie's part, a reconciling vision in which the inharmonies of her life have been, if only momentarily, transcended.

At least one additional image of the swan in Yeats's work deserves attention. In "Coole Park and Ballylee, 1931" he writes of the "mounting swan" that "like the soul" struggles toward the sky

> And is so lovely that it sets to right
> What knowledge or its lack had set awry.[25]

Welty shares with Yeats a deep sense of how the longing for knowledge can pervade, and at times torment, the human soul. The image of the swan serves as both an emblem for this struggle and as an image of beauty that serves as fully compensatory when knowledge "or its lack" sets our world awry. The book that follows is about this search.

···

Born subjective, we learn
what our own idea of the objective is as we go along.
Welty, "Words into Fiction," Eye of the Story

He found it effortless to love at a distance.
Welty, "A Still Moment,"
Collected Stories of Eudora Welty

CHAPTER I

Love and Separateness

A Necessary Distance

As early as 1944 Robert Penn Warren first wrote about the love and separateness that are now recognized as constituting a fundamental theme in Eudora Welty's fiction.[1] He based his discussion on ideas implicit in Welty's own words late in "A Still Moment": "[Lorenzo Dow] could understand God's giving Separateness first and then giving Love to follow and heal in its wonder; but God had reversed this, and given Love first and then Separateness, as though it did not matter to Him which came first" (cs 198).

Warren recognized in the two collections of Welty's stories that had then appeared (*A Curtain of Green* in 1941 and *The Wide Net* in 1943) that "almost all of [her] stories deal with people who, in one way or another, are cut off, alienated, isolated from the world."[2] The reasons for their isolation differ, but the "fact of isolation" remains the same for the majority of characters in these early stories. Through loneliness, their occupations (for example, as traveling salesmen), their states of mind (the mental limitations of Lily in "Lily Daw and the Three Ladies"), their situations (the couple's poverty in "The Whistle" and the elderly ladies' living conditions in "A Visit of Charity"), and by virtue of handicaps such as deafness (Albert and Ellie in "The Key" and Joel in "First Love"), Welty's characters experience an isolation that is exacerbated by their inability to communicate meaningfully with one another. It is in these stories, in fact, that Welty first uses the condition of deafness as a recurrent metaphor for such isolation; her deaf characters share the (illusory) assumption that genuine communication is possible among those who can hear.

Warren does not explore the second dimension of Welty's theme, the healing power of love, to the same degree, however, and for good reason: it is a subject that had only just begun to find literary realization in her stories.[3] Welty, the creator of her own fictive universe, has in a sense re-enacted the scenario Lorenzo Dow contemplated: she depicts separateness first and only gradually begins to explore how love can "follow and heal in its wonder." But Welty herself experienced love first in her life, and then, only as she grew up, did she begin to deal with the implications of separateness. Love, moreover, was never a simple solution to the problems of isolation, for the *kind* of love she knew embodied a protectiveness about which she was enduringly ambivalent.

These concepts have more than thematic significance in Welty's fiction. They play a role in her assumptions about the nature of knowledge and, by extension, influence her decisions about such matters as withholding information from and revealing it to her readers. To understand fully the relationship between the notions of love and separateness and the implications of that relationship, it is helpful to think in terms of issues raised by the work of Nancy Chodorow and Carol Gilligan. Basing their studies on psychoanalytic object-relations theory, these scholars have been able to recognize patterns of assumptions about the nature of relationship that are directly relevant to our concern with how Welty's beliefs about these matters permeate her fiction. The following brief discussion of hypotheses will be quite familiar to feminist theorists, especially those working in the area of psychoanalytic theory, but it provides a context from which to understand how Welty's assumptions about relationship and the possibilities for knowledge constitute a basis for many dimensions of her fiction.

Chodorow's *Reproduction of Mothering: Psychoanalysis and the Sociology of Gender* discusses the implications of the fact that both male and female infants in our culture are cared for almost exclusively by women. In their earliest experiences of self, people must find their identity and learn to understand themselves as separate individuals in the context of their relationship with a woman whose emotional importance in their lives is uniquely powerful. The relative absence of fathers in the lives of infants (a circumstance that has seen significant changes only in recent decades) intensifies the felt power of mothers and creates distinct patterns of response in infant boys and girls. Chodorow argues that the experiences of male and female infants are decisively different in ways that have lifelong consequences for their gender identities, producing "in daughters and sons a division of psychological capacities which leads them to reproduce this sexual and familial division of labor."[4]

Chodorow's theory accounts for the establishment of patterns that are often associated in our culture with "masculinity" and "femininity." The object-relations view of human development assumes that the developmental tasks of infants involve at least two major issues: the recognition and acceptance of one's separateness from others in the world, and the establishment of a stable and coherent sense of personal identity, including the dimension of gender.[5] Coming to understand ourselves as separate beings constitutes a paradigmatic event in each of our lives, the nature and resolution of which signals our entrance into the complex worlds of self-consciousness, symbolization, language, and, ultimately, culture. But the tasks of adjusting to separateness from the parent and establishing a sense of self-identity differ for boys and girls because of the need, psychologically, to understand their identities in the context of the mother's identity as a woman. Because their understanding of these issues emerges from within this relationship with the mother, daughters and sons have notably different experiences of these two events.

Daughters tend to find their identities as females relatively easily, Chodorow argues, because their role models are (typically) right there with them. A girl establishes her identity vis-à-vis the person who has been the most important and prominent figure in her life since it began. For her, decisive separation from the mother is not necessary for identity formation, so identification may take place rather naturally, and separation tends to occur later in her childhood than it does for a boy. For females, separation is the more problematic task. Chodorow writes that the pre-oedipal period itself is longer for girls than for boys and that the early issues of "mother-infant exclusivity" and "intensity" tend to find their counterparts in females' later affective relationships.[6] Women continue to be relatively more involved in interpersonal relationships than men are and to experience greater difficulty and ambivalence about issues of separation.[7]

For sons, in contrast, the issue of their identities as males is the more problematic one because fathers or other male role models have so often been distant or relatively absent (emotionally or actually) from infants' experience. The male child's identity has, through much of history, been formed through relationship with a male figure who is often secondary in the child's experience in the sense that he arrives on the scene after the more powerfully experienced mother. In developing a sense of gender as a male, a boy comes to understand masculinity in opposition to the powerfully felt femininity of the mother, in effect denying the degree of her power in order to embrace masculine traits and values as a stable part of the self.[8] Separation is both decisive and positively valued because it enhances the task of identity formation. Chodorow argues, however, that the denial of female power in one's life that accompanies male development is purchased at great cost: masculinity in our culture has come to be seen as a configuration of traits that are *set against* the felt characteristics of femininity. Males tend, for example, to deny their need and capacity for nurturance and to view independence as extremely valuable. They tend, as well, to idealize the absent father, in part *because* of his absence, thus building the idea of male superiority into the very definition of masculinity.[9] Moreover, the denial of maternal omnipotence through which males purchase their sense of (gendered) self has contributed to a masculine tendency to see other individuals as decisively separate from the self, as Other, and to focus on the differences separating oneself from others rather than the similarities they might share.[10] Chodorow argues that one consequence for our culture of the fact that masculinity is defined in terms antithetical to anything reminiscent of the early experience of the mother's power is the masculine hegemony that so pervasively influences our cultural values, including the devaluation of women.[11]

In thinking about these differences in relational style it is helpful to posit a continuum based *not* on gender distinctions but rather on a full range

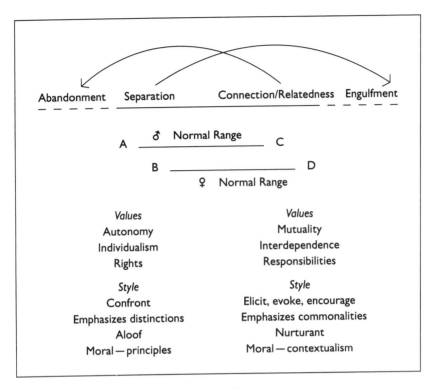

FIGURE I

of behavior in which nearly all of us participate (see fig. 1). The solid line between *Separation* and *Connection/Relatedness* is meant to indicate the relatively healthy range of possible degrees of relationship with others. For everyone, movement back and forth along this line is quite normal, a relationship with a store clerk being far to the left compared with encounters with one's parents, for example. The full span of possible relationships tends to be wide, regardless of gender. The long space between *B* and *C* (moving horizontally across the chart) shows that most men and women tend to relate with a mixture of closeness and distance, empathy and autonomy, most of the time. What Chodorow has observed, however, is that in the horizontal space between *A* and *B*, as in that between *C* and *D*, in our culture men and women, respectively, will tend to find certain of their behaviors and assumptions reflected. Men *tend* to value separation, distance, and autonomy; women *tend* to experience themselves more in terms of connection, empathy, and interdependence with others. These preferences have to a significant degree been socialized by the gender expectations of our culture, which surround people from the beginning of their lives. The male and female symbols associated with the two lines (*A* to *C*, *B* to *D*) are meant neither as statements about *innate* traits in men and women, nor as judgments about the value of the two perspectives. To the degree these patterns correspond with the felt experience of one or the other gender, they have been *constructed* as a result of the sociological and psychological contexts within which males and females grow up, and each "end" position, inflexibly held, carries with it basic dilemmas for the individual involved.

The broken lines extending to the left from *Separation* and to the right from *Relatedness* represent even more extreme experiences, the panic of troubled individuals whose relationships are precarious or otherwise threatening to the self. Such individuals often lose touch with the realities of their lives precisely by experiencing separation and relatedness in exaggerated and threatening ways. The arrows point to what may happen. Individuals who have relied upon a particular, distanced pattern of relating to others (point *A*) may, when faced with an unexpected or uninvited dependence on another, experience a distorted degree of anxiety. They may feel engulfed, smothered, or otherwise overwhelmed by the presence of the other, so that the self seems in danger of annihilation. Conversely, individuals who see their identity as embodied in their relationships with others will tend—when forced by circumstance to be alone—to feel utterly abandoned, as if the self cannot be sustained without the presence, notice, or care of those others. These two extremes reflect the province of emotionally troubled individuals, but they offer a touchstone for more normal states of relational comfort and discomfort. People who are generally located close to either *A* or *D* on the chart may resist rather vehemently a change in their habitual degrees of relationship with others. Although men and women may spend most of their time acting within the range of behavior reflected by *B–C*, there are occasions for many people when they defend their established degrees of autonomy or intimacy with others out of some deeply felt psychological imperative.

Chodorow and those who have followed her have emphasized that they are writing about *tendencies* and that we do a disservice to human complexity if we attribute these different styles of relationship too cavalierly to categories of people (by gender, for example). This idea is expressed on the continuum by showing (with lines *A–C* and *B–D*) that the ranges of healthy and acceptable behavior for men and women in our culture overlap each other a good deal. Figure 1 as a whole is intended to express visually the behavioral or "stylistic" variations that are the hypothetical consequences of how parenting in our culture is structured. Most important, it suggests something implicit throughout this chapter: that *to the degree* one's behavior falls persistently to the left or the right side of the continuum, specific clusters of interrelated beliefs and assumptions may follow (some of which are suggested in figure 1 under the headings *Values* and *Style*).[12]

Carol Gilligan has extended Nancy Chodorow's insights by applying them to a study of ethical decision making. Her provocative study *In a Different Voice: Psychological Theory and Women's Development* begins by challenging various prominent theories of moral development for not recognizing that female development toward maturity may differ in essential ways from that of males. The autonomy so often valued in masculine thought has permeated the developmental models psychologists have used to measure moral growth and maturity. The very stages of development posited by theorists such as Erik Erikson equate maturation with an ever greater autonomy, valorizing separation from others to a degree that is quite uncongenial to the usual feminine experience of ongoing relatedness with others.[13] The masculine concern with individual "rights" is paralleled by a greater feminine focus on "responsibilities" when moral questions must be decided, and Gilligan's articulateness about the implications of these shifts in perspective constitutes a decisive refutation of historically common assumptions about the moral immaturity or inferiority of women.

Her explorations into the ways males and females think about ethical dilemmas reveal a masculine valorization of individualism and self-reliance that leads to a preference for moral principles, rules that constitute categorical imperatives for what is right. Females more often work from context, asking questions about relationships and responsibilities, as they consider how to act. Little wonder, Gilligan argues, that women appear incapable (to male researchers) of making rapid, decisive choices and that they have, consequently, been assumed to "develop" more slowly and to end up achieving fewer of the stages that lead to "maturity."[14]

Gilligan also examines gender differences in various specific contexts. For example, she explores the responses of individuals who are asked to look at some relatively innocuous drawings of people alone or with others in various situations. She notes the surprising regularity with which questions of autonomy and relatedness are projected by her subjects onto these pictures in the form of their providing "stories" of confrontation, violence, aid, betrayal, or interdependence. Her analyses are particularly compelling when applied to such issues as the apparently "feminine" problem of fear of success, for its frequent corollary in those who experience it is so often a deep fear of abandonment in a person for whom relationship is central to self-identity.

The work of Chodorow and Gilligan has led to a number of studies in which feminist scholars have begun to explore what may be basic, learned differences in male and female behaviors and assumptions and to apply these concepts to various aspects of our lives. Work in such disciplines as sociology, psychology, history, philosophy, sociobiology, and political theory has proved particularly provocative for literary theory because of the light it sheds on cultural habits of thought and the ideological structures within which thought and social behavior take place.[15] Evelyn Fox Keller's work on "objectivity" in science and Carroll Smith-Rosenberg's on the nature of women's friendships in nineteenth-century America are two highly influential studies in other fields that are echoed in specifically literary scholarship. Elizabeth Abel and Judith Kegan Gardiner, for example, have used many of the same premises to address the different emotional centers of some women's fiction.[16] Two of the best critical anthologies extending these speculations into areas of literary concern such as plot, structure, point of view, and reader response are *The Poetics of Gender,* edited by Nancy K. Miller, and *Gender and Reading,* edited by Elizabeth A. Flynn and Patrocinio P. Schweickart.[17]

The theory that has found such provocative articulation in the work of Chodorow, Gilligan, and their followers may be used, however, to think productively about still other dimensions of literary meaning. Gilligan herself has suggested that the ethical distinctions she has explored might be profitably applied to Jane Austen's novels, which so often turn upon misunderstandings among the protagonists about the nature of specific moral decisions.[18] For the purposes of this book, the value of this theory is in helping to isolate and characterize important dimensions of an author's cognitive style. The theory makes it possible to speculate productively about how an author's participation in the gender-linked premises of his or her cultural time and place may reflect coherent configurations of meaning that illuminate a range of issues within the literary text.

My objective is to explore the cognitive assumptions reflected in Eudora Welty's fiction; in the course of doing so I also cite some of William Faulkner's texts as a counterpoint for the discussion of Welty's treatment of similar themes and issues. The assumption that women's perspective on relationship is different enough from men's to be meaningful is now widespread in many arenas of feminist thought, and although shared parenting may, in the past decade or two, have begun to change some basic dimensions of family life, the unspoken assumptions disclosed by these theorists still deeply affect many aspects of our cultural experience. Certainly, in the earlier, less self-conscious decades of the twentieth century—when Welty and Faulkner grew up—these assumptions were powerful, pervasive, and unanalyzed. Both Faulkner and Welty were born at a time in our culture (1897 and 1909, respectively) when gendered behavior was sharply distinguished, and both writers show significant evidence of being aware of their society's views and expectations about gender. Faulkner, for example, appears to have assimilated the gender values of his historical milieu with particular thoroughness, as I discovered shortly after completing a study of the "perceptual style" reflected in his fiction,[19] when I became familiar with the theory presented in this chapter. Many features of the style of being-in-the-world portrayed in Faulkner's stories correspond in remarkable ways with Chodorow's and Gilligan's specific conclusions about the consequences of holding a view that insists on autonomy and experiences relationship as inherently threatening. His texts so consistently express the very high valuation of autonomy characteristic of the left side of the continuum that they serve as a powerful example of the coherence of beliefs that correspond to such a position. Faulkner himself did not necessarily exemplify all of these traits, but his typical protagonists do, insofar as their moments of extreme thought and behavior regularly reflect anxiety-filled responses to the implications of relationship.

Welty's fiction does not consistently reflect either end of the continuum, although her work as a whole tends to imply the desirability of values suggested on the right, such as a recognition of our responsibilities toward one another. Her stories do deal regularly, however, with the issues involved in holding various possible positions. They tend to address the consequences of choosing different degrees of isolation or relationship vis-à-vis others. Just as Faulkner's work typically reveals a peculiarly modernist form of loneliness and alienation, linking him with other male modernists such as James Joyce, D. H. Lawrence, T. S. Eliot, and Nathanael West, Welty's texts overtly explore the difficulties and implications of various types of relationships in ways echoed by women writers of the period, such as Virginia Woolf, Edith Wharton, and Willa Cather.[20] Woolf's *Mrs. Dalloway,* for example, largely concerns the eponymous Clarissa's speculations about her relationships with her husband, her rejected suitor Peter Walsh, and various other friends and acquaintances in what seems almost a ballet of approach and avoidance regarding their expectations about her. The party she gives at the end of the novel is a metaphor for Clarissa's preferred solution, a way of giving herself the pleasure of bringing a variety of people together and enjoying their company while at the same time preserving the personal dignity and solitude that she finds so precious and necessary to her peace of mind.[21]

What I suggest in my comparisons of cognitive occasions in the fiction of Eudora Welty and William Faulkner is distinctly speculative, for a particular assumption about the nature of things may as easily reflect an idiosyncratic personality or a distinct (as, for example, a southern) ideology as it does the assimilation of a gendered way of thinking. But as a hermeneutic aid to understanding the ultimate coherence of the worldview reflected in a writer's body of work, Chodorow's theory is extremely suggestive. In many ways, this chapter is an exercise in demonstrating why this is so.

· · ·

Among the basic ideas emerging from the feminist studies mentioned above has been a recognition of the tendencies of those at the left side of the spectrum to place a very high valuation on autonomy and objectivity and to assume a decided difference between the self and others. This habit and the related one of viewing the world itself in terms of dichotomies (culture/nature, male/female, good/evil, etc.) have received particular attention from scholars because they appear to underlie the basic questions formulated by several of the academic disciplines. In "The Cartesian Masculinization of Thought," a suggestive article on Descartes's legacy to later philosophic thought, Susan Bordo explores the implications of the importance attributed to the mind/body dichotomy by Descartes and his successors.[22] The devaluation of the body in favor of "pure" mind or spirit is analogous, she writes, to the devaluation of the power of the female/maternal body, itself rooted in the dread of women that is a residue of early infantile dependence on one's mother. Descartes's radical doubt of any knowledge based in the world outside of his consciousness and the scientific objectivism that followed from it have constituted, Bordo believes, "an aggressive intellectual 'flight from the feminine' rather than (simply) the confident articulation of a positive new epistemological ideal."[23] Holding dispassion, detachment, and objectivity as the highest values to achieving accurate knowledge of the world, Cartesian thought contributes directly to "the sense of experience as occurring deeply within and bounded by a self."[24]

William Faulkner's stories offer particularly vivid examples of the felt experience of individuals existing on the far left of the continuum (see fig. 1). As I have suggested, individuals "stuck" too rigidly at either the left or right end of the spectrum will be likely to experience an event that forces them to the other side not as a normal variation but as a situation fraught with anxiety. Individuals whose patterns of response perpetually reinforce their belief in their independence from others will tend to feel engulfed or overwhelmed if they are forced to be dependent. Joe Christmas in Faulkner's *Light in August* is a striking example of a character clinging desperately to a sense of his own autonomy. Joe's experience is admittedly extreme, but it is worth noting because the *content* of his anxiety—toward women and what they represent, especially—is so clearly depicted. Joe participates in recurrent rituals of denial of his need for others by paying prostitutes or deliberately telling them that he is black when the encounter is over or by insisting that he has *taken* food rather than accepted it from others.[25] When his strategies to reaffirm this autonomy fail to reassure Joe, complete panic overtakes him, a panic re-created for Faulkner's readers in the particularly intense rhetoric Faulkner uses in narrating such incidents.[26]

Especially pertinent to Faulkner's prose is Bordo's recognition of the close relationship between this "Cartesian experience of self as inwardness" and "its corollary—the heightened sense of distance from the 'not-I.'"[27] The radical Otherness of so many figures in Faulkner's fictive world— women, blacks, the wilderness, Yankees, Snopeses, mules—is by now a critical commonplace; and readers sensitive to these categories can scarcely fail to experience the powerful mythologizing that occurs when women (for example) are characterized, especially as a group. The declarations about woman's nature in Quentin's section of *The Sound and the Fury* and in *Light in August*—where she is associated with darkness, evil, threats to the self, engulfment, filth, decay, and death—bear so little resemblance to women's actual experience of themselves that they seem most readily understood as projections of masculine anxiety.[28] The Faulknerian male characters experiencing such perceptions share a cognitive style much like that Bordo attributes to Descartes, which she characterizes as "a defiant gesture of independence from the female cosmos—a gesture that is at the same time compensation for a profound loss."[29]

A number of Faulkner's protagonists experience the fact of others' separateness in ways that echo these concerns; his characters often seem Cartesian in their insistence on the otherness, the "not-I-ness," of the other. Consider, for example, those poignant moments when young white males discover for the first time the *difference* that is to destroy their childhood rapport with a black companion. In "The Fire and the Hearth," Carothers (Roth) Edmonds, age seven, destroys the friendship and sharing—of the woman who has replaced his dead mother, of food and places to sleep—that he has known all of his life with his foster brother Henry: "One day the old curse of his fathers, the old haughty ancestral pride based not on any value but on an accident of geography, stemmed not from courage and honor but from wrong and shame, descended to him. He did not recognize it then."[30] Inexplicably, even to himself, Roth refused to let Henry sleep with him, relegating him to a pallet on the floor beside Roth's bed. Roth lies "in a rigid fury of the grief he could not explain, the shame he would not admit" long after Henry has fallen asleep.[31] The boys never again eat at the same table or sleep in the same room. "Then one day [Roth] knew it was grief and was ready to admit it was shame also, wanted to admit it only it was too late then, forever and forever too late."[32] What is salient about this example and others like it is that the protagonist recognizes in a deep and irrevocable way that once this connection has been broken, there is no going back.[33] Knowledge has somehow destroyed the possibility of reconnection, has made the shift in the nature of the relationship irreparable. It should be no surprise, then, that these passages echo the Fall from innocence, the banishment from an original bliss, and that this bliss should be associated, by Faulkner himself, with the feminine. Roth knows very well that he and Henry, and their fathers before them, had "had the first of remembering projected upon a single woman whose skin was likewise dark" and that Molly Beauchamp had provided the original security and peace in his life:

> the woman who had been the only mother he, Edmonds, ever knew, who had raised him, fed him from her own breast as she was actually doing her own child, who had surrounded him always with care for his physical body and for his spirit too, teaching him his manners, behav-

ior—to be gentle with his inferiors, honorable with his equals, generous to the weak and considerate of the aged, courteous, truthful and brave to all—who had given him, the motherless, without stint or expectation of reward that constant and abiding devotion and love which existed nowhere else in this world for him.[34]

The Otherness of race and that of gender are here conjoined in the figure—the "womanshenegro"—toward whom Faulknerian protagonists feel the deepest ambivalence.[35] When Faulkner's young protagonists inherit the cultural legacy of racist belief, they reexperience the original loss of innocence and remembered bliss associated with the mother. Knowing that this innocence is gone forever, Faulkner's protagonists fluctuate between a nostalgic mythologizing of women such as Molly, and the complete denigration of women and a denial that one needs them at all. These antithetical reactions express the decided ambivalence toward women and what they represent that is characteristic of the "autonomous," or "masculine," mindset Chodorow, Bordo, and others have explored.

Bordo argues that the scientific and philosophic worldview that has predominated since Descartes—with its high valuation of objectivity—differs sharply from the sense of self-in-the-world that existed during the Middle Ages. The medieval sense of the world was much more organic, she writes, reflecting a "relatedness to the world" based "on continuity between the human and physical realms, on the interpenetrations, through meanings and associations, of self and world."[36] The characters in Welty's fictive world make a variety of choices about the nature of relationship and identity, but in general her fictive worldview bears far more resemblance to this medieval sense of being in the world than it does to the Cartesian view.

In contrast with the stark fate of so many Faulknerian protagonists are the stories of Welty's characters, whose experience of Otherness reflects a position far to the right on the spectrum from Faulkner's. Welty's fictive world is in many respects more "feminine," in Chodorow's definition, because it suggests a meaningful, cosmic interdependence among all things. She portrays this as a multilayered universe of coexistent realms in which patterns of significance are echoed regularly from one dimension of experience to another (between sky and earth or people and animals, for example). In a scene similar to the one just considered in Faulkner—that of a child encountering for the first time a powerful sense of a companion's Otherness—Welty's text reveals a very different event. In "Moon Lake" the child Nina Carmichael discovers with awe that some of the girls with her at summer camp are orphans. The orphans have enviable rings of dirt on the backs of their necks, and nobody watches them, so they are not answerable to people the way Nina is. Observing their fascinating differences for a while, she ponders what it would be like to be someone else: "The orphan! she thought exultantly. The other way to live. There were secret ways. She thought, Time's really short, I've been only thinking like the others. It's only interesting, only worthy, to try for the fiercest secrets. To slip into them all—to change. To change for a moment into Gertrude, into Mrs. Gruenwald, into Twosie—into a boy. To *have been* an orphan" (CS 361).[37]

This passage is characteristic in that Welty's characters often make a conscious imaginative effort to understand and overcome the differences existing between themselves and others. They assume there is something there to empathize with and to understand. Moreover, the failure to empathize with the otherness of others (as in "June Recital," with the community's refusal to show compassion for Miss Eckhart, the piano teacher) is precisely the source, for Welty, of evil and of human tragedy. And although Faulkner, too, may show the failure of empathy as a source of evil—as in the deputy's complete lack of understanding of Rider in "Pantaloon in Black"—he does so in quite different ways,[38] for example by juxtaposing, and thus both separating and opposing, sections of the story that feature the two main characters' thoughts. This structural device reaffirms the thematic point that Rider and the deputy cannot imagine one another's situations; the text itself precludes any possibility for meaningful interaction between them by locking them out of one another's experience. An imaginative placement of the self in another's shoes such as we find in Welty's stories is virtually absent in those of Faulkner.[39] The isolation of his characters appears insurmountable.

Assuming their separateness—that once it has been achieved, it should be secure, as does Gail Hightower: "I have bought immunity. I have paid. I have paid"—Faulkner's characters seem startled and incredulous when they are forced to cope with the interconnections of things.[40] Consider Mink Snopes in the days following his murder of Jack Houston. Mink's life becomes a frantic nightmare as he attempts to elude the relentlessly accumulating connections, clues linking him to the crime, that close in on him, bringing his doom. Tracks, smells, the corpse, hound, shotgun, buzzards: all appear to conspire to entangle him. Mink's panic and fury are characteristic of those Faulknerian protagonists who struggle to deny connection because to them it means entrapment, in Mink's case, quite literally: imprisonment. Ironically, the tall convict in Faulkner's *Wild Palms,* another such protagonist, *chooses* prison rather than relationship. For him prison is a barrier against the dangers and felt chaos of connection.[41]

Welty's characters tend to assume something quite different—that they and the world are part of the same plenitude. In Bordo's terms, Welty's fiction reveals a sense of self-in-the-world that, in this respect, is more medieval than "modern." It is far more characteristic of Welty's protagonists to be amazed when connection does *not* happen. The boy Loch Morrison (in "June Recital"), voyeuristically enjoying the events converging in the house next door, realizes how fortunate he is: "Suppose doors with locks and keys were ever locked—then nothing like this would have the chance to happen. The nearness of missing things, and the possibility of preventing them, made Loch narrow his eyes" (CS 281). In Welty's fictive world, connection among things is perceived as the normal state of affairs; even new things that are encountered are assumed to be assimilable, to be *like* the things we already know. In Faulkner's stories, new, unknown things are perceived, by his troubled protagonists at least, as likely to be inimical. Characters run from things and are panicked by them often in Faulkner's fictive world, rarely or never in Welty's.

Faulkner's characters often use the sense of sight to try to keep track of others; it reassures them that dangerous others are not too close to the self.[42] In "The Mind's Eye" Evelyn Fox Keller and Christine R. Grontkowski argue that in the "hierarchy of the senses" implicit in Western thought, vision is especially valorized, and that this emphasis on the visual "is not only symptomatic of the alienation of modern man, but is itself a major factor in the disruption of man's 'natural' relation to the world."[43] The peculiarly spatial nature of vision *encourages* the separation of perceiver from the perceived, a separation that is characteristic of a mindset valuing autonomy and avoiding the corporeal and the feminine. This emphasis on vision is particularly evident in the modernist imagination (of which Faulkner's is a paradigm) with its focus on human isolation and the problematic nature of communication.[44]

Another of the senses, touch, has an equally intimate bearing on the problems of otherness and distance. In Faulkner's fiction, touch is momentous. All of those distinctions that characterize the ideological beliefs of the South—race, gender, class—are threatened with annihilation when touch eradicates the boundaries maintaining difference. Faulkner himself recognizes (and through his portrayal deconstructs) the tenuousness of these distinctions, here in the narration of Rosa Coldfield: "*Because there is something in the touch of flesh with flesh which abrogates, cuts sharp and straight across the devious intricate channels of decorous ordering, which enemies as well as lovers know because it makes them both:—touch and touch of that which is the citadel of the central I-Am's private own. . . . But let flesh touch with flesh, and watch the fall of all the eggshell shibboleth of caste and color too.*"[45]

Faulkner does not often mention touch, but when he does, as in describing the marriage of Isaac McCaslin and his wife, it is portrayed as something of a miracle: "in that one long-ago instant at least out of the long and shabby stretch of their human lives, even though they knew at the time it wouldn't and couldn't last, they had touched and become as God when they voluntarily and in advance forgave one another for all that each knew the other could never be."[46] It is as if in Faulkner's world (a world where separation is the only thing that leaves the self feeling safe) touch, especially gentle touch, is an extraordinary event.

In Eudora Welty's fiction, characters are often immersed in experiences of touch and texture; they repeatedly reach out to the world and to particular objects. At night in her cot at summer camp, Nina Carmichael sees that the older girl Easter's hand is held out as if to welcome the unknown:

> Easter's callused hand hung open there to the night that had got wholly into the tent.
> Nina let her own arm stretch forward opposite Easter's. Her hand too opened, of itself. She lay there a long time motionless . . . looking immovably at her hand. . . . Its gesture was like Easter's, but Easter's hand slept and her own hand knew—shrank and knew, yet offered still.
> "Instead . . . me instead . . ."
> In the cup of her hand, in her filling skin, in the fingers' bursting weight and stillness, Nina felt it: compassion and a kind of competing that were all one, a single ecstasy, a single longing. (CS 362)[47]

And Delia Farrar, the protagonist in Welty's story "A Sketching Trip," feels this:

> It was a day you could touch. It was texture she had always wanted—she was excited, a little, going under the fragrant trees—and hoped so much to learn; and surely, texture she had felt as a child at Fergusson's Wells—

then she had first put out her hand and touched what was around her— an outer world. *At the time* she knew it—that was the remarkable thing. She knew this was discovery; she had reached with her full reach, put out adoring hands and touched the world . . . a touching of the outward pulse, the awareness of a tender surface underneath which flowed and trembled and pressed life itself. It was as if this pulse became the green of leaves, the roundness of fruit, the rise and fall of a hill. (ST 62)

For Welty touches that are *not* gentle are momentous, as when Eugene MacLain slaps his wife in "Music from Spain" and spends the entire day brooding about the implications of his act (CS 393–426).

.   .   .

The cognitive styles of these two authors appear to fall at different positions along the continuum in figure 1, suggesting that Faulkner and Welty may well be working from different basic definitions of key terms reflecting human experience. That is, their implicit definitions of key terms may be pervaded by assumptions about the nature of relationship that echo their affinity for one or the other end of the continuum.

Perhaps the most salient example of this is that they view the likely nature of the *unknown* in quite different ways. Anticipating connection or relationship with something previously unknown, Faulkner's characters tend to expect the worst. The dichotomous thinking characteristic of his fictive world is part of an attempt to keep otherness decisively away from the self, expecting it to be harmful, inimical, hostile.[48] Welty's protagonists, on the other hand, expect discovery to involve recognizing commonalities in newly encountered people and things.

These contrasting attitudes toward the unknown may explain why Faulkner and Welty also seem to work with different definitions of terms such as "love," "knowledge," and even "violence." For Faulkner's characters love appears to entail an overcoming of distinctions that, however mediated by desire, involves some degree of anxiety. Harry Wilbourne in Faulkner's *Wild Palms*, for example, feels overwhelmed at times by his lover, Charlotte Rittenmeyer: "She looked at him—the unwinking yellow stare in which he seemed to blunder and fumble like a moth, a rabbit caught in the glare of a torch; an envelopment almost like a liquid."[49] As with other Faulknerian protagonists, Harry's anxiety takes the form of fantasies of envelopment, engulfment. Faulkner writes more often of the physical fascination of lust than he does any romantic notion of love, and his characters never achieve serenity in their relationships with women. Even in Faulkner's personal life, there is evidence that he felt a need to exert an unusual amount of control in being with women he loved. Meta Carpenter Wilde writes that he insisted on a particular imaginative reading of their relationship, ignoring her age and past experience with men to insist that she was somewhat younger than she actually was. It is as if this provided a version of their love relationship with which he could be most comfortable, even though Wilde herself has said that she "was confounded by his need to turn me into a sweet, tremulous girl."[50] Echoing this preoccupation with control, Faulkner's characters typically exhibit a vigilance toward others in their efforts to understand the precise degree of threat that they represent. When the Otherness assumed in others proves too formidable an obstacle, his characters reveal a poignant and compelling bewilderment about what they should do. As Harry Wilbourne talks with Charlotte's now-abandoned husband, he senses the other man's pain, and his own helplessness: "It seemed to him that they both stood now, aligned, embattled and doomed and lost, before the entire female principle."[51]

In Welty's fiction the experiences of love and knowledge are closely linked in meaning, because they both involve a willing assumption of the other's similarity with the self. The very attempt to put yourself in another's place constitutes an act of love, even as it is an act of understanding. Whereas for Faulkner a character's intellect is typically used to orient the self toward others, as a way of speculating about and keeping track of them for the sake of distance and control, in Welty's fiction the use of one's intellect is motivated by love and the desire to reach an empathic understanding. Welty does not often write about romantic love either, yet her characters, especially children, reveal a loving approach to the world that permeates such stories as "The Winds" and "Moon Lake." The passages cited earlier about characters holding their hands out to welcome new experience are exemplary; these moments reveal "compassion . . . a single ecstasy, a single longing" (CS 362). The fulfillment of love and that of knowledge are nearly indistinguishable events in Welty's fiction, and they are never accompanied by the anxiety (even terror) that often appears in Faulkner's stories. Welty's characters reflect what Chodorow describes as the "more permeable ego boundaries" of individuals on the right side of the continuum, ego boundaries that make possible a far more engaged relationship with the other and enhance a realization of the ways in which we participate in and are interdependent upon one another's lives, thoughts, and identities.[52]

Violence is a bit more problematic but still reflects the attitudes toward relationship and the unknown that are characteristic of Faulkner and Welty. Violence occurs often in Faulkner's world, especially that methodical, almost mechanical, beating of others that his most despairing protagonists participate in (Joe Christmas beating the horse or Lucas Burch/Brown; Abner Snopes hitting his mules and then his son in "Barn Burning," "hard but without heat"; and Mink Snopes striking his wife "with that slow gathering which was not deliberation but extreme and patiently indomitable and implacable weariness"[53]). The relentless, passionless nature of these acts powerfully conveys the characters' hopelessness about ever gaining control of the events in their lives. Striking relatively helpless others, Faulkner's characters try to declare their autonomy by controlling *something*. Their ritual of violence is meant to reestablish the line of demarcation between the self and the Other.

This phenomenon accords with Carol Gilligan's observations of the differences between college-age men and women who were asked to provide stories to go along with some rather innocuous pictures of people in different situations.[54] Her male subjects tended to project violence onto scenes where people were together, from apparently tranquil situations such as a man and woman sitting together on a bench near a river to more obvious occasions of interdependence, such as two trapeze artists high above a circus floor. These same male subjects tended *not* to see violence in scenes where people were alone (for example, in an office setting). While women subjects were busily imagining nets that would ensure the safety of the trapeze artists, male subjects envisioned betrayal, even murder. As Gilligan herself concludes, "it appears that men and women may experience attachment and separation in different ways and that each sex perceives a danger which the other does not see—men in connection, women in separation." Males projected "more violence into situations of personal affiliation than they did into impersonal situations of achievement," thus construing danger to exist in very different contexts than women tended to do.[55] Gilligan's male subjects tended to find connection somewhat more threatening than autonomy. Given Nancy Chodorow's premises, this should not be surprising, but the *degree* of violence expressed by Gilligan's subjects remains startling—yet consistent with the anxieties and behavior of many of Faulkner's male characters. The work of Chodorow and Gilligan suggests that violence in our culture may be in part a product of a particular stance toward relationship, leading to a territoriality and a concern with boundaries that seem far more characteristic of men than of women. Males' and females' differing relationships to violence may well be linked to such deeply felt needs and fears as those Chodorow articulates.

Possibly because in Faulkner's fictive world love for others involves an overcoming of Otherness, Faulknerian protagonists often act on their love by attempting not only to control but also to possess the loved one. The inability to control and own the actions of the loved one drives protagonists such as Quentin Compson, Gavin Stevens, and Horace Benbow to distraction. This desire to exercise one's will over the Other is seen, in both Faulkner's and Welty's stories, as most typical of the male lover. The antithesis of love—rage—occurs when the loved one does not succumb to the lover's desire for control. That there is *no rage* in Welty's texts, then, is noteworthy.[56] When her (almost always, male) characters try to control others—as do Solomon in "Livvie" and Jenny's grandfather in "At the Landing"—the young woman who is the object of such control typically accedes to what is expected of her; there is no struggle, no battle of wills, because Welty's young female protagonists begin in acquiescence and only gradually learn that there are other ways to live.[57] These situations in Welty's stories are usually resolved by external events, as when Welty frees her protagonists by having the controlling character die, leaving the woman free to explore the wider world. In contrast, the beatings committed by Faulkner's characters openly express their rage and helplessness at the Other's refusal to go along with being controlled. Rage is frequently and powerfully depicted in Faulkner's stories, revealing love's failure to mediate the differences between the self and the Other to the protagonist's satisfaction. The constant vigilance of Faulknerian characters toward one another is yet another consequence of this need for the illusion of control.[58]

Violence also exists in Welty's fictive world. There is the rare character who actually harms another (Howard in "Flowers for Marjorie"), or the character who imagines doing so (Ran MacLain in "The Whole World Knows"). Far more characteristic, however, is Welty's attention to those who are the victims of violence rather than its perpetrators. Here, she causes her readers (feminist ones, in particular) a good deal of dismay at times by depicting such events as rape in a matter-of-fact manner that refuses to judge what has taken place.

There is something of a paradox built into Welty's treatment of such events. The southern female child is surrounded by prohibitions, cautions, and warnings about the Other, imposed by her culture and intended to hold her back, circumscribe her activity, and keep her ignorant of things that would excessively frighten her. Yet repeated warnings about the "unspeakable" things that might happen if white men were *not* protecting her must themselves build up excessive fear—by being too dreadful to speak of. Strangely enough, then, the females in Welty's texts who do encounter the darkest sides of human nature—"the horror, the horror" that Joseph Conrad exposes in "Heart of Darkness"—do not seem to find them unbearable after all. Although violence and evil make themselves evident in terrible events, they are not as annihilating as the myths about them had suggested. Experience of such events as rape may alter consciousness but does not destroy it.

In "June Recital" when Miss Eckhart is attacked by a black man who jumps out from behind a bush at her, the reader is not told about the nature or context of the attack or its impact on the victim herself, but rather of the community's reaction. Miss Eckhart's neighbors would like her to leave town so they can forget what has happened there. "But Miss Eckhart stayed, as though she considered one thing not so much more terrifying than another" (CS 301). It is as if violence, too, turns out not to be totally alien or incomprehensible. It does not lead, as it so often does in Faulkner, to a reaffirmed sense of one's separateness. Despite their vigilance, Faulkner's characters are repeatedly caught off guard and overwhelmed by what they find. The horror they undergo in confronting previously unknown phenomena is much worse than anything to be found in Welty's fiction. Instead, Welty's female characters survive (one might almost say "transcend") the violence against them, as if Welty is suggesting that it is part of life and can no more be avoided than its other dimensions.[59] Not surprisingly, then, Welty does not depict characters for whom violence is a strategy for survival, and she rarely attempts to reveal the thoughts of characters committing such acts.[60] The basic attitudes toward life that her characters reveal—acceptance, curiosity, love of it—are depicted as remaining unchanged when violence occurs, even for those who are its victims.

.   .   .

The object-relations paradigm in figure 1 has an obvious importance in thinking about the theme of protective love that is basic to Welty's creative imagination. A comparison of her texts with Faulkner's in terms of the perceptual differences they exhibit suggests some of the consequences of Welty's general tendency to choose values reflected on the right side of the continuum. Her placement on the continuum is by no means static, however. Whereas Faulkner's characters (certainly his more troubled ones like Quentin Compson, Mink Snopes, Horace Benbow, and Joe Christmas) seem to hold a remarkably consistent view of the dangers of relationship and therefore value autonomy highly, whether they actually achieve it or not, Welty's characters vary widely in their choice of solutions to the question of where to place themselves along the hypothetical spectrum. Like other women writers, perpetually aware of how one's relationships entail powerful and legitimate demands on one's time and energies, Welty allows her stories to serve as an artistic vehicle for pondering the entire range of choices—from the loneliness and "freedom" of her wanderers to the comfort and potential "suffocation" of familial and community expectations. Her stories address the topic of relationship in all its varieties.

The problem of love and separateness provokes as basic a dilemma for the artist as it does for the individual, and Welty's statements about her writing of fiction and her photography reflect the complexities implicit in these issues. The question of the value of objectivity and the degree to which artists must separate themselves from their subject in order to depict it accurately are never permanently resolved, especially for the woman artist, whose inclinations to be responsive to others may conflict directly with her sense of a necessary artistic detachment. By differing from context to context, Welty's statements about these matters reflect an inherent ambivalence. She speaks on the one hand of the importance of total empathy with her characters: "I have been told, both in approval and in accusation, that I seem to love all my characters. What I do in writing of any character is to try to enter into the mind, heart, and skin of a human being who is not myself" (cs xi). But she also writes, "the artist needs and seeks distance—his own best distance—in order to learn about his subject" (es 48).

In her discussions of her photography, a purely visual medium, it is not surprising that the idea of proper distance or perspective predominates. Recalling her first journalism job, she compares it to her writing by saying that "getting my distance, a prerequisite of my understanding of human events, is the way I begin work. . . . Frame, proportion, perspective, the values of light and shade, all are determined by the distance of the observing eye" (owb 21). As a writer whose empathy is a central feature of her thought,

Welty chooses distance and perspective, when she does, only momentarily, as a way of determining the best *way in,* a means of discovering the perspective or captured moment that reveals most about the character, the gesture or behavior that embodies the character's intentions and beliefs. Welty's relationship with her artistic subjects involves a fluid movement both toward and away from them, as if trying to view them from all sides. Although she may begin "writing from a distance," her stories quickly draw her into them, lead her "closer . . . toward what [is] at the center" of them (OWB 87) so that, finally, her engagement with her story is deep, intricate, and personally compelling. Her narratives, too, often mirror this fluid, dreamlike quality as she portrays her characters' consciousnesses moving readily between the realms of fantasy and perception, toward and then away from the reality of their encounters with one another.

Welty's ideas about the implications of separateness and connection are various and complex. But in an early story with the promising title "The Key" she addresses directly the subject of the self's need for—and right to—privacy and detachment. The story concerns Albert and Ellie Morgan, a married couple, both deaf, who are waiting for a train to take them on a long-planned trip to Niagara Falls. Ellie is one of those deaf characters in Welty's fiction who assume that those who can hear experience degrees of communication she (and others who are deaf) can only imagine. She has worked and planned carefully for a long time to make the trip to Niagara Falls come about, because she has been told that in standing up close to the railing and experiencing the roar and motion of the Falls, she and Albert will feel through their bodies what it is like to "hear." And because Niagara Falls is also that most famous of honeymooners' vacation spots, Ellie has allowed her imagination of the new communication that will then be possible between herself and Albert to grow into a fantasy of perfect marital bliss.

Albert, somewhat dominated by his wife, shy, and even "effaced" (CS 30) by her greater energy, is the more serene of the two. He seems less ambitious and has gone along with the idea of the trip, it appears, as much to please Ellie as himself. He and his wife are both aware that their marriage has been based as much on the loneliness they have felt, being deaf, as it has been on love, and to some degree, Albert shares Ellie's hope that when they have seen the Falls, they may "get along better, have more understanding . . . even fall in love, the way other people have done" (CS 32). As the story evolves, however, a basic difference in what Ellie and Albert hope for is revealed. Ellie longs for closeness, communication, the kind of love in which she and Albert will share all their thoughts with one another. Yet even as Albert and Ellie speak with one another through a sign language, Ellie's participation seems urgent, almost too needy, whereas the "talking seemed rather to dishevel" Albert (CS 34).

The sudden and unexpected arrival of a key that rolls into sight at Albert's feet, unheard, brings the differences between the two into sharper relief. Albert sees in the appearance of the key a symbol for the possibility of their having "something that we deserve . . . happiness in Niagara Falls" (CS 32). As he talks with Ellie about his pleasure in finding the key, Albert discovers that it has significance for him that he does not want to share with her: "He had almost shared it with her—you realized that. He frowned and smiled almost at the same time. There was something—something he could almost remember but not quite—which would let him keep the key always to himself. He knew that, and he would remember it later, when he was alone" (CS 34). What Albert realizes is that Ellie's longing to share everything with him has left him no privacy; he feels intruded upon, as if the most delicate and special of his feelings cannot survive her knowing of them. Ellie, he feels, holds onto every limitation she perceives in their relationship as something to be worried over and analyzed, and Albert recalls how she would cling to her sense of unhappiness, "worry about it, talk about it. . . . Just try to tell her that talking is useless, that care is not needed" (CS 35). For Albert, ultimately, there is a "funny thing about talking to Ellie":

> As long as you let it alone everything goes peacefully, like an uneventful day on the farm—chores attended to, woman working in the house, you in the field, crop growing as well as can be expected, the cow giving, and the sky like a coverlet over it all—so that you're as full of yourself as a colt, in need of nothing, and nothing needing you. But when you pick up your hands and start to talk, if you don't watch carefully, this security will run away and leave you. You say something, make an observation, just to answer your wife's worryings, and everything is jolted, disturbed, laid open like the ground behind a plow, with you running along after it. (CS 35)

Albert has the capacity to enjoy life as it comes, without struggling for things he does not have. As for Ellie: "You saw by her face that she was undauntedly wondering, unsatisfied, waiting for the future" (CS 36). The narrator of the story offers a final judgment about Ellie's limitations: "And you knew how she would sit and brood over this as over their conversations together, about every misunderstanding, every discussion, sometimes even about some agreement between them that had been all settled—even about *the secret and proper separation that lies between a man and a woman,* the thing that makes them what they are in themselves, their secret life, their memory of the past, their childhood, their dreams. This to Ellie was unhappiness" (CS 36; emphasis mine).[61]

If these words were simply Albert's, one might conclude that Welty is portraying a long-felt distinction between men's and women's senses of "being with" a loved one. Psychologist Lillian Rubin has written about gender differences in perceptions of intimacy, exploring the fact that men and women may experience even being in a room alone together in strikingly different ways, the woman feeling that she and her husband/lover are truly together only if they are talking, and the man feeling that being silently there with each other constitutes intimacy.[62] Welty has chosen an omniscient narrator who assumes that there *is* an appropriate separation between people and who, therefore, interprets Ellie's wishes as *in*appropriate and overly possessive. Implicitly, then, this narrator affirms the validity of Albert's belief in some degree of separation of his thoughts and feelings from those of his wife.

In terms of the paradigm in figure 1, Welty recognizes the impossibility of holding a position of complete autonomy and isolation, just as she does the implications of too powerful an interdependence, and in "The Key," through the voice of her narrator, she advocates a love that is mutually supportive but not intrusive. She shows the desirability and importance of an ultimate privacy of the soul and depicts Ellie's vision of love as violating something essential in her husband. What Albert wants to withhold from his wife is some sense of the mystery and wonder of his own individual experience of life, the joy of the unexpected—as in the arrival of the key: "The key had come there, under his eyes on the floor in the station, all of a sudden, but yet not quite unexpected. That is the way things happen to you always. But Ellie did not comprehend this" (CS 34). Ellie, planning, wondering, brooding, seems incapable of the joy her husband experiences. Her cautious approach to life prevents any spontaneous appreciation of simple pleasures. Because Ellie's love threatens to engulf Albert, the story itself supports him in his decision to hold part of himself back from her.[63]

Welty, like many women writers, *assumes* the connections between humans and works to explore and articulate the nature of a viable distance that allows for selfhood and meaningful work, as well as for living.[64] Apart from the discomfort and threat to one's work of an interdependence with others that precludes solitude, Welty's concern with distance is enhanced by her belief in an essential mystery at the heart of human experience, a mystery that *remains* mystery only if we allow it to *be,* without analysis and attempts at communication, which her fiction suggests, in any case, seem doomed to fail.

....

Then a whole swarm of fireflies instantly flickered all
around him, up and down, back and forth, first one
golden light and then another. . . . These were the signs
sent from God that . . . his eyes were more able to see the
fireflies of the Lord than His blessed souls.
Welty, "A Still Moment," Collected Stories of Eudora Welty

Beyond the beauty and the sword's stroke and the terror lay
their existence in time—far out and endless, a constellation which the heart could read over many a night.
Welty, "The Wanderers," Collected Stories of Eudora Welty

CHAPTER 2

Fireflies and Constellations

The Types of Knowledge We Seek

The caring environment that Eudora Welty's parents provided her
as she grew up had much to do with the development of her adventure-
some approach to life and her love of knowledge. She has characterized her
parents as loving, protective, gentle people who allowed their children's
curiosities to take their course even as they firmly guided them past inappropriate goals or perceived dangers. Perhaps their most valuable gift to
their artistic daughter, however, was that they provided an atmosphere that
encouraged the growth of her rich imagination. In *One Writer's Beginnings,*
Welty writes that at one time, having been diagnosed with "fast-beating

heart," she was "put to bed" for several months. She was allowed to spend all day in her parents' double bed and, in the evenings, to fall asleep there while the two of them sat nearby, talking or reading to one another (OWB 20). With a newspaper shielding her from the glare of the lamp, Welty would drift to sleep to the sound of their murmuring voices, carried into her dreams by those reassuring sounds. The movement between waking life and dream must have been remarkably cushioned by their comforting presence, as Welty makes clear in a childhood recollection attributed to Laurel McKelva Hand in *The Optimist's Daughter:* "In the lateness of the night, their two voices reading to each other where she could hear them, never letting a silence divide or interrupt them, combined into one unceasing voice and wrapped her around as she listened, as still as if she were asleep. She was sent to sleep under a velvety cloak of words, richly patterned and stitched with gold, straight out of a fairy tale, while they went reading on into her dreams" (OD 57–58).[1]

As the language of this passage suggests, the sense of comfort and safety was so palpable that it became intertwined with her drifting imagination, her pleasure in fairy tales, and most particularly, with her emerging love for words themselves. Welty also recalls that in the mornings when she was buttoning her shoes, her parents (one upstairs and one down) would conduct a duet, whistling and humming, and fill the house with their voices. With waking and sleeping so closely associated with such sounds, it is little wonder that words, sounds, and sensuality have become fused in Welty's imagination just as they have in her narrative style. This long, protected time of childhood helps us understand the sheer power of imagination found in Welty's stories, the fluid movement between dreaming and "reality" for her characters and, through her narrations, for her readers. The imagination is as real as any material object in the lives of Welty's characters.

Protected from the sorts of knowledge for which, in her parents' view, she was not yet ready, Welty's curiosity continued to grow, even as she became aware of the ways in which knowledge was being kept from her. Clear indications of her sense of being too well protected are evident in the obvious pleasure with which she speaks of times when she was free to roam the town (not a city, then) of Jackson: "The happiness of errands was in part that of running for the moment away from home, a free spirit" (ES 332).

In interviews with Bill Ferris conducted in 1975 and 1976, Welty spoke of what Jackson was like as she was growing up: "It was so small that one knew everybody practically. Also, it was a very free and easy life. Children could go out by themselves in the afternoon and play in the park, go to the picture show, and move about the city on their bicycles and everything, just as if it were their own front yard. There was no sense of danger or things happening in town. No one had to really take care, so we felt. That was a nice way to grow up. . . . All of which is gone now, of course, because Jackson is a city" (Con 170).

The joy she expresses on occasions when she was allowed as a child to go beyond the protected space her parents tried to create around her—what I am calling a *radius of safety*—betrays her eagerness to be out in the larger world. If only obliquely, her exhilaration at these times shows her discomfort at being so protected.[2]

In terms of the Gilligan-Chodorow paradigm presented in chapter 1, Welty's natural desire to explore the wider world was perpetually affected by her awareness that her family wanted her with them. The separation that Chodorow believes is especially difficult for females was indeed so for Welty, and she never left them, it appears, without some sense of guilt. Even her college career reflects this pattern of pushing beyond one radius to another. Graduated from high school at sixteen, Welty was not ready, her parents felt, to begin college far away, so she completed her first two years at Mississippi State College for Women. Only then did she travel north to the University of Wisconsin at Madison to complete her degree.[3] That she was sent there suggests a somewhat unusual appreciation for the time of the value of a fine education for a young woman, and Welty's father was farsighted in advocating this move.

His support did not entirely obviate Welty's *feelings* about leaving, however. She was terribly conscious that although excitement awaited her, her family would be longing for her and missing her. Welty's feelings about leaving her family were *not* simply a function of her gender, however; in fact, the family was so closely knit that anyone who left (as her father sometimes did on business trips) became part of "the torment of having the loved one go, the guilt of being the loved one gone" (OWB 94). But her own experience of it is unmistakable. About traveling to New York to see her publishers, Welty has written that she would settle into her seat on the train "with an iron cage around my chest of guilt" (OWB 93). She refers to these trips as "something that had better be momentous, to justify such a leap into the dark" (OWB 94). This leap into the unknown is a recurring theme in her fiction, just as it has been in her life: "most of all the guilt then was because it was true: I had left to arrive at some future and secret joy, at what was unknown, and what was now in New York, waiting to be discovered" (OWB 94).

Throughout her stories, Welty expresses her characters' fascination with the borders of this protected zone, this radius of safety, and with the possibility of going beyond it to the unknown. In "Moon Lake," for example, the narrator speculates with apparent relish about the possibilities lurking for little girls in the lake at a summer camp:

> If they let their feet go down, the invisible bottom of the lake felt like soft, knee-deep fur. The sharp hard knobs came up where least expected. The Morgana girls of course wore bathing slippers, and the mud loved to suck them off. The alligators had been beaten out of this lake, but it was said that water snakes—pilots—were swimming here and there; they would bite you but not kill you; and one cottonmouth moccasin was still getting away from the Negroes—if the Negroes were still going after him; he would kill you. These were the chances of getting sucked under, of being bitten, and of dying three miles away from home. (CS 345)

When harm does come to a character, Welty's narrators tend to note whether the protectiveness of home has proved adequate. In *The Optimist's Daughter,* Judge Clint McKelva's friend Dr. Woodson recalls how, as a boy, Clint had cut his foot on a piece of tin and "liked-to bled to death a mile from home!" (OD 74).[4] The nature of the unknown beyond the radius of safety remains a permanent and intriguing lure for her characters, just as it becomes a feature of Welty's own narrative strategies as she determines what she will reveal to her readers.

On the other side of protectiveness and safety, then, is the joy of exploring the unknown. Welty's fervent desire to learn led her to turn to the adults around her to find out what she could from them. She recalls as a child sitting between her mother and a neighbor in the back seat of the Weltys' automobile for a Sunday afternoon ride, saying as the car began to move, "Now *talk*" (OWB 13). Her mother intervened at crucial moments, both with the neighbors and with their sewing woman, whose latest gossip about someone in town would be interrupted with the caution: "Fannie, I'd rather Eudora didn't hear that." As Welty explains, " 'That' would be just what I was longing to hear, whatever it was. . . . It was tantalizing never to be exposed long enough to hear the end" (OWB 14). The frequency with which Welty relates such scenes about her childhood reinforces our sense that she had developed very early a passion for understanding that was repeatedly deferred:

> Even as we grew up, my mother could not help imposing herself between her children and whatever it was they might take it in mind to reach out for in the world. For she would get it for them, if it was good enough for them—she would have to be very sure—and give it to them. . . . She did indeed tend to make the world look dangerous, and so it had been to her. A way had to be found around her love sometimes, without challenging *that,* and at the same time cherishing it in its unassailable strength. . . .
>
> But I think she was relieved when I chose to be a writer of stories, for she thought writing was safe. (OWB 39)

This reference to the safety of writing is ironic, because Welty's conception of how writing takes place explicitly involves the willingness to leave safety behind. In her essay "Place in Fiction" she argues that "no art ever came out of not risking your neck. And risk—experiment—is a considerable part of the joy of doing, which is the lone, simple reason all writers of serious fiction are willing to work as hard as they do" (ES 130). She notes that even though writers often write best about what they know, it is "not for safety's sake . . . writing of what you know has nothing to do with security" (ES 130): "For the artist to be unwilling to move, mentally or spiritually or physically, out of the familiar is a sign that spiritual timidity or poverty or decay has come upon him; for what is familiar will then have turned into all that is tyrannical" (ES 129).

The fact that, for Welty, writing entails a deliberate movement into the unknown is confirmed in another of her essays on writing, where she repeats—in speaking of her art—an image she has used (OWB 94) to describe her trips away from home: "This very *leap in the dark* is exactly what writers write fiction in order to try" (ES 134; emphasis mine). Welty's childhood and, indeed, lifelong experience of conflict between the safety her parents tried to foster and the adventure she longed for may have led directly to this conception of her art as a risk-taking in which all of the self is centrally involved. Experiencing her writing in this way has allowed Welty both to meet her family's needs and expectations of closeness and to enjoy the exhilaration of venturing into the challenging unknown of her fictive imagination. Her strong sense of independence and love of risk are fulfilled by the act of writing itself, as is apparent when she describes how she feels when she writes: that no story you have written prepares you for the challenges of the next story you try to write;[5] that risk and taking chances are implicit in writing; that writing is utter pleasure. And surely an understanding of how writing enables her to meet both needs—for family involvement and responsibilities as well as finding opportunities for adventure—accounts for the sheer pleasure she finds in writing. Welty is not someone who could have left her family behind for long, much as she loves to travel. In terms of the continuum presented in chapter 1, she cannot remain comfortably or exclusively at *either* end of the spectrum. Her aesthetic theory allows her to experience deeply the freedom of adventure. It is most appropriate and telling, therefore, that she ends her autobiographical essays by writing: "As you have seen, I am a writer who came of a sheltered life. A sheltered life can be a daring life as well. For all serious daring starts from within" (OWB 104).

.   .   .

Welty's imagination and curiosity were basic features of her childhood and took the form, in large part, of a passion for reading that was nearly insatiable. Her mother guided this hunger, whose indiscriminateness Welty describes in an amusing short essay entitled "A Sweet Devouring" (ES 279–85), by adding her rules to those of the librarian to limit what the child was allowed to read. Some books were *not* to be checked out to her for her own good. *Elsie Dinsmore* was among the forbidden texts, because her mother thought Eudora was too impressionable to remain unaffected by Elsie's passionate reactions to the events of her young life (OWB 29). Histrionics were an inappropriate role model for a young lady.

The librarian added to the impression that one had to be "ready" for certain kinds of knowledge. In addition to rules about wearing enough petticoats so the sun would not shine through one's skirt, Welty encountered the inevitable injunctions on every wall demanding SILENCE, signs that the librarian herself blithely ignored. Worse, still, were the librarian's own rules about the books: "You could not take back a book to the Library on the same day you'd taken it out; it made no difference to her that you'd read every word in it and needed another to start. You could take out two books at a time and two only; this applied as long as you were a child and also for the rest of your life, to my mother as severely as to me" (OWB 30).

But although Welty found herself, as a child, surrounded by parents, teachers, and librarians who controlled her access to new experiences, and although she was well aware that they kept some things from her, she also benefited from their appreciation of knowledge and the imagination, of books and the arts. Her parents seem not to have imposed on her any early or urgent demand to give up the richness of her imaginative life in order to face harsh reality. She was not forced, as children often are, to abandon her imaginative flights for the sake of practical objectives. Instead, her imagination was allowed to grow alongside her acquisition of more pragmatic lessons. As Richard Coe writes, the truly original artist may differ from the rest of us precisely in being able to retain throughout life something of the special quality of childhood experience, a texture, richness, and vividness that most of us have lost in growing up. Coe agrees with Jean-Jacques Rousseau that "the child's fundamentally *irrational* modes of being—instinct, sensual awareness, above all fantasy and imagination—are the very stuff of which poetry is made, and, therefore, that the child's experience is richer, profounder, more varied and, in the broadest sense, more *poetic,* than that of the 'finished being' who, by comparison, is limited, impoverished, and confined to that dreary routine of sterility which consists in never seeing anything save that which actually exists."[6] Welty's luxuriant deployment of sensual detail and the fluid movement into realms of fantasy and dream that are characteristic of so many of her stories attest to the legacy of imaginative freedom and richness from which she has always been able to draw.

The children's texts of the period played important roles in her development, as well, not only by feeding her imagination with stories but also by conveying a particularly benign view of the nature of reality. Welty's characters often reveal a longing for harmony and order in their lives. Many of them, especially in the early stories, experience the world as a place tending to disorder, where bewilderment and loneliness predominate. Yet beyond the sublunary world, they sense a realm of order, reflected in such images as the constellations. Welty's introspective characters, in particular, look frequently at the stars as if to find answers there.

The mythology that attributes meaningful stories to heavenly configurations has long been recognized as important to Welty's texts. Like her characters Cassie Morrison and Virgie Rainey in "June Recital," Welty appears to have seen the stars as making up "a constellation which the heart could read over many a night" (CS 460). One source for this fascination was undoubtedly a collection of books Welty received as a child. In volume 1 of the multivolume *Our Wonder World: A Library of Knowledge,* the names of the chapters suggest that knowledge *is* entirely orderly, to be read and assimilated systematically like the successive pages of a book. One chapter is entitled "The Earth a Storybook," another "The Earth a Wonderbook," and the one pertaining to the sky is "The Open Book of the Heavens" (its subtitle: "How People Read it of Old and How They Read it Now"). This latter chapter discusses the planets from a scientific point of view but also features the constellations and the stories associated with them. An illustration of the figures in the constellations reveals many of Welty's favorite mythic characters: Pegasus, the Twins (Gemini), Cassiopeia, Taurus the Bull, Perseus and the head of Medusa, and, as if caught in the stream of the Milky Way, the image of the Swan. The book urges children to make "friends of the stars" by learning to locate and name some of the constellations.[7] It was here that Welty probably first learned that the word "planets" means "wanderers."[8] The geniality of this entire series characterizes the search for knowledge as the systematic acquisition of pleasurable new understandings of the various features of the world.

The classical worldview also typically turns upon the interplay of order and disorder. Ancient stories and myths are frequently cautionary tales about how to avoid getting into trouble. Michael Kreyling argues persuasively that the twin impulses of Apollo and Dionysus are prominent in Welty's fiction,[9] suggesting that the myth of Apollonian order is recurrently balanced in her stories by the fructifying appearance of a godlike Bacchic, or Dionysian, figure, such as Troy Flavin in *Delta Wedding,* Billy Floyd in "At the Landing," and Cash in "Livvie." In the latter story the perfect orderliness and symmetry of the home old Solomon creates for his young wife, Livvie, is literally shattered by the stones Cash throws as he breaks the bottles in the bottle trees.

McGuffey's Fifth Reader, another text Welty knew as a child, also conveys the unequivocal impression that orderliness, good behavior, virtue, and rewards go hand in hand. Characters in these stories and poems, as in much of the children's literature of the time, find themselves living with the terrible consequences of having made the wrong decision—choosing beauty over utility, for example, or putting one's desires before one's duties. The content and tone of these texts offer plentiful evidence of the conflict between virtue (duty, loyalty, deference to adults) and adventuresomeness that the young Welty seems to have experienced, and a very specific set of lessons for "proper" behavior is promoted throughout.

The palpably encouraging atmosphere of Welty's home included a dictionary and encyclopedias in the dining room to help answer questions raised during family dinner conversations. Her father kept various instruments—telescope, magnifying glass, gyroscope, kaleidoscope—in a table in the library to "instruct and fascinate" and used them to introduce his children to the mysteries of the wider (and the smaller) worlds (OWB 3). Welty retains the sense that such objects constitute windows to new worlds when she refers to such magical objects as the stereopticon and telescope in her fiction. But although access to these instruments constitutes sheer pleasure for her young protagonists, Welty's narratives themselves tend to recall the ubiquity of parental caution. In "June Recital," for example, Loch Morrison is given permission to use his father's telescope while he is confined to bed with malaria. In his memory of a time when the whole family had waited to see an airplane fly over "with a lady in it," we are told that "the telescope had been gripped in his father's hand like a big stick, *some kind of protective weapon* for what was to come" (CS 277; emphasis mine).

These objects may have conveyed to children the idea that knowledge was accessible and benign, the world ordered and meaningful, but Welty gradually realized that the sorts of information they revealed did not actually answer the kinds of questions she had begun to formulate about life. The dictionary and encyclopedia offered only facts; the instruments only data. Welty's early reliance on their being there gave way to her later recognition that the knowledge they offered did not illuminate the questions that truly concerned her: human motivations, communication, relationships, mystery, the allure of the beauty around her, the functioning of memory and imagination. What had been offered to her as answers—fascinating though the data might be at times—was only part of the truth.

This lesson came suddenly to Welty with her first awareness of the pain and sorrow that can make up the darker side of life. An episode recorded in her essay "The Little Store" tells of her childhood knowledge of a Mr. Sessions, the proprietor of a store to which her mother sometimes sent her on errands, and of the Sessions family, who lived upstairs from the store with their unknown lives—"but I think we children never thought of that" (ES 333). Never having seen this family in any of the contexts in which she came to understand the families of her friends, such as sitting as a group around a dinner table, the young Welty had been quite unprepared for the revelation of how events had altered the basic facts of their existence.

> The possibility that they had any other life at all, anything beyond what we could see within the four walls of the Little Store, occurred to me only when tragedy struck their family. There was some act of violence. The shock to the neighborhood traveled to the children, of course; but I couldn't find out from my parents what had happened. They held it back from me, *as they'd already held back many things,* "until the time comes for you to know."
>
> You could find out some of these things by looking in the unabridged dictionary and the encyclopedia—kept to hand in our dining room—but you couldn't find out there what had happened to the family who for all the years of your life had lived upstairs over the Little Store, who had never been anything but patient and kind to you, who never once had sent you away. All I ever knew was its aftermath: they were the only people ever known to me who simply vanished. (ES 334; emphasis mine)

The secret was never disclosed, and Welty was left with only a glimpse of some deeper and unfamiliar reality, "early news of people coming to hurt one another" (ES 335).

A more personal example of how adults withheld crucial truths from children occurred after the episode in which Welty challenged her mother to tell her where babies come from. As Welty writes, "Not being able to bring herself to open that door to reveal its secret, one of those days, she opened another door" (OWB 16). Discovering two nickels in one of her mother's boxes kept in a bottom bureau drawer, Welty wanted to spend them immediately, and to quiet her, her mother was forced to tell her the truth, that there had been a baby brother who had died before Eudora was born, a baby never spoken of by his parents because, as Welty quickly realized, it was too painful for them. The nickels "had lain on his eyelids, for a purpose untold and unimaginable" (OWB 17). In remembering them, Welty conflates these two adult secrets, the one she longed to understand and the one she would never have guessed: "She'd told me the wrong secret—not how babies could come but how they could die" (OWB 17). In recognizing the significance of her brother's death, Welty was given the key to understanding the *degree* of protectiveness her parents felt toward her and their many precautions for her and her younger brothers' safety. The infant's death may account, too, for the paradox that Welty's parents served *both* as models for adventure—each of them having traveled so far to begin their marriage in Mississippi—*and* as the ardent protectors of their three children. Her mother's revelation of this secret, however, and the secrets in other families that Welty gradually became aware of may have led her to believe, as her fiction so often suggests, that the truths worth knowing are beneath the surface of the truths we are given.

Welty's childhood, her reading habits, and her relationships with adults suggest a basis for her beliefs about the nature of knowledge. Thus far, I have treated knowledge in the most general sense of the word, as standing for the way things are in the "real" world, and it is this conventional sense of the term in which Welty's characters believe. Welty does not begin with any systematic set of epistemological assumptions but rather from what she grew up observing around her. There is a basic difference, however, between the worldview of most of her characters and that of Welty herself. As Guy Davenport has noted, she has made her subject, to a remarkable degree, the minds and imaginations of essentially inarticulate people who rarely understand what happens to them.[10] Welty herself, in contrast, is concerned with showing the traps people create for themselves when they do not question their premises. In a very real sense, her fiction explores the implications and consequences of holding such unrecognized assumptions about life, about others, about language, and about knowledge.

Welty's characters do not begin their understanding from a position of innocence. By the time they are capable of introspection—Welty considers the age of nine to be pivotal (ES 47)—they have already unwittingly assimilated an enormous body of information, assumptions, and interpretations from the people they have known. What they come to realize is that bits of knowledge they have learned from the adults around them do not "fit" their own experience and observations. Thus the acquisition of new knowledge comes in the form of recognizing the falsity or distortion of what one thought one already knew. The flaws or limitations of our present knowledge are laid aside in favor of some more-nearly-adequate view of things. Consequently, while we may believe we are moving toward some truer vision—our Platonic longing for the truth behind ephemeral phenomena remains strong—Welty recognizes the fact that each new piece of information we think we have achieved is itself likely to be replaced. All understanding is tentative.

One of the stories that best exemplifies the situation of a young person raised in such a manner is "A Memory," in which the unnamed girl who is the protagonist experiences both an insatiable longing to know more about life and a vulnerability born of the fact that she has not been prepared to encounter its uglier dimensions. Welty's protagonist recalls that when she was younger, she had a passionate need "to watch everything about me" (CS 75) in the belief that important truths were waiting to be uncovered: "It did not matter to me what I looked at; from any observation I would conclude that a secret of life had been nearly revealed to me—for I was obsessed with notions about concealment, and from the smallest gesture of a stranger I would wrest what was to me a communication or a presentiment" (CS 76). The young Welty in *One Writer's Beginnings* and her many young protagonists poised on the threshold of new knowledge share an insistent desire to understand what is taking place around them. Welty frequently portrays her protagonists as inquiring children, leading them—and her readers— through the anticipation of learning, its frustrating delays, and glimpses of deeper understanding. In "A Memory" the protagonist's adolescent intensity as she longs for things she only dimly understands creates a compelling picture of how one may be forced to confront one's own ignorance.

The story begins with the girl's admission of how urgently she wants to understand things beyond her limited experience: "I do not know even now what it was that I was waiting to see; but in those days I was convinced that I almost saw it at every turn" (CS 75). She is well aware that her understanding has been limited by parental love:

> I was at an age when I formed a judgment upon every person and every event which came under my eye, although I was easily frightened. When a person, or a happening, seemed to me not in keeping with my opinion, or even my hope or expectation, I was terrified by a vision of abandonment and wildness which tore my heart with a kind of sorrow. My father and mother, who believed that I saw nothing in the world which was not strictly coaxed into place like a vine on our garden trellis to be presented to my eyes, would have been badly concerned if they had guessed how frequently the weak and inferior and strangely turned examples of what was to come showed themselves to me. (CS 75)

As the imagery of this passage suggests, the parents have drawn a protective border around their child, meant to present to her only a benign and comprehensible world. The carefully guided vine on the garden trellis is echoed in other Weltyian stories by pictures in frames, mirrors, and the idea of framing in general, which imply keeping *in* what is safe and keeping *out* what is undesirable or unseemly. Such frames are yet another image for the radius of safety within which a child is protected. Eventually, however, the frame fails, and some truth is glimpsed.

The dilemma the girl faces concerns a boy she has been in love with for the past year, someone who has never spoken to her and about whom she knows so little that she is tormented, feeling a "constant uneasiness" as she speculates "endlessly on the dangers of his home" (CS 76), the characters of his parents, and his own apparent obliviousness to the dangers around him. A sudden nosebleed that he experienced in class confirmed all of her fears: "This small happening which had closed in upon my friend was a tremendous shock to me; it was unforeseen, but at the same time dreaded; I recognized it, and suddenly I leaned heavily on my arm and fainted" (CS 76).

On the day of the story, the girl watches a noisy, vulgar family that destroys the quiet of a lakeshore where she is sunbathing. The grotesqueness of this group, "inflicting pinches, kicks, and idiotic sounds" (CS 77) upon one another's "ugly bodies" (CS 79), breaks through her reverie in a way that permanently dispels her romantic dream. Trying to resume her thoughts about the boy, she finds that the memory refuses to come back; it has been annihilated, supplanted by this display of physical ugliness. Welty implies that the too-sudden interruption of the girl's childhood illusions by a vulgar reality—the rough physicality she observes—has the power to contaminate her dream of love. All she can think of now is how vulnerable the boy she loves is as she imagines him (in the last words of the story) "solitary and unprotected" (CS 80).

Beyond the idea that love conceived of as protection prevents access to truer forms of knowledge by isolating individuals in a protective "space," Welty demonstrates in "A Memory" and elsewhere that love, contrary to what we desire, *fails* to protect loved ones from harm. What Madelon Sprengnether has called the "stunning vulnerability" of Welty's characters is seen again and again regardless of whether love is present.[11] As central to our lives as loving others and being loved ourselves may be, the idea that it can keep us safe is illusory. This harsh truth is particularly evident in "A Curtain of Green," in which the protagonist, Mrs. Larkin, suffers overwhelming despair because she was unable to protect her husband when a tree fell and killed him. She had whispered "'you can't be hurt.' But the tree had fallen, had struck the car exactly so as to crush him to death" (CS

109). She tries to repeat the "protective words . . . so as to change the whole happening. It was accident that was incredible, when her love for her husband was keeping him safe" (CS 109). Mrs. Larkin and the girl in "A Memory" both realize that the inability to protect the one you love is a basic source of the terror of loving.

In her novel *The Optimist's Daughter,* published in 1972, Welty fully addresses the implications of this view of love as protection. This is the novel in which Welty's own family memories are most clearly revealed, and the time when she wrote the novel—shortly after the deaths of her mother and her only living brother—suggests a searching through her own experience to understand the role that love has played in her life. Late in the story, Laurel McKelva Hand recalls what her husband had tried to teach her: "Until she knew Phil, she thought of love as shelter; her arms went out as a naive offer of safety. He had showed her that this need not be so. Protection, like self-protection, fell away from her like all one garment, some anachronism foolishly saved from childhood" (OD 161). Coming to see the view of love as protection as "naive," Welty, through her protagonist, hints of the need to grow beyond the childhood experience, the preoccupation with safety that parents sometimes instill in us. In this novel Welty creates a dialectical relationship between two key terms—"protect" and "protest"—to explore the implications of a love that emphasizes safety at the expense of a freedom to explore the unknown (see chapter 5). The lessons of this novel about the need to allow oneself and one's memory to remain vulnerable to new experience and understanding are the culmination of an interior debate that emerged from Welty's own childhood (and lifelong) experience of a love that had a hard time letting go.

. . .

The protagonists of "A Memory" and "A Curtain of Green" are, in effect, artist figures.[12] Both are placed in a position where they try to understand the complexity of the reality around them and yet are hampered by misunderstandings about the protective power of love. The girl in "A Memory" has been taking painting lessons and makes "small frames with [her] fingers, to look out at everything" (CS 75). Her desire to find aesthetic harmony in what she looks at—by locating and framing scenes—is an unwitting continuation of her parents' protective vision, noted in the image of the vine they coaxed onto a garden trellis. At the same time, it reflects the acts of selection and composition that a photographer undertakes in looking through a viewfinder, a reminder of Welty's experiences with photography and her emphasis on the importance of perspective and distance in beginning to work (OWB 21, 87). In any art form, the creative impulse expresses itself in part, at least, as a desire to find and depict pattern or structure in essentially random phenomena, to convey the illusion or perception of meaning. Welty would find the Nietzschean vision of art as an interplay of Dionysian chthonic energy and passion with the Apollonian imposition of order to be entirely congenial,[13] for she has written that the "work of art is . . . an achievement of order, passionately conceived and passionately carried out" (ES 58) and that "discovering a shape or pattern to some set of experiences, is the way we all take of imagining what life is up to" (ES 26). It is this order and structure, created by the writer, that the reader comes away with in finishing a story or novel "so that he feels that some design in life (by which I mean esthetic pattern, not purpose) has just been discovered there" (ES 144). Welty does not believe that the author reveals some a priori order inhering in external reality, but she *does* consider it basic to the artist's task to impose an aesthetic order that conveys the artist's idea of meaningfulness onto the work of art itself.

In "A Curtain of Green" Mrs. Larkin, whose notions of the orderliness of life have left her unprepared for the shock of her husband's death, cultivates an especially unruly garden "plot" after he is killed, as if she is experimenting with letting things overreach "their boundaries" (CS 108). Distraught at the failure of her love to protect her husband's life, "she seemed not to seek for order, but to allow an over-flowering, as if she consciously ventured forever a little farther, a little deeper, into her life in the garden" (CS 108). The total collapse of her (Apollonian) beliefs in the orderly nature of things—and of the illusion of safety her love had brought into her life—causes Mrs. Larkin to plunge into a world of Dionysian fecundity, chaos, and boundlessness. Within her garden, Mrs. Larkin has left "civilization" behind; she nourishes her flowers according to no principle of organization that her neighbors (from their windows overlooking her garden) can begin to recognize. Her garden, like her hair, becomes tangled and unkempt; she wears faded men's overalls; she doesn't welcome her neighbors' visits of condolence—all of the old forms are now meaningless to her. She enters into this state of mind in which nothing matters and comes close to enacting the random destructiveness of Dionysian frenzy in her impulse to strike Jamey, her garden helper, dead with her hoe. Then there is a moment of silence, of suspense, after which rain falls, an event that Mrs. Larkin appears to experience as a sign, perhaps a blessing, certainly a cleansing. That this rain has interrupted a moment of madness in which she might have lost the last traces of her humanity in an act of violence seems significant and timely, and Mrs. Larkin faints, almost in relief, one feels, at being connected again with the natural world and its rhythms.

Mrs. Larkin's task of controlling the unruly, her necessary detachment from the social expectations of her neighbors, her immersion into dangerous, boundless realms where she must choose what to include and what to exclude from her plots, her decisions about what to leave alone and what to cut back—all reflect the situation of the writer and make of this story a kind of parable of artistic endeavor.[14] Emerging from a world that had been characterized by her love for her husband, a love that failed to protect, Mrs. Larkin struggles to find a viable relationship with the natural world. As an artist she must reveal (by pruning back and exposing) or impose (by organizing) patterns that signify meaning she can believe in. As an image of her spiritual chaos, the garden is a labyrinth of tangle and disruption. This is the world artists must confront, eschewing the meanings others would impose on them in order to create their own.

.　.　.

The benignity of the world one usually experiences in Welty's texts is conveyed not only by her characters' expectations of order and meaning but also by narrative techniques—particularly the use of similes—that convey the notion that correspondences exist throughout the universe. Her figurative language regularly gives the impression that events happening here on earth mirror things in the sky, that human behavior parallels that of birds and animals, that microcosms have their counterparts in macrocosms.[15] Her character Audubon (in "A Still Moment") is not alone in feeling humbled by the patterns he views around him: "He felt again the old stab of wonder—what structure of life bridged the reptile's scale and the heron's feather? That knowledge too had been lost" (CS 196). Persistent analogies among phenomena constitute a basic feature of Welty's descriptive passages:

> The luminous ranges of all the clouds stretched one beyond the other in heavenly order. They seemed to be the streets where Joel was walking through the town. People now lighted their houses in entertainments as if they copied after the sky. ("First Love," CS 161)

The night insects all over the Delta were noisy; a kind of audible twinkling, like a lowly starlight, pervaded the night with a gregarious radiance. (DW 240)

On either side of their horses' feet the cotton twinkled like stars. (DW 30)

Directly below Loch [up in a tree] a spotted thrush walked noisily in the weeds, pointing her beak ahead of her straight as a gun, just as busy in the world as people. ("June Recital," CS 317)

Each tree like a single leaf, half hair-fine skeleton, half gauze and green, let the first suspicious wind through its old, pressed shape, its summer-time branches. ("The Wanderers," CS 439)

All life used this [Natchez] Trace, and he liked to see the animals move along it in direct, oblivious journeys, for they had begun it and made it, the buffalo and deer and the small running creatures before man ever knew where he wanted to go, and birds flew a great mirrored course above. ("A Still Moment," CS 193)

Welty's reliance on similes, in general, far exceeds her use of metaphor and enhances the reader's sense that everything in her world is *like* every-thing else. Whereas metaphor blurs the distinctions between objects, simile gives them equal place, equal importance. Each thing retains its own iden-tity yet is analogous to other things in what can become a nearly infinite sequence of correspondences. Thus it might be argued that her use of simile *embodies* a balancing of separateness and connection that expresses in an especially vivid way a successful resolution of the relational dilemmas posited in chapter 1.[16]

The plenitude of Welty's fictive world—where nature teems with sounds, sights, smells, and textures—combined with her characters' sensuous ap-preciation of natural processes such as the growth of fruits and flowers, the decay of structures (for example, old houses), the fragility of the physical in a world of passing time: all express an ongoing, accepting relationship with the natural world in which the self finds pleasure and strength rather than alienation.[17] The tendency of Welty's characters to find, or expect to find, familiar and congenial things when they encounter the unknown stands them in good stead.[18] Even on occasions of partial understanding or genuine bewilderment, her characters retain a striking capacity to find pleasure in the world they inhabit. The achievement of knowledge is so important and valuable to her characters that even when that knowledge is of something troubling or violent, they assimilate it quickly and with little evidence of trauma. New understanding—whatever its nature—brings its own kind of joy, the intellectual pleasure of coming closer to what one believes is truth.

A number of Welty's images evoke in her characters (and by extension, in her readers) the sense that the joy of understanding is at hand. They promise fulfillment, and the fact that they do not often provide it is secondary, for it is in their function as *promises* that they have importance for her characters. Her stories often feature boxes or chests, letters, newspapers, telegrams, and post offices, all serving to indicate characters' interactions with and expectations about the unknown and, in the case of mail and post offices, their communication (or lack thereof) with the world beyond their typically circumscribed environments. Unlike what is found in Faulkner's stories, where his depiction of boxes and images of containment tends to recall the myth of Pandora's box—likely to be full of evil or threats to the self and meant to be approached, at the very least, with caution [19]—Welty's references to various types of containers are to objects full of promise, mystery, and delight.

Welty's mother "kept treasures of hers in boxes," which in turn were kept in her bottom bureau drawer (OWB 16), creating a box-within-a-box of successive surprises for her daughter to explore. Welty recalls this pleasure in characterizing Laura, a child in *Delta Wedding,* as someone "who loved all kinds of boxes and bottles, all objects that could keep and hold things" (DW 136). Lily Daw's hope chest, with its carefully packed washcloth and two bars of soap (CS 6), is a basic image in "Lily Daw and the Three Ladies," where it seems to embody the community's beliefs about the best possible fate for a girl like Lily; Welty's decision to let the hope chest be carried off on the train without Lily constitutes a gentle satire of the romantic plot her friends imagine for her. In "June Recital" Loch Morrison does not recognize a "small brown wooden box" as a metronome, and so he imagines it as the best thing it could possibly be: "the box is where she has the dynamite" (CS 285). Numerous stories involve telegrams (such as the one Powerhouse receives), mysterious and unexplained letters like the one peeking out of King MacLain's pocket in "Sir Rabbit," and post offices so clearly standing for "secret hope or joy" (CS 205) that they constitute an unbearable reminder to Miss Sabina in "Asphodel" that her life is over, so that she tears her town's post office apart just before she dies. And finally, Grady, a little boy in "The Wide Net," looks wistfully (as perhaps any child would do) at this scene: "Far away a long freight train was passing. It seemed like a little festival procession, moving with the slowness of ignorance or a dream, from distance to distance, the tiny pink and gray cars *like secret boxes*. . . . Tears suddenly came to Grady's eyes, but it could only be because a tiny man walked along the top of the train, walking and moving on top of the moving train" (CS 175). The train itself with its evocation of far away places, the idea of a procession, and the box cars are all examples of the allure of mystery felt by Welty's characters, a powerful longing to experience something new.

.   .   .

The milieu in which Eudora Welty grew up—her parents' beliefs and predilections, her formal education, her reading—encouraged an early vision of the world as harmonious and orderly, and this impression was carried into her fiction through her characters' assumptions about the nature of things. But although Welty's *characters* tend to believe in the Platonic notion that knowledge in this world corresponds in some important way to a more permanent sort of truth, Welty herself views this all-too-human tendency to find harmony in the world as being illusory, born of need rather than accurate observation. Her stories continue to reflect this belief in an orderly universe, long after Welty reached far different conclusions, precisely *because* she has continued to be concerned with understanding how such unquestioned assumptions interfere with our reaching more nearly adequate views of what happens in our lives.

Welty's fascination grew as she recognized the motivations behind people's insistence on seeing the world in particular ways. She came to see other reasons, beyond the protectiveness of adults, for their frustration of her passion to understand. She believed that her parents never lied, that indeed they "*couldn't* lie" (OWB 16), but they could and did withhold things from her. And although her parents had established it as a basic rule that there was no lying in their home, Welty was intrigued to discover that lies took place all the time in other children's homes. She soon realized that what parents and other adults say to children is often suspect; their answers to questions, for example, are typically only partial answers.[20] Moreover, vigilance in grasping what people are *not* saying is as important to understanding as listening to what *is* said.

It took me a long time to realize that these very same everyday lies, and the stratagems and jokes and tricks and dares that went with them, were in fact the basis of the *scenes* I so well loved to hear about and hoped for and treasured in the conversation of adults.

My instinct—the dramatic instinct—was to lead me, eventually, on the right track for a storyteller: the *scene* was full of hints, pointers, suggestions, and promises of things to find out and know about human beings. I had to grow up and learn to listen for the unspoken as well as the spoken—and to know a truth, I also had to recognize a lie. (OWB 15)

Adult manipulation of the truth may often have occurred through the best of motives—to protect the child from unseemly, painful, or incomprehensible information. But this was not always so, and Welty came to see that much of what people say to one another (and not only what adults say to children) consists of fictions that disguise, distort, or interpret events for quite personal and (particularly to a child) mysterious reasons. Welty seems to have created a large number of child protagonists for some of the same reasons her friend Katherine Anne Porter did so—because the question of how adults have "betrayed" children and one another with their versions of reality and of how we must distance ourselves even from beloved adults in order to see more clearly is a recurrent theme.[21] For these writers the characters capable of seeing things newly tend to be children who have begun to think about and compare the world they observe with the world as adults have characterized it to them. It is children who possess qualities that make them far more likely than adults to recognize and appreciate different possible understandings; it is children who reveal curiosity, wonder, openness, and a willingness to question the premises behind what they are told. This ability to discern the gaps between the publicly sanctioned view of things and what we observe is, for all too many people, lost in the course of growing up.

Welty's idea of knowledge, then, is *not* the achievement of some unquestioned truth, for all knowledge is ultimately unverifiable. The most one can hope for is to illuminate and eliminate as many distorted beliefs as possible, to reach an understanding that seems truer than what one had believed. Welty is concerned throughout her fiction with how people create stories to explain their lives to themselves and others. This *use* of language to generate personally meaningful versions of reality fascinates her as she addresses how lies, silences, and fabrications constitute the knowledge passed on from one human being to another. She knows how thoroughly perceptions are mediated by desires and how people simply do not observe phenomena that fail to correspond with their preconceived notions of the ways things are.

Welty's attempt to understand how knowledge can occur in a world in which so much is withheld, only partially revealed, distorted in the revelation, transformed into myth, and otherwise rendered "suitable," especially when intended for children's ears, is a major, lifelong preoccupation. It is her sense—again a legacy of childhood—that knowledge is *everywhere* and yet the means for getting to it are just out of reach that pervades her images, the scenes in her stories involving children, and the ways in which she maneuvers through issues of point of view, narrative voice, and revelation in her fiction. In her essay "Looking at Short Stories" (ES 85–106) she observes "that the finest story writers seem to be in one sense obstructionists. As if they held back their own best interests. . . . What is stranger is that if we look for the source of the deepest pleasure we receive from a writer, how often do we not find that it seems to be connected with this very obstruction" (ES 105). In her various stories Welty plays all the roles of her childhood vis-à-vis what might be learned: sometimes she is the parent revealing (for mysterious parental reasons) partial truths or appearing to modify her truths to make them appropriate for our ears; sometimes she is the child (as character), bewildered by what is seen, and misinterpreting it, only gradually (if at all) beginning to grasp more accurately what is there. At times, too, Welty makes her readers long to know something and then leaves it "obscure," perhaps because she believes the sort of knowledge everyone seeks *is* ultimately mysterious, and she intends for readers to feel what she has felt about this unreachability, even as they take on a readerly involvement in needing to know.[22] Fascination with what can and cannot be known motivates Welty's fiction as well as informs it, and the act of exploring how language can be used both to reveal and to conceal constitutes, for Welty herself, much of the pleasure of writing.

Welty's treatment of these themes can be seen in the story "Old Mr. Marblehall," which reveals, through an ironic narrator, an elderly man's attempt to give meaning to his life through the stories he tells himself. Mr. Marblehall is a nondescript figure who, like other very quiet figures in Welty's fiction (for example, Mr. Fergusson in "A Sketching Trip"), longs for life to come along and sweep him off his feet (ST 69).[23] At the age of sixty or so, apparently realizing that his life is empty, he marries and has a son, fulfilling at least one acceptable plot that implies purposiveness and import in his existence. But, perhaps because this change in his life seems anticlimactic, Mr. Marblehall does something more to give extraordinary meaning to his life: he marries a second woman and has another son, nearly identical with the first. Now he is a bigamist, undiscovered, who can relish the community's likely reaction if they were to find out about his double life. Mr. Marblehall (whose name suggests cold emptiness) does not seem to expect emotional fulfillment in either of his marriages; there is no hint that his relationship with either wife or either son promises him inner peace. His passivity over many years has led him to an isolation that apparently renders even marriage incapable of meeting his spiritual needs. Rather, he longs for some *public* recognition that will establish and affirm his sense of identity.

Mr. Marblehall creates a life that he sees as not only meaningful but doubly so, because it involves risk and a defiance of his community's values. He fantasizes that one of his sons will find out about his other family and expose him, persuading himself that people would be shocked and amazed *if they knew*. The secret Mr. Marblehall believes he is protecting—the fact of his double life—is one he can never admit to, for although it might lead to public acknowledgment of his uniqueness, thus lending an importance to his life that he has never felt, it also protects him from a revelation he cannot risk: he might discover that people aren't amazed at all and simply don't care. The secret of his loneliness and isolation is hidden within a more dramatic secret in a series of embedded stories whose degree of reality remains ambiguous.[24] Welty's tale offers such details as Mr. Marblehall's bedtime reading of *Terror Tales* and *Astonishing Stories* (CS 95) to affirm the fictionality of his perceptions and desires and his need to create a plot for his life. Yet the story as a whole confirms Welty's notion that the secrets we would admit, if pressed, are screens for truths we would find harder to face, even within ourselves. We bolster our illusions by multiplying our disguises. Mr. Marblehall is able to believe in his uniqueness because he doubly masks his ordinariness and thus forestalls the recognition (revealed by the story's narrator) that "nobody gives a hoot about any old Mr. Marblehall" (CS 93) and, beyond that, the deeper truth that his life *has* been uneventful.

The specter of meaninglessness lies behind many of the stories humans hold on to, for we would much prefer that our lives have importance—even an unpleasant importance—than to admit to emptiness and insignificance. In "Keela, the Outcast Indian Maiden," the badly abused black man, Little Lee Roy, actually seems to enjoy the conversation that two characters, Steve and Max, have about his past because that past mattered; it happened, and it characterized his life, and these strangers have cared enough to be upset about it. Throughout the discussion of Steve's complicity in mistreating him, Little Lee Roy smiles, giggles, and behaves in a manner that might be considered entirely inappropriate except that he is "excited almost beyond respectful silence" (CS 39) by the two white men who are recalling his abuse.[25] When there is a pause in the telling, "Little Lee Roy held his breath, for fear everything was all over" (CS 42). The relative insignificance of his existence apart from this atrocious victimization is suggested at the end of the story when Little Lee Roy's children treat him disdainfully as he tries to tell them of the visit of the white men who had come to talk about "de ole times when I use to be wid de circus—"; they tell him to "hush up, Pappy" (CS 45). Perhaps they have heard the story before. In any event, they are not prepared to allow him the sense of significance his narration might restore.

Steve also locates the meaning of his life in his "story"; his soul-searching and guilt have, after all, been the occasion for this trip to find Little Lee Roy. When Max does not share his view of the enormity of what happened—and, in fact, scoffs at him by suggesting that *he* would have known what was going on—Steve punches Max in the jaw. A moment later he explains: "I had to hit you. First you didn't believe me, and then it didn't bother you" (CS 44).

Even Welty's unselfconscious characters need to generate stories that give their lives significance. Another such figure is given an unexpected glimpse of the possibility and appeal of an alternative plot for her life. Ruby Fisher in "A Piece of News" becomes conscious of her commonplace existence by a happenstance that shows her how different her story might have been. Finding an item in an out-of-state newspaper about a woman named "Ruby Fisher" who "had the misfortune to be shot in the leg by her husband this week" (CS 13), Ruby first experiences a moment of awe and confusion as she tries to understand how the news could be true and then imagines what such an event in her own life might be like.

Ruby's revised version of the newspaper story as applied to her life embellishes it by adding precisely those features—romance, melodrama, and passion—that are missing in her life with the gruff and somewhat insensitive Clyde, who takes his wife utterly for granted.[26] Imagining her life as being so crucial to him that he is frantic with remorse for having shot her "through the heart," Ruby acts out and savors the fantasy of her final moments: "Ruby began to cry softly, the way she would be crying from the extremity of pain; tears would run down in a little stream over the quilt. . . . She lay silently for a moment, composing her face into a look which would be beautiful, desirable, and dead" (CS 14).

This story is particularly powerful in showing how people who are rarely, if ever, introspective about their experience may be jolted into an awareness of entirely new possibilities. Holding this awareness like a secret, Ruby is "filled with happiness" (CS 15). When she shares the article with Clyde, he is at first defiant, and then the two of them are momentarily "filled full with their helplessness" and inability to understand: "Slowly they both flushed, as though with a double shame and a double pleasure. . . . Rare and wavering, some possibility stood timidly like a stranger between them and made them hang their heads" (CS 16). Clyde is too threatened, however, even to contemplate this new vision, and he seizes the first opportunity to point out that the newspaper is from Tennessee and "that he had been right all the time" (CS 16). Ruby, on the other hand, has seen a magical something else—possibility.

The versions of our lives that we generate tend, not surprisingly, to reflect our individual resolutions of the dilemma of separateness and connection that we all, more or less consciously, come to terms with. Our decisions about the meaning of our lives naturally entail particular conclusions about the nature of our relationships. Thus Ruby Fisher adds the element of passion to her relationship with Clyde in her death bed fantasy. Mr. Marblehall, by adding the illusion of familial involvement to the story of his life—as if denying his isolation and loneliness—through the fantasy (or fact) of his double life, frees himself to be a somewhat detached participant in both of his families. One suspects that a fear of intimacy may have been behind the long decades of his life in which he allowed nothing to happen.

.   .   .

One of Welty's most elusive stories, "A Still Moment," concerns three historical figures who meet briefly on the Natchez Trace, where they see a white heron descend to feed in the waters of a marsh. For each man the moment is significant, potentially transfiguring, yet what happens to each of them is already fully implicit in his perceptions. Throughout this complex text, Welty explores how the preconceptions underlying the stories people create about their own lives filter and, thus, determine the nature of what they perceive.

Lorenzo Dow, the first character introduced, is an "itinerant Man of God" who spends his life on the road, traveling quickly from place to place as he tries to save souls for the Lord. His deeper motive, however, is to find a sense of mystical harmony with Him. He is looking for the fulfillment of a faith he is still struggling to develop, a faith he envisions as an unquestioning acceptance of God's protection of his mortal vulnerability. Dow's problem is that in moments of great danger, he hears voices that tell him how to save himself, and he instinctively follows those voices, changing himself into various forms (playing dead to fool a bear, for example) and only realizing after he has been saved that the voice he heard was not that of God but the Devil's. He has been tempted—and succumbed—to the instinct to save himself rather than trust in God to do so, and he recognizes his failure of faith as the influence of the Devil: "But all the time God would have protected him in His own way, less hurried, more divine" (CS 190).

What Dow does not recognize is that his own conception of love is part of the problem, as Welty implies in describing his marriage to Peggy, whom he has left in Massachusetts while he travels throughout the South. He has spent only "a few hours of time" with his bride (CS 190) and in proposing marriage to her had made it clear that his work would keep them apart for long periods of time. When Welty writes that "he could look at the flowering trees and love Peggy in fullness, just as he could see his visions and love God" (CS 189), the reader begins to understand how he subverts his own apparent intentions in choosing distance and safety, making it impossible for the union with God he longs for to take place. It is of Dow that Welty writes, "he found it effortless to love at a distance" (CS 189).

Dow's metamorphoses, undertaken to keep himself safe, constitute a "humiliation of his faith" because he does not ultimately trust that God's love will take care of him in the ways he (Dow) desires. He cannot embrace the involvement, daring, or vulnerability of real love either with Peggy or with God. Instead, he projects onto the world—and onto his relationship with God—his own preoccupation with safety. He sees his purpose in speaking to his congregation as bringing them "divine love and sufficient warning of all that could threaten them" (CS 191). Moreover, he interprets the singing of birds as being about the "divine *love* which was the one ceaseless *protection*" (CS 190; emphasis mine), revealing the equation implicit in his definition of "love." Even in his compassion for his congregation, which inspires him, as he rides, to send them "a premature benediction," he spreads his arms out toward them "one at a time for safety" (CS 191). In terms of the image of the labyrinth to be discussed in chapter 3, Dow does not see himself as living *within* the complexities of human existence on earth; rather, he wishes "to brood *above* the entire and passionate life of the wide world" (CS 191; emphasis mine). His desire for distance and immunity from turmoil and his wish to look down upon God's design make him a timid disciple for a fallen world.

It is paradoxical, given Dow's longing to transcend secular concerns, that he can never, until it is too late, stop himself from acting on mundane knowledge to save his fleshly self. His instincts are tuned to the wrong kind of knowledge, knowledge of this world rather than faith in God. His tendency to mistake one sort of knowledge for another is imaged in the fireflies that "instantly flickered up all around him" (CS 189). Lights of this sort are distractions that take the place of truer knowledge, and they serve this function here: "These were the signs sent from God that he had not seen the accumulated radiance of saved souls because he was not able, and that his eyes were more able to see the fireflies of the Lord than His blessed souls" (CS 189).

The second character introduced, the outlaw James Murrell, is, in his tormented way, as interested in the secret of life as Lorenzo Dow. His is a much darker vision, which does not even pretend to encompass love, but seeks rather to confirm his cynical view of mankind, in part, no doubt, because it justifies his behavior in robbing and murdering lone travelers along the Natchez Trace. After the killing of the heron at the end of the story, Murrell "looked about with satisfaction, and hid. Travelers were forever innocent, he believed: that was his faith. He lay in wait; his faith was in innocence and his knowledge was of ruin; and had these things been shaken?" (CS 197–98). Murrell's dark vision—even his eyes are dark and "narrowed to contract the heart" (CS 195)—is left intact despite the promise that had been implicit in the beatific vision of the bird.

Whereas Lorenzo Dow looks to the *future,* when he hopes his soul will be capable of communion with God and his ministry will be of genuine help to his congregations, and James Murrell tries to create a *past* version of events that lets him feel in control of moments of death and to glimpse the meaning of life in his victims' eyes, John James Audubon, the third character to appear, tries to live in and preserve the *present* moment. Like

Welty's other wondering characters, he relishes the beauty around him. "Great abundance had ceased to startle him, and he could see things one by one" (CS 194), and he tells "himself always: remember" (CS 193). His journal notes, of one particular day of beauty: "Only sorry that the Sun Sets" (CS 194).

That the white heron's existence sharply contrasts with that of the men is part of what they feel in observing it. Like the animals that move in their "oblivious journeys" along the Natchez Trace (CS 193), the heron seems timeless, unhurried, unreflective, at peace. Unlike human beings with their tortured awareness of time and frantic movement through space, the bird "has nothing in space or time to prevent its flight," undoubtedly a large part of its fascination and appeal. A "single frail yearning seemed to go out of the three [men]" (CS 196) toward the unselfconscious, unimaginably free bird.

Audubon is the character most able to understand this. Indeed, Welty's narrator attributes such sensitivity and perceptiveness to him as to create a very sympathetic figure, and the reader is prepared to contrast his love for life in all its richness with the limited preoccupations and perceptions of Lorenzo Dow and James Murrell. Consequently, Audubon's sudden killing of the bird is especially shocking, even more so in view of his recognition of how beauty and utter vulnerability coexist in the bird: "He felt again the old stab of wonder—what structure of life bridged the reptile's scale and the heron's feather? That knowledge too had been lost. He watched without moving. The bird was defenseless in the world except for the intensity of its life, and he wondered, how can heat of blood and speed of heart defend it?" (CS 196).

What, then, should be made of the violence in this story, both the senseless murders Murrell has committed and Audubon's unexpected killing of the heron? Welty herself has said little to help readers interpret this dimension of the story; she only emphasizes that she was writing "about three attitudes of looking at life" (Con 20). She does not pretend to say anything about life itself, but about human *perceptions* of life, about interpretations that have consequences for what people are able to experience. Although these three men are together, each of them might well have been alone in seeing the heron, for none of them appears changed in the least by this potentially transformative experience. Each goes on with his life in the same way as before.

Carol Gilligan's hypotheses about how differently males and females tend to experience relationships may be as provocative for thinking about Murrell and Audubon as they are for considering Lorenzo Dow's predilection for distances and safety. If Dow deludes himself about the nature of his relationships with God and with his wife, then Murrell would seem to deny relationship entirely, to find it unbearable. Gilligan writes that "if aggression is conceived as a response to the perception of danger . . . the danger men [in her studies] describe in their stories of intimacy is a danger of entrapment or betrayal, being caught in a smothering relationship or humiliated by rejection and deceit." Aggression may then be seen as "a signal of a fracture of connection, the sign of a failure of relationship" in which safety comes to be found in separateness.[27] Murrell chooses to be alone, and his encounters with others are always carefully orchestrated to provide him the illusion of complete control. Yet his unnecessary killing of his victims appears to be motivated by a fear that he is missing life itself and that these men know about human experience in ways he does not. The text suggests that he knows only a terrible loneliness and a terror that he is barely alive at all, yet at the same time a fear of relationship so great that he must ritualize his meetings with others. "Destroy the present!— that must have been the first thing that was whispered in Murrell's heart— the living moment and the man that lives in it must die before you can go on" (CS 192). Thus Welty's narrator writes about Murrell; but Murrell has given himself loftier motives: "Murrell in laying hold of a man meant to solve his mystery of being. It was as if other men, all but himself, would lighten their hold on the secret, upon assault, and let it fly free at death. In his violence he was only treating of enigma" (CS 192).

Murrell believes that he views something true about human experience at the moment in which a fellow traveler's defenses are all stripped away, the instant of his recognition of impending death. Murrell himself may sense the degree to which people's lives are composed of fabrications, stories, and behaviors constituting personae they wish to project rather than some authentic, true, vulnerable self. He may feel that in breaking through such facades, he will learn something about life that he has missed. He would concur with the ironic truth of Emily Dickinson's lines, "I like a look of Agony, / Because I know it's true—."[28] Yet oddly enough, Welty characterizes Murrell several times as not looking or not seeing (CS 191, 192, 195), just as she says that Dow does not always hear (CS 192).

Audubon is the most difficult figure to understand, because he looks "with care" and can even "see well in the dark" (CS 194, 198), just as he notes "all sights, all sounds, and was gentler than they as he went" (CS 198). His killing of the heron has been viewed positively by many of Welty's critics, as representing a violence necessary to the fulfillment of art.[29] I find it troubling, however, that Audubon commits this act despite the fact that his experience has taught him that his art cannot, even in his own eyes, fulfill his vision of nature's beauty:

> It was undeniable, on some Sunday mornings, when he turned over and over his drawings they seemed beautiful to him, through what was dramatic in the conflict of life, or what was exact. What he would draw, and what he had seen, became for a moment one to him then. Yet soon enough, and *it seemed to come in that same moment* . . . he knew that even the sight of the heron which surely he alone had appreciated, *had not been all his belonging,* and that never could any vision, even any simple sight, belong to him or to any man. He knew that the best he could make would be, after it was apart from his hand, *a dead thing* and not a live thing, never the essence, only a sum of parts; and that it would always meet with a stranger's sight, and never be one with the beauty in any other man's head in the world. As he had seen the bird most purely at its moment of death, in some fatal way, in his care for looking outward, *he saw his long labor most revealingly at the point where it met its limit.* (CS 198; emphasis mine)

In his seeing the bird "most purely at its moment of death," Audubon is very like Murrell, who searches for truth at the moment of *his* victims' deaths. Moreover, Audubon's action cuts short the very moment in which all three men might have glimpsed some other pattern to their lives in an apprehension of mystical unity, a moment of connection with nature that would have allowed them to overcome their individual isolation. Welty's characterizations make clear why her reader's intuition of the possibilities inhering in the still moment has been only an illusion.

Another way of understanding this moment of violence, however, may reside in the story's emphasis on a failure to love and in a second reference to failure that Welty offers: early in the story, her narrator speaks of Lorenzo Dow's remembered "failure in Ireland" (CS 191) when he was a missionary there. Such a visit did, historically, take place, but Welty may recall it here for still another reason, as a way of hinting at a wider reading of the story's events.[30] In this portrait of Christian ineffectuality, Welty may be echoing William Butler Yeats's concerns about the end of the Christian era. Yeats had created a thoroughgoing cosmology in which he argued that history consists of two-thousand-year-long cycles. The first "antithetical era," initiated by the encounter of Leda and the swan, was the classical age; it was succeeded by a "primary era," the two thousand years of Christianity now drawing to a close, an era whose annunciation involved the appearance of the dove to Mary. In *A Vision* Yeats anticipates the beginning of a forthcoming age, yet another "antithetical" era comparable to the classical age. As Northrop Frye explains, "we are now in the last century of the Christian era, at the very nadir of primary abstraction, and are approaching the return of an antithetical age. . . . Yeats prophesies the time when Christianity will give place to an opposing culture of proud beauty and invincible violence. . . . The dove and the virgin are to go and Leda and the swan are to come back, in the form of the watchful and ironic heron of the Irish marshes and his fanatical priestess."[31]

J. Hillis Miller writes of Yeats's belief that "evil is the increase in violence and unreason *threatening all orders of law and art,* but preparing, it may be, a new annunciation, a reversal of the gyres whirling out new right and wrong." The "absolute violence of the center," Miller notes, is at an "unnamed crossroads,"[32] implicit in the "great forked tree" (CS 193) at which Welty's three wanderers meet and observe the heron. Directly after the heron is killed, Welty offers an image: a "new moon, slender and white, hung shyly in the west" (CS 199). As Helen Vendler observes, "symbolically speaking, when the primary cycle ends . . . the heron's cycle will come round in the new crescent moon."[33] Welty's heron and the shy moon that accompanies it may signal a new millennium, especially inasmuch as the act of violence at the emotional center of the story—Audubon's destruction of the heron—suggests a role for violence in the new age. As Northrop Frye noted, violence is implicit in Yeats's characterization of "antithetical" ages.

That Welty subscribes to Yeats's metaphysical schema as a whole seems doubtful. But this story does seem to reflect the depleted energies of Christian enthusiasts, and Welty's allusion to Ireland may be a clue that she has Yeats's vision in mind. The story's title, "A Still Moment," may itself indicate this, for Yeats's most famous poem about the advent of a new age, "Leda and the Swan," is also regularly viewed by critics as pivoting on a single moment in time in which great changes have their beginning.[34]

If the characterization of Audubon is read as a story about a failure of love, so that even Audubon misunderstands what love and art require of him, then an application of Yeats's prophetic vision to this story makes sense. Both religion and art, in this reading, have failed to fulfill the promise in love, the overcoming of separateness that might be the healing of our era's sorrows. Perhaps the ultimate irony in this story lies in each man's belief that in this quiet moment he has glimpsed a truth that, in fact, he merely uses to justify what he already knew about his life. Each traveler's a priori interpretations remain intact.

The paragraph toward the end of the story that occasioned Robert Penn Warren's essay on the themes of love and separateness in Welty's fiction can now be understood more fully. Lorenzo Dow, shaken by the killing of the bird, rides away:

> Suddenly it seemed to him that God Himself, just now, thought of the Idea of Separateness. For surely He had never thought of it before, when the little white heron was flying down to feed. He could understand God's giving Separateness first and then giving Love to follow and heal in its wonder; but God had reversed this, and given Love first and then Separateness, as though it did not matter to Him which came first. Perhaps it was that God never counted the moments of Time; Lorenzo did that, among his tasks of love. Time did not occur to God. Therefore— did He even know of it? How to explain Time and Separateness back to God, Who had never thought of them, Who could let the whole world come to grief in a scattering moment? (CS 198)

The version of human experience Dow expresses—that love comes first and then separateness—corresponds to the psychoanalytic understanding of our emergence as human beings from that early childhood drama of separation and individuation. We begin, as Welty certainly did, from within a context of love. Carol Gilligan notes that Freud and his followers have always interpreted this experience as the story of "an initial fracture of connection leading through the experience of separation to an irreparable loss, a glorious achievement followed by a disastrous fall."[35] Indeed, the individual's experience has been seen to recapitulate the more broadly human myth of the Fall in Eden, with an eternal punishment consisting of separation from that original bliss. Freud concludes that aggression "forms the basis of every relation of affection and love among people," but he offers a telling qualification: "with the single exception, perhaps, of the mother's relation to her male child."[36] As he often does in his writing, Freud uses the term "people" when he means "males"; women, as Gilligan notes in discussing this passage, remain anomalous "by demonstrating a love not admixed with anger." In studying her male and female subjects' differing responses to issues of relationship, Gilligan finds that masculine experience, emphasizing the search for autonomy and the tendency to wish for control of the other, continues to be linked to both assertion and aggression, thus threatening civilization itself. Female experience, though, traces a different path; the narratives of Gilligan's female subjects suggest that even during their painful sense of deprivation, they continue to stress continuity in ways that allow connection to be restored. She argues, therefore, that women's experience seems to authorize the ongoing importance of attachment and continuity in ways men's experience does not.[37]

The excerpt from Welty's story also reveals that not only separateness needs to be explained "back to God," but time, as well. Just as humans are presumed to experience loss through physical (that is, spatial) separation from an early sense of well-being and bliss, they are also susceptible to the loss—into the past—of precious things that do not endure through the course of time. These temporal and spatial separations are the source of much, if not all, human pain. God presumably experiences no loss because His vision and knowledge are of plenitude, continuity, and wholeness, just as all of time is simultaneously present to Him.[38] How, then, Dow wonders, can He understand the "grief" that can pervade the human soul?

I suggest that Welty has quite deliberately attributed these particular doubts to Lorenzo Dow. His sense of love as protection and his concern with distance and safety have led him to isolate himself from true involvement with others. In his own way, his encounters with his congregations are as formal and ritualized as Murrell's with his victims. Allowing himself to identify with the heron as to one of God's particularly beautiful creatures—believing himself to have been granted a moment of grace in his love for the bird—Dow is shattered when it is suddenly destroyed. But as we have already noted in coming to understand how he persistently defends himself against loss, Dow cannot imagine getting *through* grief back to connection. So, as with the other two men, his view of his life and its meaning is momentarily shaken, but quickly restored as he rides off to his next sermon "on the subject of 'In that day when all hearts shall be disclosed'" (CS 199), as his so clearly has been to Welty's reader.

"A Still Moment" offers a clearer understanding of Welty's ongoing fascination with the archetypal figure of the wanderer. Whether she is speaking of historical wanderers such as Audubon, Dow, and Murrell or (in "First Love") Aaron Burr; her traveling salesmen, Tom Harris in "The

Hitch-Hikers," R. J. Bowman in "Death of a Traveling Salesman," and King MacLain in *The Golden Apples;* or such mythic figures as Odysseus, whose fate entails wandering for decades, such characters allow Welty to explore the virtually implicit trait they share of avoiding human involvement and commitment. The jobs many of these characters have chosen require leaving behind family responsibilities, and King MacLain's very motive for wandering is to abandon those responsibilities. The fates of these characters reflect Welty's fictive consideration of a lifestyle that she was drawn to because of its promise of new experience, although she ultimately concludes that it seems always to end in a poignant loneliness.

It was funny how sometimes you wanted to be in a circle
and then you wanted out of it in a rush. Sometimes
the circle was for you, sometimes against you,
if you were It. Sometimes in the circle you longed for
the lone outsider to come in—sometimes you
couldn't wait to close her out. It was never a
good circle unless you were in it.

Welty, Delta Wedding

CHAPTER 3

Circles and Labyrinths

The Characteristics of the Perceiver

Two essential images in Welty's fiction pertain to the contexts in which she believes understanding can take place. They express a condition—often social or psychological, sometimes spatial—necessary in the perceiver or seeker of knowledge. The circle and the labyrinth suggest ways in which characters may be excluded from knowledge or included within it, enclosed within some social definition or "free," entangled in their own obfuscating assumptions or placed where vision is possible. There is no simple equation in Welty's imagination between being inside a circle (as, for example, a family) and attaining full knowledge. Finding oneself within a radius of safety, however well-intended, can lead just as easily to frustration and suffocation as to understanding. Nor does status as an outsider guarantee perceptual accuracy. When Welty's characters become outsiders, they seem not so much free to observe as lost and without anchor. What she says of the traveling salesman Tom Harris in "The Hitch-Hikers" is true of anyone who chooses to remain distant from others: "He knew he would not be held by any of it. . . . None of any of this his, not his to keep, but belonging to the people of these towns he passed through, coming out of their rooted pasts and their mock rambles, coming out of their time. He himself had no time. He was free; *helpless*" (cs 72; emphasis mine).

Writing about her own travels and the sense she has of when she knows a city well enough to write about it, Welty has spoken about how valuable shifts in perspective can be to the perceiving self. She commented in an interview with Linda Kuehl that place is no less than

> my source of knowledge. It tells me the important things. . . . It helps me to identify, to recognize and explain. . . . To my mind, a fiction writer's honesty begins right there, in being true to those two facts of time and place. . . .
>
> You can equally well be true, I feel, to an *impression* of place. A new place seen in a flash may have an impact almost as strong as the place you've grown up in, one you're familiar with down to the bone, and know what it's like without having to think. I've written about place from either one extreme or the other, but not from partial familiarity or guessing—there's no solidity there. . . .
>
> ["Music from Spain," situated in San Francisco, is] written from the point of view of the stranger, of course—the only way to write about a strange place. On the other hand, I couldn't write a story laid in New York, where I've come so many times—because it's both familiar and unfamiliar, a no man's land. (Con 87–88)

But although Welty can write about a new *place* based on her vivid early impressions of it, she portrays her characters as needing a fuller experience of *situations* before understanding can take place. R. J. Bowman, in "Death of a Traveling Salesman," significantly misinterprets what he finds in the shotgun house nearby after his car rolls into a ditch. He believes he has met a mother and her grown-up son when, in fact, they are a young married couple about to have a baby. The woman's shapelessness has fooled him. Whereas part of the cause for his misunderstanding is a recent illness that has left him weak and "almost childlike" (CS 121) in his vulnerability, Bowman's loneliness and isolation ultimately account for his failure to recognize "a marriage, a fruitful marriage. That simple thing" (CS 129). Having failed ever to create a close relationship in his life, Bowman is shocked at his discovery, which drives him from the house back to the road, where he collapses, aptly enough, from heart failure.

Welty believes that understanding a situation most typically involves holding a dual position, not so completely enmeshed in the context as to be blind to its dynamics, yet not so much a stranger to it as not to know what is being seen. Ideally, one has had occasion to be *both* insider and outsider, to have seen the situation from both perspectives. Observing, from outside, what the limitations of an interior view of something might be allows one to reach a wider and more accurate apprehension of it. The recurrent contrast in Welty's stories between the wanderer and the one who stays at home reflects this dilemma. Those characters who move away, like Eugene MacLain in *The Golden Apples,* look longingly back at what they have left, as if staying might have been a wiser choice, and those who remain at home assume that they might have found more meaning for their lives had they chosen to leave.

The idea that if we are to understand something fully, it is best to have both an insider's knowledge of its intricacies *and* an outsider's perspective based on additional experience is developed with special vividness in Welty's story "Kin," which records a young woman's visit to relatives in an unnamed town in Mississippi "several hours by inconvenient train ride from Jackson" (CS 539). Dicey Hastings has lived in the North long enough now to have the perspective of an outsider to the world her Aunt Ethel and cousin Kate inhabit, even while she retains an insider's knowledge of that world. Her dual status proves crucial to her ability to recognize the discrepancies between what the family says about itself and some of what has actually happened.

The very first word in the story announces Dicey's momentary forgetting of the name of the family home, Mingo: "for the first moment I didn't know what my aunt meant. The name sounded in my ears like *something* instead of *somewhere*" (CS 538). Quickly oriented again, Dicey becomes aware of how her own perceptions have come to differ from those of her aunt and cousin. With a fiancé up North, Dicey considers herself "as having a great deal still waiting to confide" (CS 542), yet her desires are postponed by her aunt's and cousin's living "as if they had never heard of anywhere else, even Jackson" (CS 539) and their consequent assumption that Dicey should "keep up in spite of being gone almost [her] whole life, except for visits" (CS 538).

The difference between what Dicey and her cousin Kate (who is about the same age) comprehend is intimated early in the story in Dicey's recognition that they tend to use different adverbs: "I was thinking, if I always say 'still,' Kate still says 'always,' and laughed, but would not tell her" (CS 546). Phrasing her questions to the family in terms of whether or not something is still the same ("Uncle Felix! Is *he* still living?"), Dicey implicitly proclaims how much has happened in her life beyond this family and her bemusement that things here seem never to change. Using "always" to refer to the way things are, Kate unwittingly expresses the stability and sameness through the years of *her* world. Dicey notes this difference—as she does others during the story—but she does not tell Kate, who she feels would not understand. This perceptual distinction sets the stage for Dicey's and Kate's very different capacities to comprehend what has been happening in Uncle Felix's life.

The two young women are sent to visit their uncle, who has been ailing and is now being cared for by Sister Anne, a cousin of some sort whom Dicey at first does not remember and about whom even Kate is somewhat confused:

> "Mama, what is she?" asked Kate. . . . "I may be as bad as Dicey but I don't intend to go out there today without you and not have her straight."
>
> Aunt Ethel looked patiently upwards as if she read now from the roof of the tester, and said, "Well, she's a remote cousin of Uncle Felix's, to begin with. Your third cousin twice removed, and your Great-aunt Beck's half-sister, my third cousin once removed and my aunt's half-sister, Dicey's—"
>
> "Don't tell me!" I cried. "I'm not that anxious to claim kin!" (CS 540)

Aunt Ethel's response, especially the word "patiently," suggests that she sees her role as that of teaching the younger generation the family's values, in particular, the value of family itself. Even her reminiscences involve lessons the young women are meant to assimilate: "'When your mother was alive and used to come bringing you, visits were different,' said my Aunt Ethel. 'She stayed long enough to make us believe she'd fully got here. There'd be time enough to have alterations [of dresses], from Miss Mattie, too, and transplant things in the yard. . . . Our generation knew more how to visit, whatever else escaped us, not that I mean to criticize one jot'" (CS 541).

As a member of that older generation, Aunt Ethel herself acts in accordance with her society's requirements that ladies not speak of other people with open disparagement. Instead, she only obliquely hints at "truths" Kate and Dicey would never be told directly but are meant somehow to understand. Thus Aunt Ethel is willing to state a few facts about Sister Anne: "She never cooked nor sewed nor even cultivated her mind! She was a lily of the field." But beyond that, "'She has no inner resources,' confided my aunt, and watched to see if I were too young to guess what that meant" (CS 544). Welty exposes here the social use of language to conceal as well as reveal, to approach the boundaries between what can and cannot be said.

When the young cousins arrive at Uncle Felix's house, they are bewildered to see carriages and people gathered, and Kate concludes that Uncle Felix must have just died. Her dismay increases when Sister Anne's welcome provides no acknowledgment of the family's loss, until finally Kate bursts into tears, and the truth comes out. Felix is not dead; rather, Anne has turned the house over to an itinerant photographer who is taking photographs of people in the neighborhood. The parlor is all lit up, and everyone is dressed for the occasion "like Sunday and Election Day put together" (CS 550). Uncle Felix has been stashed in a small room at the back of the house where apples used to be stored in the winter, out of the way of the intruders and the truth of what is taking place in his home.

Led back to see him, Dicey is filled with memories of what the house was like when she visited it as a child ("always silvery . . . cypressy and sweet, cool, reflecting, dustless" [CS 557]), especially on Sunday afternoons after dinner, while the rest of the family napped, when she would bring Uncle Felix's stereopticon to him on the porch and he would share "pictures of the world" with her. These moments of happiness—Uncle Felix's sharing with the little girl his joy in thinking about the world beyond—have remained her most vivid memory of the time and have served as a foreshadowing of her adulthood, which she is living far from the southern community where Felix still has his home. Some of the adults in charge of Dicey's upbringing, her aunt in particular, are unaware that Uncle Felix has initiated her into this larger world. Dicey remembers how he would fold his coat and place it on the porch beside him, sitting in his shirtsleeves next to the child. Yet when she mentions to Aunt Ethel that he "had red roses on his suspenders," her aunt protests: "When did he ever take his coat off for you to see that? . . . He was a very strict gentleman all his life, you know, and made us be ladies out there, more even than Mama and Papa did in town" (CS 541). "Being ladies" appears to have involved being protected even from the sight of a gentleman without his jacket, and Aunt Ethel may well have felt, had she known, that Dicey should not have been shown those slides of far away, exotic places.

Instruments like the stereopticon, as we have seen, were favorites of Welty's father, and they serve in her stories (as in her imagination) as almost magical vehicles for glimpsing new dimensions of the world. But what little girls are to know about *is* distinct from the larger body of knowledge, and even the slides are marked with this in mind: "The slide belonging on top was 'The Ladies' View, Lakes of Killarney'" (CS 557). Dicey recalls:

> Some places took him a long time. . . . He handed each slide back without a word, and I was ready with the next. I would no more have spoken than I would have interrupted his blessing at the table. . . .
>
> It's strange to think that since then I've gone to live in one of those picture cities. If I asked him something about what was in there, he never told me more than a name, never saw fit. (I couldn't read then.) We passed each other those sand-pink cities and passionate fountains. . . . Yet there were things too that I couldn't see, which could make Uncle Felix pucker his lips as for a kiss. (CS 558)

Even Uncle Felix holds back some of the slides from Dicey, selecting those that he will allow her to see. Because these included some "passionate fountains," the thought of what he might have been withholding is tantalizing, even to Dicey's adult memory. At the time of this story the old man is unable to talk, but he seems to recognize Dicey and, recollecting perhaps their long-ago sharing of the pictures, he writes a cryptic message on the torn-out page of a hymnbook.

On their way out of the house, Dicey and Kate stop by the parlor to see Sister Anne take her turn at having her picture taken. In the parlor, which has been set up for pictures, Dicey notices the absurd version of reality depicted on the photographer's backdrop, which has itself been placed in front of the only portrait at Mingo, "the romantic figure of a young lady seated on a fallen tree under brooding skies: my Great-grandmother Jerrold, who had been Evelina Mackaill" (CS 561). Dicey remembers the picture now, even more vividly than if she could see it: "And I remembered—rather, more warmly, *knew,* like a secret of the family—that the head of this black-haired, black-eyed lady who always looked the right, mysterious age to be my sister, had been fitted to the ready-made portrait by the painter who had called at the door" (CS 561).

The falsification built into this portrait, with its "forest scene so unlike the Mississippi wilderness (that enormity she had been carried to as a bride . . . where she'd died in the end of yellow fever)" (CS 561), and Evelina's submission to the painting of her portrait in so unrealistic a milieu make Dicey feel a strong affinity for the woman, based on their both being aware of the stories that people insist on making of their own and others' lives. Dicey believes that she and Evelina share the same innocence of what was to come and the same courage to continue to look when faced with the truth. Despite the fact that "none of it, world or body, was really hers" (CS 561), Dicey believes that she sees in Evelina's eyes the truth of the hardship of her life and her "unknown feelings" about it. "Those eyes . . . saw out, as mine did; weren't warned, as mine weren't, and never shut before the end, as mine would not. I, her divided sister, knew who had felt the *wildness of the world behind the ladies' view.* We were homesick for somewhere that was the same place" (CS 561; emphasis mine).

Meanwhile, for her own photograph, which is her payment for allowing the photographer to use the parlor, Sister Anne chooses to hold an archaic fan covered with forget-me-nots "languidly across her bosom" as her picture is taken against the "absurd backdrop" (CS 562). She is, it seems, quite willing to be remembered as she never was. Now the photographs and portrait are seen in light of the fabrication they embody, the stories people and their families allow to be told and passed on—and the stories they (implicitly) hide. That Sister Anne should be excited about having her picture taken in such a manner, when as far as Dicey can imagine, there is no one to whom she could possibly give it, suggests her poignancy as a member of a family that has little sense of what makes up her life ("She has no inner resources" [CS 544]) and that views her, therefore, as anomalous, someone to be pitied.

But after these two reminders of the discrepancies between what people present to the world and the reality of what they are, Dicey finds herself ready to understand Uncle Felix's message that he seemed to urge her to hide from Sister Anne: "River—Daisy—Midnight—Please" (CS 561). Because his wife's name had been Beck, Kate doesn't even understand at first that Daisy is a woman's name. "I don't believe it," she declares when she glimpses the possibility that Uncle Felix might have had other experiences beyond what the family knew about (CS 563). Dicey doesn't completely understand either, but she comprehends the important part of it, the feeling conveyed. Consequently, when Kate says, "I expect by now Uncle Felix has got his names mixed up, and Daisy was a mistake," Dicey cannot so easily dismiss the knowledge she has glimpsed: "It was the 'please' that had hurt me. . . . Some things are too important for a mistake even to be considered. I was sorry I had showed Kate the message" (CS 564). Even the photographer, inured, one might expect, to the illusions people cling to, races from the house like an escaping Yankee at the intensity of falsehood. Dicey notes, "I felt the secret pang behind him—I know I did feel the cheat he had found and left in the house, the helpless, asking cheat. I felt it more and more, too strongly" (CS 564). Kate and Dicey end by laughing helplessly at Sister Anne's commonness and the vulgarity of what they have seen, but Dicey now knows irrevocably how different her understanding is from that of her cousin. As they ride back to Aunt Ethel, Dicey's thoughts turn back to the outer world, as she wonders if her fiancé is writing to her.

The pleasure of those glimpses into the still-unknown world that Dicey shared with Uncle Felix and the adult withholding of knowledge that a child is not supposed to know are paradigmatic moments in Welty's fiction. They help establish Welty's sense that the achievement of knowledge is a stripping away of the facades behind which adult truths have been held.

．　　．　　．

A number of critics have noted that Welty's stories feature characters who are outsiders facing the difficulties of becoming part of social groups, particularly families.[1] They are liminal figures, in Victor Turner's sense of the term, because while they may now have become part of the group in name, they have still not accepted or assimilated the family's value systems, which, characteristically, involve a way of being in the world that resists the ideas and desires of its new members.[2] The most typical such figure is the young wife of a major character, often from a different social class, who does not want to be absorbed into her husband's family entirely, but to keep him treating and valuing her as a separate and special individual. Wanda Fay (Chisom) McKelva in *The Optimist's Daughter,* Gloria (Beecham) Renfro in *Losing Battles,* and Robbie (Reid) Fairchild in *Delta Wedding* all struggle against their new families' implicit pressure to subordinate their personal priorities to those of the group they have entered.

The results may be comic, as with Wanda Fay McKelva's idea of elegance in decorating a complete bedroom in peach satin, or ominous, as with Gloria Renfro, an orphan who endures a rough initiation when some of her new relatives force pieces of watermelon down her throat to make her "admit" that Sam Dale Beecham (her husband's uncle) may have been her father (LB 259). In all such cases, however, even when one despises the character's behavior, as many readers do that of Wanda Fay, Welty shows the poignancy of being placed in such a position: longing, on the one hand, for a truly personal existence with the husband and, on the other, being pressured into assimilation in a family network that seems more interested in conformity than acceptance.

Delta Wedding makes the situations of outsiders particularly vivid, in part because of the very size and solidarity of the family depicted there and in part because of the characterization of Ellen Fairchild, who has been in the family for decades but is still somewhat detached. Ellen is the family's emotional center, yet at the same time she is able to view its members as if from a distance, slightly apart because her status as a Fairchild is through marriage. More obvious outsiders are nine-year-old Laura McRaven, who is visiting her Fairchild cousins; Robbie, the young wife of the family favorite, George Fairchild; and Troy Flavin, who marries Dabney Fairchild during the novel. Carol S. Manning rightly argues that this novel serves as a turning point in Welty's work. Whereas her earlier stories featured often strikingly lonely protagonists, shut out permanently (so it would seem) from meaningful communication and relationship with others, as well as dreamy, unusual, or even grotesque scenarios, "with *Delta Wedding,* the Southern family and community replace the isolated individual and the abnormal one as Welty's favorite focus."[3] It is as if Welty deliberately moves from her consideration of isolation and autonomy in their various guises to a text centering on characters' movement into the intense web of relationships within an extended family. Those outsiders who have recently married into the family are seen as rather tentatively and ambiguously related to the Fairchilds: Troy Flavin and Robbie Reid are both members of "lower" social classes and are seen as threatening the somewhat aristocratic self-image the Fairchilds would like to preserve. Yet, as Louise Westling notes, the insularity of the Fairchilds' way of life is implicitly doomed, and Troy and Robbie bring into their marriages a healthy and much-needed vitality.[4]

Laura's mother, born a Fairchild, died the previous year and left her to live alone with her father in Jackson. Those portions of the novel focusing on her perspective record the ambivalence she feels about this family whose self-sufficiency makes it seem so formidable. As the child views them, the Fairchilds are such a powerful force, a single entity, that she is ultimately overwhelmed at the prospect of being absorbed into the circle of their love. Thus, at the end of the novel, when Ellen invites her to stay on and become part of the family—something Laura had seemed to long for from the beginning—the child intuitively decides against doing so: "Laura felt that in the end she would go—go from all this, go back to her father. She would hold that secret" (DW 237). In this novel Welty begins to explore at length a theme that pervades much of the fiction she wrote thereafter: what it means to cross that threshold into a closed circle of relationship—what is left behind, and what is now possible. Troy's reaction is not depicted, but the novel does imply that both Robbie and Laura find something claustrophobic there, and it hints, as well, that the family's eldest daughter, Shelley, will leave, choosing another way of life.

．　．　．

Welty's story "First Love" presents another young protagonist, a deaf boy named Joel Mayes, who finds himself at the edge of a circle he longs to enter. As she did in "A Still Moment," Welty uses historical figures— this time, Aaron Burr and Harman Blennerhassett—as characters, but the central point of view, the consciousness the reader comes to know, is Joel's. Welty chose to make Joel deaf, she has said, because she knew little about Burr's personality and did not want to falsify it, so she created a protagonist whose own understanding would be limited to what he could see and infer. Beyond this very pragmatic concern, Joel's deafness also serves as a particularly apt metaphor for his isolation and loneliness.[5] Joel believes that everything would be clear to him if only he could understand the words that people speak to one another, but Welty recognizes and conveys to the reader that this is an illusion. Conversations may reveal remarkably little that is true, and Joel learns all he needs to know simply by watching. Although he does not understand the discussions he witnesses between Burr and Blennerhassett, he observes and interprets something crucial about them—the tone of urgency and significance the two participants bring to their conversations.

Before now, Joel's life had been dominated by a single event. His parents were lost the previous summer in the forest along the Natchez Trace, "cut off from him, and in spite of his last backward look, dropped behind" (CS 154), apparently taken by Indians. The boy's life was saved by the group's leader, Old Man McCaleb, who hid Joel and his fellow travelers in a canebrake to save them from discovery by approaching Indians. Watching McCaleb kill an excited dog with the blunt end of an axe to save their lives, Joel learned "what silence meant to other people" (CS 155). Yet in the canebrake he also experienced an oppressive interdependence: "Through the danger he had felt acutely, even with horror, the nearness of his companions, a speechless embrace of which he had had no warning, a powerful, crushing unity" (CS 155). Having undergone a particularly abrupt and dramatic separation from his parents, followed closely by the forced, total reliance on others—thus experiencing the sense of abandonment and of suffocation associated with the paradigm discussed in chapter 1—Joel much prefers the quiet privacy he now knows as boot boy at an inn in Natchez, where others sleep while he gathers and cleans the guests' boots. His painful experiences of vulnerability through the loss of loving parents and the necessity of relying on others for his safety have left him appreciating peace, safety, and relative isolation from others: "It seemed then that his whole life was *safely alighted*, in the sleep of everyone else, like a bird on a bough, and he was alone in the way he liked to be" (CS 156; emphasis mine).

From this peaceful seclusion Joel is awakened in his small room behind the saloon by the appearance of Burr and Blennerhassett, who arrive repeatedly in the middle of the night to discuss Burr's plans. Joel's position at the periphery of this inner circle of conspirators is visually emphasized by the lamp on the table, which reveals the two men's faces to Joel while leaving him just at the edge of the darkness, a detached observer.[6] Joel does not understand the content of the mystery shared by the two men, but he watches their faces and sees the intensity, "ardor," and commitment that Burr, especially, radiates: "All his movements and his looks seemed part of a devotion that was curiously patient and had the illusion of wisdom all about it. Lights shone in his eyes like travelers' fires seen far out on the river" (CS 159). Through images of fire, light, and rushing water, Welty builds her characterization of Burr, whose almost reckless passion captures the imagination of the mesmerized boy. The very fire in the fireplace would "flame up" as Burr talked (CS 159), while Joel looked out from the shadows, "the lone watcher of a conflagration. The room grew warm, burning with the heat from the little grate, but there was something of fire in all that happened. It was from Aaron Burr that the flame was springing" (CS 158). Noting the radiance of Burr's face, Joel sees how unconcerned with safety the older man seems to be in his preoccupation with his plans, so much so that Joel himself comes to feel protective and fatherly toward his visitors (CS 160).

One morning, observing the winter river break through frozen chunks of ice, releasing a "torrent of life," Joel is held motionless, "watching over it like the spell unfolding by night in his room" (CS 160). Joel sees in the churning river an image of the strength and passion he finds in Burr and tries to anticipate his fate: "Was any scheme a man had, however secret and intact, always broken upon by the very current of its working? One day, in anguish, he saw a raft torn apart in midstream and the men scattered from it. Then all that he felt move in his heart at the sight of the inscrutable river went out in hope for the two men and their genius that he sheltered" (CS 160).

What Joel feels move in his heart is, simply, love for the two men. They have brought into his life an awareness of a passion that is beyond safety and taught him implicitly that a concern with safety precludes passion because it precludes the kind of commitment that risks everything for the sake of what is loved. Although Joel had felt love for his parents and anguish at their loss, the title of this story, "First Love," reflects the *kind* of love that Joel observes in Burr and comes to feel himself—love that is full of possibility and willing to place everything on the line.

One night Blennerhassett's wife appears in the room and eventually takes her husband away with her, but before they go, she plays a fiddle. Her strange motions as she plays and the atmosphere brought into the men's eyes by her music recall to Joel a memory from his childhood—a flowering mimosa tree at his parents' home in Virginia. The "feathery puffs" of the tree had seemed "like thousands of paradisiacal birds all alighted at an instant," as if the tree lighted up the entire garden with brightness (CS 163), just as now, to Joel, Burr's presence seems full of fire, magnifying the light in his room. The image of birds as emblems for human aspiration— glimpsed earlier in the reference to Joel's peaceful, safe solitude, "like a bird on a bough" (CS 156)—will recur with a significant difference at the end of the story.

Matters take a distinct turn when, on "a 'false spring' day" (CS 166), Joel watches Burr's trial. Burr's grace, eloquence, and charm are all evident once again, but this time he uses them for "explaining away, smoothing over all that he had held great enough to have dreaded once. He walked back and forth elegantly in the sun, turning his wrist ever so airily in its frill, making light of his dream that had terrified him. And it was the deed they had all come to see" (CS 166). This betrayal of his dream is reenacted the following night, when Joel sees Burr disguise himself, blackening his once "radiant" face with shoe polish and putting on shabby clothes and a cap of turkey feathers. The narrator notes that the "youngest child in Natchez would have known that this was a remarkable and wonderful figure that had humiliated itself by disguise" (CS 167). Burr had "eluded judgment, that was all he had done" (CS 168), but he has also left Joel bewildered and disenchanted about the possible outcome of anyone's dreams. At the end of the story Joel wanders along "the Liberty Road" but sees there "the bodies of the frozen birds [that] had fallen out of the trees," and he weeps (CS 168). The dead birds remind the reader of the duality throughout this story of the cold, frozen, snow-benumbed landscape and the warmth of Burr's fiery passion. Human aspiration, for Joel, has been betrayed and killed by the chilling effects of falsity, the self-betrayal in Burr's ultimate decision to save himself by denying his dream. As with Lorenzo Dow in "A Still Moment," Burr's dream is ultimately sacrificed to a desire to be safe. Joel is left to question whether his glimpse of a love that was not about protection— what he thought he found in Burr's apparent passion for his project—was an illusion after all.

.　.　.

Another of Welty's characters finds herself permanently excluded from experience she longs to understand. The title character in "Circe" is hampered by her own immortality from understanding the secret of human lives, a mystery that particularly haunts her when she encounters the hero she is destined to love, Odysseus. Caught in the realm of eternity, outside the circle of human time, Circe is unprepared: "Oh, I know those prophecies as well as the back of my hand—only nothing is here to warn me when it is *now*" (CS 532). The story of Odysseus's visit to Circe's island is couched in terms of these two experiences of time. For Circe, for whom time is endless, the visit seems very brief, yet what in Circe's view (and from the text's perspective) has seemed to be overnight, has for Odysseus and his men been a year. Circe perceives their eagerness to leave as the blackest ingratitude.

This is not the only part of the men's behavior that bewilders her, however. When Circe restores Odysseus's men to their human form, they embrace, and she speculates: "Reunions, it seems, are to be celebrated. (I have never had such a thing.)" (CS 534). She knows that there is a "mortal mystery" (CS 533), but, ironically, her perspective is too wide to allow her to grasp the implications of finitude. Reunions are celebrated because mortals experience time as limited, and it is always possible, therefore, that one may never again see one's friends. To come together again is felt as a triumph, certainly an occasion for joy. Circe has all of time in which to experience or reexperience such encounters—depending on whether one views eternity as the eternal copresence of all experiences or as infinite time in which all things may happen again and again. By any definition, however, Circe does not understand the emotions that follow from human finitude: the poignancy of what might have been, the sorrow at what is now over, the pleasure at what is (because it might not have been), and the urgency brought into human lives by our awareness of the transitoriness of most of what is important to us. As Circe observes, somewhat bitterly, "ever since the morning Time came and sat on the world, men have been on the run as fast as they can go, with beauty flung over their shoulders" (CS 535). They have, she believes, no capacity to appreciate beauty, not having the leisure to contemplate it.

Instead, men tell themselves and each other stories about their lives, another human trait that Circe finds quaint and incomprehensible. She contrasts these men with the other male in her life: "I thought of my father the Sun, who went on his divine way untroubled, ambitionless—unconsumed; suffering no loss, no heroic fear of corruption through his constant shedding of light, *needing no story,* no retinue to vouch for where he has been—even heroes could learn of the gods!" (CS 533; emphasis mine).

In referring to human motivations, this passage clarifies some of the existential consequences of time-bound as opposed to timeless existence. Humans need stories to give the illusion of importance to finite lives, whose special urgency is that they might be lived without meaning (as in "Old Mr. Marblehall"). Because time is limited, humans are subject to loss; it is possible to consume time foolishly, to waste it. Human beings must choose how to live their lives (thus the notion of heroism, for which the gods have no need), and they feel a need to "vouch for" their use of the time they are given. All of this, Circe notes, is based in human frailty, yet without that frailty, mortals would be incapable of the *degrees* of joy and sorrow that make up human experience. In immortality as Welty envisions it, there is no capacity for the deepest grief or, consequently, for ecstatic joy. The enchantress wishes "for grief" when Odysseus leaves her, but "it would not come" (CS 537). In one sense, then, this story urges readers to contemplate the human consequences of living within time and to appreciate that much of the unique tenor of human experience relies upon a factor often considered an unhappy limitation. For Circe, it is a tantalizing secret: "Only frailty, it seems, can divine it—and I was not endowed with that property. They live by frailty! . . . Only to possess that one, trifling secret, I would willingly turn myself into a harmless dove for the rest of eternity!" (CS 533).

Another perspective for thinking about this story involves seeing the relationship of Circe and Odysseus as that of a woman and a man, and the question of how many of their differences are accountable to these terms and how many to their being, also, a goddess and a hero. There is humor in Circe's characterization of the men as greedy ("sizing up the household for gifts" [CS 531]), sloppy and dirty ("treading on their napkins, tracking the clean floor with honey" [CS 535]), and ungrateful. Beyond this, however, the story addresses an interplay of values ostensibly held by each gender. Circe is concerned with neatness, cleanliness, providing for the future (growing grapes), and making things (bread, broth, sewing), whereas Odysseus and his men rival one another and fulfill their love for adventure and excitement. The men's urgent experience of time, moreover, expresses a preoccupation much more characteristic of men than of women—certainly as it is depicted in most modernist fiction.[7]

Julia Kristeva is among those who have suggested that women's experience of time may, indeed, differ from men's because of how women's physiological experience is anchored in biological rhythms. Men tend to experience "time as project, teleology, linear and prospective unfolding; time as departure, progression, and arrival—in other words, the time of history."[8] This is the time, also, of wanderers, of those who need stories to account for their use of lives and opportunities that will never return. Here, in the linearity, the movement away from things, of this experience of time, Kristeva sees a re-creation of that decisive separation from otherness that Chodorow and Gilligan found so problematic for the "masculine" worldview. As Kristeva explains, "this temporality renders explicit a rupture, an expectation, or an anguish which other temporalities work to conceal."[9] Here, too, is an explanation for the urgency time places on human lives.

Women, though obviously mortal and therefore vulnerable to the anxiety that an awareness of the passage of time may generate, may be blessed by additional, alternative experiences. Kristeva argues that women may come to know two additional varieties of temporal experience:

Female subjectivity would seem to provide a specific measure that essentially retains *repetition* and *eternity* from among the multiple modalities of time known through the history of civilizations. On the one hand, there are cycles, gestation, the eternal recurrence of a biological rhythm which conforms to that of nature and imposes a temporality whose stereotyping may shock, but whose regularity and unison with what is experienced as extrasubjective time, cosmic time, occasion vertiginous visions and unnameable *jouissance*. On the other hand, and perhaps as a consequence, there is the massive presence of a monumental temporality, without cleavage or escape, which has so little to do with linear time (which passes) that the very word "temporality" hardly fits. . . . [This temporality is] all-encompassing and infinite like imaginary space.[10]

Thinking of what life would have been like for a woman "condemned to live forever" by her immortality,[11] Welty may have recognized an apt occasion for exaggerating the commonplace assumptions about the differences in men's and women's awareness of time. The humor of her story resides largely in the reader's recognition of those exaggerations "whose stereotyping may shock" but that nevertheless seem to reflect some of the felt differences people intuit when they consider what they know about the other gender. Circe's participation in "cosmic time" has left her ignorant of particular features of human, time-bound experience. If women experienced *only* these alternative varieties of time, and never the finitude and poignancy of mortality, then surely their ability to understand the consciousness of men would be so diminished as to leave men and women irrecoverably lost to one another. Caught in such a position, Circe feels, at the end of her story, how bitter is "the soft kiss of a wanderer" (CS 536). Pregnant with Odysseus's child, she is now part of the inevitable biological process that will bring forth their son, but the vision of her watching as he sails away is, perhaps, particularly moving to Welty's women readers. Like Snowdie MacLain in *The Golden Apples,* who waits for years for a husband who may or may not ever return, Circe may reflect Welty's acknowledgment of the waiting that is so deeply a part of some women's lives.

Such conflicting experiences of time are also a prominent feature of

Welty's story "Flowers for Marjorie." The protagonist, Howard, has come to feel shut out of the world of his pregnant wife and, as a consequence, quite alone in his despair that because he cannot find a job, they are in danger of starving. The illusion of physical self-sufficiency that Marjorie's pregnancy has given her constitutes a physical space that, like a protective circle, refuses to admit him: "Away at his distance, backed against the wall, he regarded her world of sureness and fruitfulness and comfort, grown forever apart, safe and hopeful in pregnancy, as if he thought it strange that this world, too, should not suffer" (CS 101). As he hears the ticking of the clock grow "louder and louder . . . feeling new desperation every moment" (CS 100), Howard's tortured consciousness drives him to violence. His despair so distorts his perspective that he views Marjorie and her understanding of reality as permanently lost to him ("forever apart"). He kills her, suddenly, unexpectedly, and only then does he think to throw the ticking clock out the window.

Howard's act may be viewed—as suggested in chapter 2 in the discussion of violence in "A Still Moment"—as having been brought about by a fracture of relationship, for Howard has been made to feel smothered by Marjorie's presence and his responsibility for her and yet, simultaneously, hopelessly alone.[12] Near her "he drew deep breaths of the cloverlike smell of her tightening skin . . . as he buried his face against her, feeling new desperation every moment in the time-marked softness and the pulse of her sheltering body" (CS 100). Yet in the moment just before he stabs her, he feels that "they were now both far away, remote from each other, detached" (CS 101). In a bizarre twist of circumstances, Howard seems to have killed not only Marjorie but her differing perspective on time, and he is thrust irrevocably into a linear time in which relentless changes take place, as if to mock Howard's belief that everything in the world had stopped except for her pregnancy. Everything that follows mocks Howard's sense of time and hints at how right Marjorie had been to have hope in the future. His "fortune" is reversed: he wins the jackpot at a slot machine; he is given roses and the key to the city as the ten-millionth person to enter Radio City; and traffic seems to stop when he wants to get by, while people "seemed to melt out of his way" (CS 105). Marjorie's murder, committed to free him from his sense of entrapment in a situation he could not face, becomes the act that traps him once and for all in the lonely consequences of his mortal choice.

．　．　．

If the image of the circle says something about the existential position of the seeker of knowledge, that of the labyrinth conveys many of the same connotations and elaborates upon them by reflecting the entangling dimensions of human consciousness or of the situations in which people find themselves. In her study *The Idea of the Labyrinth from Classical Antiquity through the Middle Ages,* Penelope Reed Doob notes that the richness of the labyrinth as a symbol results from its essential duality, its "embodiment of simultaneous artistry and confusion, order and chaos, product and process, depending on the observer's (or the writer's) point of view."[13] The image is especially appropriate for Welty's purposes because it embodies the interplay of order and disorder that so frequently underlies her stories. Even more centrally, the fact that one's experience of the labyrinth depends entirely upon one's perspective on it emphasizes her sense of the importance of the position of the observer, who must be ready in both a physical and a psychological sense to understand what is seen.

From within the labyrinth, one's experience is diachronic. The wanderer experiences successive turns and alternatives as choices that must be made if any progress is to occur. The maze may seem *impenetrable,* if the interior goal toward which one is moving seems elusive, or *inextricable,* if one is trying to escape from some sense of danger or entanglement felt to exist at its core. Labyrinthine impenetrability has often been seen as an allegory of Christian experience—pilgrims trying to avoid decisions that will cause them to be mired in sin and to find, instead, the one true path to salvation. Inextricability has been especially emphasized in the twentieth century as writers have attempted to show how humans create their own forms of personal and cultural entrapment.[14] The images associated with the interior experience of labyrinths include any that convey bewilderment and confusion, a need to make choices, and the absence of a clear path leading to freedom. Welty uses several of the images Doob lists, including crossroads, forest, ocean, and a series of caves, all reflecting the difficulty of making choices, just as in "A Still Moment" she used a forked tree as a meeting point, a crossroads, for her characters. The wandering so regularly featured in her stories entails the idea of poor judgments and choices; Doob associates "wanderings" with *errores,* as in "going astray."[15]

From outside the labyrinth, in contrast, one sees the whole pattern, and the human response tends to be not the confusion of the interior view but rather an aesthetic appreciation for the artistic design and complexity of the maze itself. The emphasis is on the maze as product rather than as process, and comprehension of the nature of the design—of how apparent disarray is in fact intricate design—is intellectually and aesthetically satisfying. The reader of difficult texts may first experience a stumbling, tentative, linear movement through the text, and then, in retrospect, come to see, in a synchronic moment of comprehension, the pattern of the whole. Welty's characters typically remain within their self-generated mazes, whereas her reader is offered clues to the wider perspective.

The labyrinth has temporal as well as spatial significance. The choices that it forces us to make are poignant because they take place within time. Our realization that any choice we make precludes others, because we do not have an infinity in which to try every choice, makes our decisions momentous. From outside, under the aspect of eternity, any one choice is perceived far differently. In the story "Circe" the goddess notices that her visitors are not as impressed by metamorphoses as is she, who can perform them: "That moment of transformation—only the gods really like it! Men and beasts almost never take in enough of the wonder to justify the trouble" (CS 531). Mortals cannot appreciate the aesthetic pleasure ("the wonder") of transformation because, from their perspective within time, transformation or change so often entails loss. Circe's artistic enjoyment is a function of her living in eternal time, during which everything is possible (or possible again), and no loss is necessary. The situation is analogous to the spatial experience of the labyrinth: from beyond finitude, it is possible to appreciate the labyrinth as a beautiful artifact; from within, it is only possible to understand it one turn at a time, never knowing what the next will bring.

For hundreds of years the labyrinth has stood as a powerful image for human lives. It is part of a configuration of images that, together, mirror human speculations about the nature of earthly existence.[16] Like the cave, the labyrinth or maze reflects the mundane world; set in opposition to it are the sky and images such as the temple, suggesting human aspirations toward a more celestial knowledge. The image of the dome has a dual purpose, signifying either the *outer* limits of human existence and understanding or the *inner* boundary of the heavenly realm, depending upon the poet's perspective. Two poets' uses of the dome image reveal the rich ambiguity of its liminal position. In "Byzantium" Yeats indicates that the domelike heavens offer a serene view of the labyrinth that is our mortal existence:

> A starlit or a moonlit dome disdains
> All that man is,
> All mere complexities,
> The fury and the mire of human veins.[17]

Conversely, as G. Wilson Knight observes, Shelley's use of the dome in "Adonais," instead of reflecting the eternal, contrasts with it: Life like a dome of many-colour'd glass / Stains the bright radiance of Eternity.[18] Throughout the long tradition extending back to Boethius and even to Plato, pairings of images express, as Peter Elbow phrases it, the opposition between "the cave and the sky . . . the two most famous and resonant epistemological metaphors from ancient times: slaves chained in Plato's cave, and the soul of Scipio Africanus looking down upon the tiny earth from the upper heavens. . . . Above all, the cave is associated with complexity and multiplicity, the sky with simplicity and unity."[19] Angus Fletcher, discussing Coleridge, offers a different pair of images with virtually identical meanings; he writes that "temple and labyrinth provide the models of sacred stillness and profane movement."[20]

Welty follows her poetic predecessors with her own variations on the dome image of the Romantic poets, even Coleridge's originary "pleasure-dome" in "Kubla Khan." In her story "The Purple Hat," one of the protagonists works in the Palace of Pleasure in New Orleans, where his job is to monitor events below him from "a little catwalk along beneath the dome." His perspective is far different from that of the Palace's customers, who are in the middle of the noisy commotion of a gambling house. For him, "somehow all that people do is clear and lucid and authentic there, as if it were magnified. . . . I can see everything in the world from my catwalk" (CS 224). Like the detached god or godlike artist, this unnamed protagonist has "the feeling now and then that you could put out your finger and make a change in the universe" (CS 227). Lorenzo Dow in "A Still Moment" longs for this same type of heavenly perspective, "to brood *above* the entire and passionate life of the wide world" (CS 191; emphasis mine). For the most part Welty's narrators alone have such a perspective. Her characters (with the rare exception of someone like Circe) are wanderers in the complex labyrinthine paths of the sublunary world beneath those domes.

. . .

Welty's most thoroughgoing exploration of the labyrinth image occurs in adjacent stories about the twin brothers Ran and Eugene MacLain in *The Golden Apples*. Whereas all of the remaining stories in her intricately structured collection feature female protagonists—and a community whose very name, "Morgana," conveys the idea of a feminine realm[21]— the stories of Ran and Eugene focus on the frustrations and ineffectuality of two brothers who have created for themselves the mazes that entrap them. As is so often the case in Welty's stories, these two characters are distinguished, on the surface, at least, in terms of one's decision to wander and the other's to remain in his hometown. Ran remains in Morgana; Eugene has left and moved to San Francisco. Although each assumes that his brother must have found something better in life, both, in fact, carry their entanglements within themselves. Looking at how these two stories mirror each other helps us to understand how the notion of labyrinthine entanglement functions in Welty's imagination.[22]

Ran's and Eugene's respective tales—"The Whole World Knows" and "Music from Spain"—differ in basic ways, but several parallels invite a comparison of the brothers' dilemmas. In each story the protagonist is estranged from his wife and unable to communicate his feelings of distress. The two wives, in turn, appear unconcerned by their husbands' malaise. Symbolizing their sense of imprisonment, Welty depicts both men as working behind bars—Ran as a bank teller and Eugene as a repairer of watches in a jeweler's shop. Both men are associated with running, which is explicit in Ran's name and in Eugene's childhood nickname, "Scooter." Each of them enacts real or imaginary violence against his wife: Eugene slaps his wife, Emma, on the morning of his story; Ran imagines shooting his wife, Jinny, at point-blank range with a pistol. Both young men echo the sins of their father, King, in leaving their wives, only to return later. In despair, they each choose to spend time with a stranger or near-stranger with whom there is no true relationship. For Eugene, this is a Spanish guitar player he saw perform the night before. For Ran, it is a young woman, Maideen Sumrall, whose "company was the next thing to being alone" (CS 377). Their companions are associated with femininity and gracefulness. Even the "big Spaniard . . . for all his majestic weight proved light on his feet, like a big woman who turns graceful once she's on the dance floor" (CS 401). Moreover, although both Maideen and the Spaniard are linked with dancing and music, the two brothers are not,[23] and for Welty—as for Yeats—this says something about the soul's despair.

Each brother travels with his companion toward a body of water (the Mississippi River, the Pacific Ocean); each hovers on a bluff overlooking the water, where he is in some jeopardy; and each backs away from it. If water signifies the possibility of rebirth, then both Ran and Eugene fail to take advantage of this opportunity for baptism or renewal into a new way of being. Elsewhere in *The Golden Apples* Welty uses water to suggest precisely such potentials. The early, staged drowning of King MacLain and the actual drowning of Mr. Sissum are followed in "Moon Lake" by Easter's survival from near-drowning and in "The Wanderers" by the luxuriant and restful swim of Virgie Rainey. Eugene himself once nearly drowned (CS 420). The three characters in the collection who have the potential for higher levels of understanding are each explicitly and positively associated with water: Virgie, Easter, and Loch Morrison, the junior lifesaver in "Moon Lake."

In both stories Welty has hinted at the circuitous nature of Ran and Eugene's obsessive thoughts by proliferating images of twisting and circularity that suggest getting nowhere. The MacLain brothers fail to become heroes of their own stories by failing to overcome their self-generated confusion and despair and by missing the opportunity each has to see his life from a new perspective. In the first of the two stories, "The Whole World Knows," Welty sets the stage by using images that are rarely found elsewhere in *The Golden Apples*. References to circles abound: Randall inscribes circles by repeatedly and obsessively driving back and forth along the main street of Morgana, in a movement much like the turning around and retracing of steps found in labyrinthine motion; there are references to his "*walking around in a dream*" (CS 380), to the Circle of ladies who gossip about his dilemma in dealing with an unfaithful wife, and to Jinny's faithlessness as being a "thing of the flesh," an "endless circle" (CS 381).[24] There are also references to locks of hair being cut, to spider webs (CS 383), and to the pigtails of the "little Williams girl" (CS 382), all reinforcing the connotations of the frequently mentioned croquet games and the crochet hook wielded by Jinny's mother, Lizzie Stark. "Croquet" and "crochet" both derive from the Old French word (*croc*) meaning hook, twist, bend, or curve.

These images are even more evident in "Music from Spain," where Welty treats the entire city of San Francisco as a kind of honeycomb of intricately connected—and dangerously interdependent—buildings, a physical labyrinth mirroring Eugene's emotional state. Even when Eugene manages momentarily to see the city from a more detached perspective, it is still portrayed as a labyrinth, differing from one occasion to the next precisely in terms of whether Eugene feels caught within it or outside somehow and able to view its aesthetic dimensions: "The city was so ugly at close quarters and so beautiful down its long distances" (CS 413). But Eugene's brief glimpses of San Francisco's beauty are all immediately qualified by his perception that this is a city of walls (CS 407). Suggestions of confinement, deception, and masking are ubiquitous, implied even by the trusses, braces, false teeth, false bosoms, and glass eyes that Eugene sees advertised in windows along Market Street (CS 397). During his day of wandering in the city, he sees images of corkscrews, twisting, and entanglement all around him: he vividly recalls his daughter, Fan, who (like the little girl in "The Whole World Knows") had worn pigtails; he stops to look in a shop window at "a double row of salmon steaks placed *fan*-wise on a tray, and filets of sole fixed this way and that down another tray as in a *plait*, like *cut off golden hair*" (CS 398; emphasis mine). He also notices a rhinestone Pegasus in a jeweler's window, the winged horse suggesting the idea of flight and, perhaps, by extension, those other winged figures from Greek mythology Daedalus and Icarus, who flew away from (and so escaped) the labyrinth at Crete.

The use of these images reaches a crescendo in a passage immediately following Eugene's acknowledgment of his despair and helplessness at the death (for which he blames his wife) of his daughter, Fan:

Each rounded house contained a stair. Every form had its *spiral* or its *tendril*, outward or concealed. Outside were fire-escapes. He gazed up at the intricacies of those things; sea gulls were sitting at their heads. How could he make a fire-escape if he were required to? The laddered, tricky fire-escapes, the *mesh* of unguarded traffic, *coiling springs,* women's *lace,* the *nests* in their purses—he thought how the making and doing of daily life *mazed* a man about, eyes, legs, ladders, feet, fingers, like a *vine*. It *twined* a man in, the very doing and dying and daring of the world, the citified world. He could not set about making a fire-escape to his flat in Jones Street, given all the parts and the whole day off. (CS 413–14; emphasis mine) [25]

Much of the wandering of Eugene and his Spanish companion is visualized as the traversing of labyrinthine paths, as in the "entire maze" of the big hotel through which they search for the men's room, with its "caves" of adjoining cubicles (CS 411). As the two leave the bluff overlooking the Pacific, Welty writes that "they looked together for the thread of the way back" (CS 424). The idea of following threads or clues appears regularly in Welty's writing, fiction and nonfiction alike, as does the image of the maze itself. In "No Place for You, My Love," for example, two unhappy characters, near strangers to each other, try to leave their troubles behind by driving south from New Orleans. Welty's narrator comments, "The stranger in New Orleans always sets out to leave it as though following the clue in a maze. They were threading through the narrow and one-way streets" (CS 467).[26]

The MacLain twins are too caught in timidity and self-delusion to find ways out of their dilemmas. Their situations and preoccupations link them imaginatively to that famous obsessive figure of southern fiction, Quentin Compson in Faulkner's *Sound and the Fury*. Rebecca Mark argues persuasively that "The Whole World Knows" deserves explicit comparison to the section on Quentin in Faulkner's novel:[27] for example, Quentin's obsessive concern with the watches in a jeweler's window, the reference to a little Italian girl in pigtails who follows Quentin around Cambridge on the last day of his life (is this William's girl in pigtails? [CS 382]), and the structure of the section itself, which involves Quentin's dialogue with his absent father. Ran conducts imaginary dialogues with his own absent father, although at times they encompass his brother as well ("Father, Eugene! What you went and found, was it better than this?" [CS 392]). Moreover, he recalls actual conversations with his mother that Welty records in the italics used so effectively in *The Sound and the Fury*.

Welty may indeed have been rethinking the dilemma of one of Faulkner's most Prufrockian characters, doubling Quentin's story into the tales of Ran and Eugene.[28] Quentin's circumstances are mirrored in *both* MacLain brothers' stories through parallels that pair two or all three stories in myriad ways. All three young men are obsessed with an absent woman (Caddy, Emma, Jinny); all wander near bodies of water, accompanied at least part of the time by a stranger; all talk to a father figure (Quentin and Ran to absent fathers, Eugene to the explicitly "fatherly" Spaniard [CS 415], absent in the sense that he speaks and understands only a foreign language). Quentin and Eugene are both associated with their residence in a faraway city, taking trolleys on a day when they play hooky from their "jobs." The correspondences between Quentin and Ran are just as striking, for both of them attempt suicide (Quentin successfully), both fantasize about (but ultimately fail at) killing their rival, and both are accused of sexual misconduct with a stranger (Quentin with the little Italian girl and Ran with Maideen). If *The Golden Apples* is to be taken as reflecting Welty's position on this matter, then she seems to share with Faulkner, and numerous other modernist writers, the sense that males have a difficult or impossible task in finding ways to be heroes in the modern world, which is to say, metaphorically, that they cannot find or generate meaningful "stories" for their lives.[29]

The content of Ran and Eugene's malaise involves a sense of entrapment, but the particular sort of entrapment they experience is that of relationships, specifically relationships with the women in their lives. Their father, King, had simply run away from his marriage to Snowdie. Ran and Eugene do so *internally*, finding their commitments to their wives claustrophobic, although neither of them seems to recognize why this is so. But the possible cause is hinted at. Snowdie herself, abandoned by her husband and seen as a saint by the citizens of Morgana, is revealed in "The Whole World Knows" as, intentionally or not, placing additional emotional pressure on Ran: "*Have you been out somewhere, son?*—Just to get a little air.—*I can tell you're all peaked. And you keep things from me, I don't understand. You're as bad as Eugene Hudson. Now I have two sons keeping things from me.*—I haven't been anywhere, where would I go?—*If you came back with me, to MacLain Courthouse, everything would be all right*" (CS 375).

This, too, is a legacy from their father. The exaggerated poignancy of their mother's life appears to carry over into their own marriages. For example, Eugene slapped his wife when she "said some innocent thing to him—'Crumb on your chin' or the like" (CS 393). Although he was "without the least idea of why he did it," it seems evident that Emma has made the mistake of *presuming* their relationship. Her wifely comment takes as a given the stability and affection of their tie to one another, and Eugene suddenly feels smothered. Although he has abandoned Morgana for San Francisco and, thus, would seem to be a wanderer, Eugene is precisely like his brother in having internalized the oppressive sense of relationship that apparently motivated King to leave his family time and again. The brothers' ultimate failure to dispel these feelings of entrapment is quietly reinforced in the fact that the final word in each character's story is, simply, his wife's name.

Eugene's feelings, in particular, are projected onto his experience of San Francisco, which he sees as a city of walls precariously interdependent on one another. His worst fear is that these walls might collapse, as in another catastrophic fire: "It would be terrifying if walls, even the walls of Emma's and his room, the walls of whatever room it was that closed a person in in the evening, would go soft as curtains and begin to tremble. If like the curtains of the aurora borealis the walls of rooms would give even the illusion of lifting—if they would threaten to go up. . . . But the thing he thought of wasn't really physical" (CS 407–8). The thing he is thinking of is psychological. The most fearful thing he can imagine would be no walls between himself and Emma, his complete vulnerability to her wifely assumptions, as if he does not have a strong enough self to withstand her. The walls of the labyrinth in Eugene's mind are paradoxical in that they intervene between himself and others (thus guaranteeing a measure of distance and safety) and simultaneously make him feel isolated, caught in lonely, inhibitory paths. He fears the dissolution of these walls as much as he does their presence.

The notion of Eugene, in particular, as a potential hero is strengthened by a number of details and allusions in Welty's story. His name itself is suggestive; it means "well-born" or "noble," implying someone favored by the gods. His nickname, "Scooter," emphasizes his running and suggests two opposing implications: first, the idea of running away from one's problems and from relationships (as both Eugene and Ran do), and second, the idea of running as a characteristic behavior of heroes. The theme of running is particularly relevant to a collection of stories entitled *The Golden Apples,* which has as a basic mythic source the story of Atalanta, famous for her speed and for being distracted by golden apples flung in her path. Being "fleet of foot" (CS 403) is a trait of heroes, and it is worth noting that the protagonist Virgie Rainey is frequently said to be running in the early stories.[30] Eugene's own closest approximation to heroism consists of his running to push the Spaniard out of the way of an approaching automobile: "He did not have time to think, but sprang forward as if to protect his own" (CS 401). This is crucial, of course. Eugene does not have time to be cautious, to brood or worry, and so something spontaneous can come out of him. He is exhilarated by the sudden, unanticipated event. "With his hand, *which could have stormed a gate,* he touched the Spaniard's elbow"

(CS 403; emphasis mine). But the heroism is short-lived. Later in the story Eugene and a crowd simply watch as a woman is struck down and killed by a trolley: " 'She's dead, I'm pretty sure,' Eugene said, but determined to keep his single voice a *cautious* one" (CS 410; emphasis mine).

The winged horse Pegasus served as a friend and aide to the hero Bellerophon, a potential role Eugene does not seem to recognize. In contrast to the power of this winged horse, a favorite of the Muses that brought forth a spring on their mountain (Helicon) by stamping its hoof, we find this meaningful juxtaposition in Welty's story. Immediately after Eugene notices some fallen eucalyptus leaves and "his shoes suddenly stamped them hard as hooves," Welty's narrator records this scene: "A quarrel couldn't even grow between him and Emma. And she would be unfair, beg the question, if a quarrel did *spring up;* she would cry. That was a thing a stranger might feel on being introduced to Emma, even though Emma never proved it to anybody: she had a *waterfall of tears* back there. He walked on" (CS 395; emphasis mine). There is nothing adventitious in this sequence; Welty is pointing to Eugene's ineffectuality by suggesting that the only thing he can cause to spring up are his wife's tears, so different from life-affirming waters.

An additional mythic substructure inviting the reader to see Eugene as a failed heroic figure consists of Welty's evocation in "Music from Spain" of two bullish figures associated with the Cretan labyrinth: the Minotaur itself and the bull-god Dionysus. Among various qualities attributed to the Spaniard, he is regularly seen as being bull-like. With his large, shaggy head, revealing a smile like that "on the face of a beast," the Spaniard exhibits a gigantic appetite when he orders vast amounts of food and (presumably like the Minotaur after his annual feast) spits out bones, leaving a pile of them behind when his meal is done (CS 407, 409). Eugene envisions him "with horns on his head," breathing fire, as indeed he seems to do when he smokes cigarettes and smoke comes "out of his nostrils in a double spout" (CS 408); again, one might think of Bellerophon, who, with the help of Pegasus, slew the Chimera, another fire-breathing monster.[31] Standing at the bluff at Land's End, overlooking the Pacific, the Spaniard wags "his enormous head," lets out a "bullish roar," and then "a bellow" (CS 421, 423)—at the moment Eugene hovers precariously above him.

The two bull figures serve as emblems for mythic roles Eugene might choose to play, either of which might enable him to generate new life and vital energy and to leave behind his spiritual malaise. Eugene might, that is, choose to become a hero, either a scapegoat or a savior, in his relationship with the Spaniard.[32] If the Spaniard is viewed as a possible avatar for the Minotaur, then Eugene might become a hero (Theseus-like) who destroys him and takes over as newly crowned king (replacing the older king, as suggested by his father's name). Eugene's intuition that this might be possible takes place on the bluff overlooking the Pacific—evoking an image of the island of Crete—when he realizes that just a small push would topple the Spaniard into the sea. Conversely, he might let the Spaniard throw *him* into the sea, assuming the role of scapegoat to save the land. In either case, the journey through the labyrinth has led Eugene and the Spaniard directly toward this potential for conflict and resolution, but Eugene backs away, and they leave (and eventually part) with Eugene still caught in the mazy paths of his own making.

The second figure evoked by the Spaniard is Dionysus, a bull-god particularly associated with fertility and a passionate vitality that is the antithesis of Eugene's passivity. On the streets of San Francisco, among many exotic and odd incidents, Eugene notices a lovely woman who is marked all over by shadowy patches: "Curves, scrolls, dark brown areas on light brown, were beautifully placed on her body, as if by design, with pools about the eyes, at the nape of her neck, at the wrist, and about her legs, too, like fawn spots, visible through her stockings. She had the look of waiting in leafy shade" (CS 404). In Euripides' play *The Bacchae,* Dionysus and his followers are dressed in fawn skins, and the god joins his Bacchae in "their whirling dances" in nearby forest glens.[33] Eugene is especially anxious that the Spaniard not see the woman, as if he recognizes her potential as a Bacchante, who might be carried away in celebration of the god: "something made him afraid of the Spaniard at that moment" as if the Spaniard "might pounce upon her" (CS 404) and she be too susceptible to him. In addition to his connection with fertility, as basic as that of the goddess Demeter, Dionysus is known for revelry, for transformations (he often appears in disguises and masks), for prophecy, and for a frenzied destructiveness that (in an Apollonian context) constitutes utter chaos.[34] Little wonder that the obsessively precise and careful repairer of watches—Eugene—is unable to join a Dionysian companion in an impassioned self-transformation, letting go of all caution and even of the self for the sake of some greater incarnation of fertility.

The woman Eugene observes is "marked as a butterfly is, all over her visible skin" (CS 404), an image that recurs several times in Eugene's story.

A stranger who passes him has a butterfly tattooed inside his wrist, causing Eugene to think about how vulnerable the spot is and how the tattoo had "come perilously near to piercing the skin" (CS 400). And the single specific word spoken by the Spaniard in this story is "Mariposa," the Spanish word for "butterfly." The cocoon of the butterfly obviously forms another of those corkscrew-shaped, confining spaces from which Eugene *might* emerge with the new life so often symbolized by the butterfly. But it is entirely characteristic of him that whenever he sees this image, his thoughts turn to safety.

In a narrative strategy that Welty uses often, she withholds the name of the Spanish guitar player until very late in her story, as if to provide the final piece of a puzzle. In doing so, she evokes the myriad sacrifices to the gods recorded in ancient literature and, in particular, those involving the sacrifice of bulls. The creation of the ancient labyrinth at Crete was a result of Minos's failure to sacrifice a particularly beautiful white bull to the god Poseidon. As a punishment, Poseidon caused Minos's wife, Pasiphaë (whose name is a title for the moon), to fall in love with the bull and, as a result of their coupling, to give birth to the Minotaur. Minos commissioned the artisan Daedalus to create the labyrinth where the monstrous offspring was to be kept. The horns of the bull are associated with the crescent-shaped moon, and the moon in turn has always been associated with women and fecundity, so that the powerful sexuality of the bull, conflated with these other images, constitutes a myth whose ultimate meaning has to do with new life. At the end of the story, the Spaniard "seemed to be looking in the sky for the little moon" (CS 425), and Eugene returns to his wife at home, where they have wine and grapes for supper (CS 426).

The sacrifice most relevant here involves rituals that emerged from these ancient stories. Robert Graves writes: "White bulls, which were peculiarly sacred to the Moon . . . figured in the annual sacrifice on the *Alban mount* at Rome, in the cult of Thracian *Dionysus,* in the mistletoe-and-oak ritual of the Gallic Druids . . . and . . . in the divinatory rites which preceded an ancient Irish coronation." [35] Welty's name for the guitar player—Bartolome *Montalbano* (CS 426)—seems a direct reference to the rituals of renewal associated with the "Alban mount," especially since she might so readily have named him after the musician she herself had seen perform: Andrés Segovia (OWB 86). The convergence of bulls, fertility rituals, the moon, Dionysus, and the scene of struggle on the cliff overlooking the Pacific Ocean suggests a way of understanding the story as a whole—as the chronicle of Eugene's opportunity to be a hero by grappling with a monstrous figure or sacrificing himself to the battle, either of which might have led to some radically new form of life or understanding.[36]

Welty's use of mythology is reminiscent of Freud's well-known image of the human past as an ancient city buried beneath the foundations of the city we can see.[37] The buried city provides strength and substructure and affects in little-known ways the architectonics of the city now existing. Human memory, in Welty's view of things, is similarly structured; nothing we deeply assimilate remains irrelevant to later ways of knowing. Thus, although Welty has said that she has tended to use mythology in her fiction, at times, rather too liberally ("I just used them as freely as I would the salt and pepper" [Con 331]), in an effort to understand the various levels of coherence of many of her stories, especially the more elusive ones such as "Music from Spain," mythology sometimes offers our only clues to recognizing the principles organizing the text. In our efforts to understand the richness of allusion and implication in Welty's stories, we ignore the "ruins of Athens" (cs 213, 313) that are glimpsed there at the risk of remaining in unnecessary darkness.

....

I know, I feel
the meaning that words hide;

they are anagrams, cryptograms,
little boxes, conditioned

to hatch butterflies . . .
H. D., Trilogy

Names were nothing and untied no knots.
Welty, The Robber Bridegroom

CHAPTER 4

Fictions, Names, Masks

Surfaces and the Hiddenness of Truth

In her essay "Words into Fiction," Eudora Welty tells of how as a child and "an unwilling sightseer" she went with her family to visit Mammoth Cave in Kentucky. They experienced there an utter contrast between the cold dark in which they first stood and the blinding light that then plunged them into "a prism" of color in which nothing could be seen because everything was "blotted out by radiance." The guide gave his memorized speech about bats, and they were sent back into darkness as the light was put out. Welty felt only "how right I had been in telling my parents it would be a bore" (ES 136).

In this essay Welty creates her own allegory of the cave—strikingly different from Plato's—in order to speak of what life, "fiction's territory . . . the so-called raw material is *without its interpretation;* without its artist" (ES 136). For Welty the cave ultimately offered a lesson:

> Without the act of human understanding . . . experience is the worst kind of emptiness; it is obliteration, black or prismatic, as meaningless as was indeed that loveless cave. Before there is meaning, there has to occur some personal act of vision. And it is this that is continuously projected as the novelist writes, and again as we, each to ourselves, read.
>
> If this makes fiction sound full of mystery, I think it's fuller than I know how to say. . . . The mystery lies in the use of language to express human life.
>
> In writing, do we try to solve this mystery? No. . . . In very practical ways, we rediscover the mystery. (ES 136–37)

At least two dimensions of this anecdote deserve close attention. First, and easiest to see, is Welty's emphasis on the importance of mystery in life *as mystery,* as a permanent lure for all of us in our desire to understand. The image of the cave in her fiction often serves to suggest a dark innerness to life itself toward which we are drawn, especially when such lights as fireflies hint at the possibility of seeing. Perhaps because in the South the sun's brightness is so intense that the dark, welcoming shade of trees seems particularly appealing, Welty finds in such contrasts of light and dark a master trope in which she can speak of the possibilities for knowledge. Her characters are often drawn in toward darkness rather than out into harsh light. Loch Morrison, for example, views a magnolia tree with his telescope: "The magnolias were open all over the tree at the last corner. They glittered like lights in the dense tree that loomed in the shape of a cave opening at the brought-up-close edge of the Carmichael roof" (CS 277).

For Plato, being freed to leave the cave promised a clearer vision, but for Welty, the cavelike coolness and darkness echoed in such phenomena as trees both recall that domelike world in which she sees us living and offer a glimpse of a mystery she wants very much to preserve, for she sees it as the magnet that draws us. Welty does not intend to *solve* the mystery but to *reveal* it; courting it is one of the pleasures she and her characters share. And while she often, in all of her writing, uses expressions such as "according to our lights" (ES 154) to indicate the conventional meaning, "according to our understanding," light—and in particular, bright light—can also signify the opposite of understanding when it blots out all subtleties. Thus, in discussing her story "No Place for You, My Love," which takes place in the heat and glare south of New Orleans, Welty notes "that secret and shadow are taken away in this country by the merciless light that prevails there. . . . I was writing of exposure, and the shock of the world" (ES 112–13).

The images of light that Welty evokes in her nonfiction essays are the gentler, more tentative lights of such objects as stars, which she uses to suggest visually the degrees of knowledge people sometimes achieve. Her essays on other writers, especially, reveal a tendency to characterize their work in such terms. She writes that Katherine Anne Porter's moral convictions stand at the center of her work: "They govern her stories down to the smallest detail. Her work has formed a constellation, with its own North Star" (ES 33). The novels of Jane Austen form a "constellation of six bright stars" deeply embedded in the crowded sky "of English literature" (ES 3). And in characterizing those dimensions of experience realized in Chekhov's fiction, she observes that "reality is no single, pure ray, no beacon against the dark. It might be thought of as a cluster of lesser lights, visible here on earth like the windows of a village at night, close together but not *one*—some are bright, some dim, some waywardly flickering" (ES 63). Welty rarely envisions comprehension in terms of the brightness of daylight.[1]

The second feature to note in Welty's allegory of the cave is her emphasis on the meaninglessness of all experience before human beings attend to it and begin to interpret it. She understands that human beings alone have the capacity to bestow meaning on experience. Moreover, the only way to share with one another our sense of the kind of meanings things have for us is through language. Yet language itself is problematic; words never simply convey what we intend in choosing them. As Welty has written, "we start from scratch, and words don't; which is the thing that matters—matters over and over again" (ES 134).

Welty has come far from her early beliefs about language. In childhood she had a sense of almost magical possibilities inhering in words to reveal the truth. Of her early love of words, she has said: "I live in gratitude to my parents for initiating me—and as early as I begged for it, without keeping me waiting—into knowledge of the word, into reading and spelling, by way of the alphabet" (OWB 9). In her reminiscences are several episodes in which language took on new dimensions for her, as on the evening when the moon turned from flat to round and *became* its roundness in her mouth as she spoke the word "moon" (OWB 10). To an unusual degree, her sensuous awareness of the resonances of language has remained vivid throughout her life, as all of her fiction attests. Yet her understanding of language is by no means naive. She does not assume any simple correspondence between words and what they signify, her experience with the word "moon" notwithstanding. Rather, as she came to understand how people use language to tell themselves and others stories about their lives, she realized that language is as often a vehicle for hiding and obscuring truths as it is for revealing them. Welty has said that she was disappointed when she first discovered "that books were not natural wonders, coming up of themselves like grass" (OWB 5), but were actually produced by people, including, to her amazement, a young classmate of hers ("illusion-dispelling was her favorite game" [ES 282]). Having begun with an idealistic belief in what she would find in books, in what words could achieve,[2] she was taken aback but also fascinated as she learned how language points both toward and away from accurate understanding. Not surprisingly, then, the fabrications and evasions that language makes possible constitute a recurrent theme in her stories. Welty is perpetually concerned with how language misleads people and falsifies experience—not merely as examples of the limitations of language itself, although she shares this postmodernist awareness—but because of the misunderstandings and pain she reveals in characters who trust it, as she once did, to provide a reliable basis for knowledge and for action.

It is impossible to pinpoint precisely when (in her life or her fiction) Welty's understanding of language shifted from the representational view her early experience taught her—that words stand for something real in the world—to a recognition that language "makes" truths rather than "pointing to" or "finding" them.[3] At least since she wrote *The Golden Apples* in the 1940s, however, her preoccupation with the problematics of naming suggests that she has long understood the tentativeness of words and the ways in which language embodies *interpretations* of reality rather than anything objectively verifiable.

The philosopher Richard Rorty has characterized in a particularly helpful way how each of us uses language to perpetuate our idiosyncratic ways of thinking about reality: "All human beings carry about a set of words which they employ to justify their actions, their beliefs, and their lives.

These are the words in which we formulate praise of our friends and contempt for our enemies, our long-term projects, our deepest self-doubts and our highest hopes. They are the words in which we tell, sometimes prospectively and sometimes retrospectively, the story of our lives. I shall call these words a person's 'final vocabulary.'"[4]

Rorty goes on to characterize the position of the "ironist," who, like Welty, recognizes the contingency of language.[5] Ironists, he notes, are people who realize that the final vocabulary they use is the result of individual experiences in a particular time and place, their assimilation from their social and intellectual environments of specific ways of thinking about their lives. We each rely on final vocabularies, but ironists are aware enough of the contingency of all language to have doubts about any one person's final vocabulary, including their own. Ironists remain open to an appreciation of others' vocabularies, recognizing that they may prove to be impressive in accounting for dimensions of experience that their own vocabularies fail to make as accessible.

In her attention to language, Welty recognizes its inherent failure to address anything essential about the realities it purports to describe, even as, paradoxically, she remains captivated by its richness and evocativeness. Language characterizes *versions* of reality by exploiting currently valorized metaphors that explain, more or less effectively, what is likely to happen in a given situation. That is, we choose to adopt newer vocabularies based largely on their predictive value vis-à-vis those aspects of reality that matter most to us. Whatever the essences of things may be, language is not a successful means of reaching them.[6] Language tells us much more about our perceptual "styles" and preferences than it can about objective phenomena—but it is no less fascinating for all that. Language is how we *constitute* our world; it shapes and structures what we are able to see. Experiences unaddressed by our vocabulary are experiences we are scarcely able to assimilate, and Welty's characters often search for words to make events comprehensible and real. As she observes in *The Golden Apples,* "some performances of people stayed partly untold for lack of a name" (CS 296). This chapter focuses on Welty's increasing awareness of the tenuousness of language, of how humans *use* language for a number of ends that have little to do with seeking truth, and of how language becomes, therefore, another of many surfaces that we must take into account in recognizing the fictions that permeate our cognitive lives.

Welty's persistently ironic vision of the import of words is evident in her story "A Sketching Trip" in which a simple mistake in pronunciation sets the stage for the revelations to follow. The story begins with the spoken words "Violence, violence," vividly recalled by the protagonist, Delia Farrar, as she passes the gates of Fergusson's Wells, where she and her mother had come twenty years earlier to vacation and drink the benevolent well waters. Holding up handfuls of violets, some children had offered "Violence, violence" to the girl and her mother, their mistake announcing—more truly than they could have realized—what was to be found at the Wells. Delia, now an adult, returns to spend an afternoon at this old site, where her memories reveal a truth to her about a family's pain and an act of violence that she only dimly understood at the time.

The story focuses recurrently on the surfaces that adults create—stories, appearances, masks—that provide children with a benign vision of reality and effectively postpone their understanding of life's complexities so that only much later, as with Delia, does a character begin to understand how events that have been observed actually fit together. The innocent misnaming by the children holding the flowers corresponds to Delia's own childish understanding of the events of that long-ago time. Her ignorance of the implications of what she witnessed as a child is seen in the fact that whenever she has thought back to Fergusson's Wells and her visit there, it has been with "an undisturbed belief that the greatest happiness had quite naturally occurred here, some magnificent festivity, a spectacle of beauty" (ST 62). Her childhood memories reveal that the vividness, beauty, and texture of the place made up most of her experience. Much of what she saw seemed dreamlike, almost too pleasurable to bear: "She stood *in deep bliss* with her hand moving upon the trunk of a cedar tree, with its purple-green above her dense like the breast of a bird" (ST 66; emphasis mine).

Even the act of violence she witnessed has been remembered only insofar as it contributed to the general excitement of a vacation during which the child had been allowed to "run wild" (ST 63) while her mother rested. Not understanding what she sees, the young Delia is witness to Mr. Fergusson's shooting of Mr. Torrance. The reader recognizes that Torrance humiliates Fergusson during a magic act in which he takes his rival's hat and pulls a rabbit from it, just as he has been implicitly mocking him in his attentions to Fergusson's wife. What Delia enjoys about the moment of crisis is the scene of ladies fainting "one after the other, as if they were weak" into the arms of nearby men (ST 69). Sensing that what is happening may offer her a glimpse of something *real* about adults, Delia tries to get closer by pushing through the barrier of adults: "In a moment some hand was going to stop her, but while she could she wanted to see" (ST 68). She is, of course, picked up and carried away; the next morning she and her mother leave Fergusson's Wells, and the "incident had never been mentioned again" (ST 69).

As a child Delia failed to understand how adults create facades whose purpose is to disguise what is actually taking place. As a young adult in the present time of the story, she has learned to recognize that there are complex relationships between surfaces and what lies beneath, as is seen in her observation of the meadow as she arrives at Fergusson's Wells. An artist deeply moved by the beauty around her, she muses about how impossible it is to capture with her painting what she feels in reaching out to the world, a joy that is "only a touching of the outward pulse, the awareness of a tender surface underneath which flowed and trembled and pressed life itself. It was as if this pulse became the green of leaves, the roundness of fruit, the rise and fall of a hill, when she began to paint, and could have become—anything" (ST 62).

Several images in Welty's narrative show that surfaces were there to see, if the child had been able to recognize them *as surfaces*. Mr. Torrance, that philanderer, presents a face "as perfect as wax fruit" (ST 65) and, as he plays the magician, dramatically lowers his eyes "as if he put on a mask and watched them through little holes" (ST 68). Mrs. Fergusson, who has so much to hide, bewilders young Delia with her remarkable imperviousness: "She was a creature of a baffling and terrifying sameness" (ST 64). She calls all of the children and even the rabbit Mirrabel "Precious," "never once [transforming] herself, even in her voice, by saying one thing to this person, another thing to another" (ST 64). Delia is fascinated, for little about Mrs. Fergusson seems natural or comprehensible: "Mrs. Fergusson's reddish-gold hair was shaped on her head like the paper in a Christmas bell. Her brows were thin and perfect, and over them were tiny holes in the skin as though she had been pricked with the thorns of roses. . . . When she walked . . . she smelled like all the sweet of the world" (ST 63).

The reader understands that Mrs. Fergusson's relentless femininity and cheerfulness are for Mr. Torrance's sake (she later runs off and marries him).

For Delia, however, her appearance and behavior are "a kind of outrage with a promise to it" (ST 64), the promise of looking behind a veil to find out what is being kept there.

A second image that Welty explores throughout this story is that of water—a universal emblem for life—to suggest (once again) the discrepancy between surfaces and reality. The Wells themselves, with their restorative waters, suggest that this is a place for renewal, although the water turns out to be "warm and smelly" (perhaps hinting at a moral failure in the place) and not everyone drinks it. The dreamy pleasure of Delia's childhood visit permeates her memories: "On the green grass at twilight the croquet balls moved slow as leviathans through a deep sea" (ST 64). Now, twenty years later, she sees the guest house as a "dilapidation . . . elaborate as a ship" with an "enormous veranda [that seems] tilted, about to sink, like a waterlogged boat in a dead-quiet bayou" (ST 63). Such images of dead water suggest the decay and stasis that Delia now finds at the house, where an abandoned Mr. Fergusson lives alone. The contrast between the meek Mr. Fergusson and his rival, Mr. Torrance, is suggested in the homonym "torrents" that implies a particularly passionate kind of force that carries away Fergusson's wife. While the poor husband looks around the room— at the moment preceding his humiliation by his rival—with his single good eye, "like a lighthouse," showing his isolation and his futile hope of avoiding disaster, his wife hides her face "as well as a curtain" behind her rapidly moving fan (ST 68).

Using the strategy of doubling of which she is so fond, Welty depicts two houses in the story, which, mirroring one another, allows her to suggest that houses, like people, attract stories to account for their fate.[7] In addition to the main house at Fergusson's Wells, where the family and guests stay, is a "haunted house" nearby that had belonged to Mrs. Fergusson's ancestors. Twenty years ago the children staying at the Wells had been taken by Miss Adella Mews, the old-maid half-sister of Mr. Fergusson, to visit the haunted house, where she told them of shocking events in its past that led a betrayed husband to murder his wife and then die, along with her lover, in a duel. The exuberant children are not prepared to accept the solemnity with which Miss Mews tells her tale; unequipped as they are to recognize the meanings of even the events they personally witness, such as Mr. Torrance caught in the parlor as he is about to kiss Mrs. Fergusson, the children fail to learn the "lesson" Miss Mews has in mind: "I gave them a lesson in history! Which *all* would do well to heed" (ST 67). Her admonition is too late, however, for this is the evening when everything comes crashing down as Mr. Fergusson shoots Mr. Torrance with his rabbit gun.

Through a poorly painted picture of the haunted house that Delia now notices hanging "like a parent portrait" (ST 66) over a mantel at the main house, Welty establishes multiple visions of the old place at three different times in its existence. At the same time, she encourages its comparison with the Wells house itself, both twenty years earlier and as seen in the present, dilapidated and fading.[8] The painting shows a pristine new house that, by the time Delia first saw it, had already fallen to shambles, with part of the roof collapsed and one of its wings gone except for "a shell of front wall" (ST 66), a skeleton that laid bare how the rooms opened off into one another and so revealed how the story of the murdered wife evolved. The "anatomy of the story" (ST 67) was visible in the exposed structure of the house: "you saw the structure all laid bare—it was no mystery as in other houses" (ST 67). In this tale about secrets that we create surfaces to conceal, Welty uses the two houses to suggest that the passage of time strips away all facades, leaving stories bare. The haunted house, when Delia now sees it, has nearly disappeared, except for its "solitary chimney," yet in this emblem of former fire (and, by implication, passion), Delia believes she sees something transcending "all that went astray in sight of it. . . . Not the house as it had once stood, but something before that, some exuberance of its inception, seemed hovering about it" (ST 70).

The Wells house itself now seems well on its way toward the decay that ultimately claimed the haunted house. Indeed, the presence of the faded, passive Mr. Fergusson and his old servant, Reuben, who make a game each day of hunting for a bottle of bourbon that will dull Mr. Fergusson's memories, makes this house, too, a haunted house. As if the two structures follow one another, through different moments of time, with their similar fates, Welty suggests the ultimate futility of trying to hide secrets that time and change will inevitably expose.

The ruins of another house serve as the setting for Welty's story "Asphodel," which centers on three women who create and perpetuate for their community what Patricia Meyer Spacks calls "mythic gossip, the kind that solidifies the traditions of a family or a wider group."[9] In her illuminating study *Gossip*, Spacks gives rightful importance to this tale of three interfering women who live vicariously through Miss Sabina as her marriage to a scoundrel, Don McInnis, deteriorates and collapses. Even as the catastrophic events take place, Cora, Phoebe, and Irene, "all old maids"

(CS 200), run to tell Miss Sabina the bad news, building as they do a virtual myth about McInnis's exploits that makes any resolution of his marital problems unlikely, if not impossible. They even prophesy that this marriage will be tragic by declaring McInnis "a man that would be like a torch carried into a house" (CS 202).

It is not always easy to determine when this Greek chorus of women is recording local history and when they are creating it through the very medium of their gossip. Welty writes of some of their speculations, "we whispered it among ourselves later when we embroidered together, as though it were a riddle that young ladies could not answer" (CS 202). To "embroider" means not only to provide ornament for a fabric but also to embellish a narrative with fictitious details or exaggeration. Believing that they are merely passing on part of their community's history, the trio may, in fact, be contributing to it by insisting on particular interpretations of what they observe.

Miss Sabina, the unwilling bride of the willful McInnis, does seem doomed. When the children she gives birth to die and her husband is revealed as being unfaithful to her, she drives him out, becoming eccentric and eventually mad. Her demise occurs on a day she enters a door she had never entered before, that of the post office. The fact that she has never received a letter in her life reveals the isolation that makes her personal experience unbearable, and she tears everyone else's letters to pieces, "having attempted to destroy the emotions and connections she cannot share."[10] Miss Sabina collapses, and the three protagonists search through the lexicon in which their community describes its experience for the proper term: "'A stroke.' That is what we said, because we did not know how to put a name to the end of her life. . . ." (CS 206).

After Sabina's death, Cora, Phoebe, and Irene travel to McInnis's home, Asphodel (the flower's name means "my regrets follow you to the grave"), for a picnic. Looking up at what seem to be the ruins of the passion that has destroyed the couple, the three women see the remnants of Greek columns left after the house burned down. But what they find actually functions as a mirror as they look "modestly upward to the frieze of maidens" (CS 200) that is, perhaps, a "freeze of maidens" whose sexual inexperience and coldness may account for their voyeuristic participation in Sabina's sexual life with the tantalizing and dangerous McInnis.

In this story Welty shows how not only individuals but also communities acknowledge just those experiences that can be accommodated by their specific vocabularies. The rest is forgotten or never acknowledged. The women sense the power their assumed roles have given them. As Cora observes, "We told the news. . . . We went in a body up the hill and into the house, weeping and wailing, *hardly daring to name the name or the deed*" (CS 203; emphasis mine).

Their picnic is interrupted by the figure of a naked man appearing from among the Doric columns. "Naked as an old goat" (CS 207), he may well be Don McInnis; mythically, however, he recalls Pan, whose noontime rest the women have interrupted, or Dionysus (they have been eating grapes and drinking wine). In either case, the figure represents forces of (sexual) chaos that shatter (like the bottle of wine) their complacency and send them scurrying away, chased by the little goats of the goat-god.

. . .

"A Sketching Trip" makes particularly evident Welty's concern with how surfaces disguise and obscure the realities that lie beneath. "Asphodel" exemplifies the power of communal myths to determine how experience is understood and even, at times, to set particular events in motion. Both stories point to a world of appearances that bears a somewhat tenuous relationship with the reality of experience, yet the interpretations imposed on these appearances have remarkable force. The shared meanings that members of a community implicitly generate characterize experience in specific ways idiosyncratic to the group *and* effectively preclude other possible interpretations.

Paradoxically, although most of Welty's characters participate in creating their community's body of acceptable meanings, they are themselves shocked when these interpretations fail. Like Wilbur Morrison (in "June Recital"), they share a tendency to rely too much on those surfaces and the meanings they encourage: "If there was anything that unsettled him it was for people not to be on the inside what their outward semblances led you to suppose" (CS 327). As a consequence, when their expectations about someone are thwarted by what actually happens, they feel betrayed. The very idea of being "cheated" in Welty's fiction entails this disjunction between what one expects based upon what appears to be true, and some different outcome that belies that appearance. In "Death of a Traveling Salesman," for example, when R. J. Bowman discovers that the couple whose hospitality he has accepted are not lonely individuals, as he had thought, but married and fulfilled, he is "shocked": "Somehow he felt unable to be indignant or protest, although some sort of joke had certainly been played upon him. . . . He felt that he had been cheated" (CS 129). In "The Whole World Knows," Ran MacLain first feels betrayed by his wife, who refuses to acknowledge the pain his behavior and their separation have caused her and plays, instead, at indifference: "When I couldn't give her something she wanted she would hum a little tune. . . . Then I loved her a lot. The little cheat" (CS 385). Later, after his emotional cruelty toward Maideen Sumrall and his seduction of her, he is too self-absorbed to recognize the shock and despair she feels that lead ultimately to her suicide: "How was I to know she would go and hurt herself? She cheated, she cheated too" (CS 392). He blames both women for his own failure to understand what lies behind their behavior.

A major reason why child characters appeal so strongly to Welty is that their perceptions in some respects exist *prior to* that thorough assimilation of ways of thinking about experience so typical of older characters. Adults increasingly accept the adequacy of their own conventions and categories because they are protected thereby from a need to grapple with uncongenial or disconcerting facts. Their loss is that they can rarely understand true novelty when it occurs. Children are much more likely to allow their patterns of thought to change when something new happens. They do not yet know that, through the language they are learning, adults are making some readings of events possible while shutting out others. And they have as yet no sense that language may sustain and perpetuate a community's most cherished illusions about itself.

Welty's story "Ladies in Spring" makes such adult illusions—and the role they play in maintaining benign fictions—especially clear. Dewey Coker, the young boy who is the protagonist of this story, is invited by his father to play hooky from school and go fishing with him. On this particular day, Dewey would actually prefer to be in school because his teacher has "promised to read them about *Excalibur*" (CS 519), but it is clear that his father, who has brought along two fishing poles, expects him to come along. Blackie, his father, knows that as a parent he ought not to endorse his son's absence from school, so as he arrives at the schoolhouse where his son cannot help but see him, he announces, "Scoot. Get on back in the schoolhouse. You been told." When Dewey hesitates, he says, "But I can see you're bound to come" (CS 519), thus deciding the matter. On their way to the river, they notice Miss Hattie, the rainmaker, walking ahead of them, and rather than catch up with her and have to conform to social expectations that they be polite and visit with her, Blackie urges Dewey to hold back. Somewhat later in the story, when they do encounter Miss Hattie, Blackie insists that Dewey behave with the respect due to a lady, just as he does himself. Miss Hattie orders the two under her umbrella because of the rain, and they have to comply or be considered rude. Thus Blackie teaches his son the outward formulas for gentlemen's behavior toward ladies.

The story of *Excalibur* that Dewey missed that day would, by its very nature, have confirmed the lesson that gentlemen owe particular, solicitous attention to women, for had he been in school Dewey would have heard about King Arthur, the knights of the Round Table, their adventures, and their virtues of courage, honesty, reverence, and respect. He would have heard of knights rescuing ladies in distress and treating them with the greatest courtesy. The lessons of *Excalibur* and of Blackie's father, however, become suspect as the reader discerns what is really happening in the story, the meaning behind events that Dewey only dimly understands because of his youth.[11] Blackie, it turns out, is something of a scoundrel where women are concerned. His fishing trips disguise a deeper motive that he wants no one to suspect; when Dewey asks if his father has been to the river before, Blackie tells his son, "Might as well keep still about it at home" (CS 519). While Blackie and Dewey are perched on a bridge, fishing, a young woman, Opal, appears at the river's edge and calls Blackie's name. He deliberately ignores her. Again and again, she tries to get his attention, without success. Later in the story, when it has begun to rain, Blackie, Dewey, and Opal are all caught under Miss Hattie's big umbrella, and it becomes clear to the reader (if not to Dewey) that Opal and Blackie have had a relationship that he now wants to end. Indeed, the trip to the nearly dry river with his son appears to have been Blackie's sign to Opal that she has no real claims on him. She knows that it would be improper and unforgivable for her to approach him with his son present. His appearance at a site where they (apparently) rendezvoused combined with his conscious refusal to acknowledge her presence is his way of cutting off any hopes she may have. Dewey notices only that she is grown up and "plump as ever" (CS 524). His general misunderstanding of what he has been seeing suggests that Opal may be pregnant—especially in light of the images of fecundity that permeate this story after the rain begins. But whether or not Opal is pregnant, Blackie's behavior toward her reveals a lack of responsibility that is the antithesis of the chivalry he supposedly wants to encourage in his son.

Dewey's mother, surrounded by his four younger siblings and watching over a newborn calf, seems almost an earth mother figure as she works at home while her husband and son take the day off. She expresses exasperation with them when Dewey offers her his fish and she realizes they have been fishing. Welty's imagery links Opal and Dewey's mother together and suggests that Blackie has betrayed them both. At the end of the walk back to town, during which Blackie has not said a word to Opal despite their being forced by Miss Hattie into close proximity, Dewey notices her wet cheeks (tears, but he thinks it is the rain) and the blue violet in her dress (CS 526). And when the boy arrives home and runs to see his mother, the narrator notes that "the big sky-blue violets his mother loved were blooming, wet as cheeks." Because blue violets signify faithfulness, Welty's reference to them points up Blackie's violation of both women's trust and loyalty. Blackie, meanwhile, is "off at a distance, on his knees—back at mending the fences" (CS 529). As well he should be. This story makes clear the active role that adults assume, and the major investment they make, in perpetuating a benign and decorous surface (cover) story of male solicitude toward "ladies." Dewey does not recognize that he is being socialized into accepting a false version of what life in his community is like.

Welty enhances her message about Blackie's true nature with some playful allusions to the adjacent short story in this collection (*The Bride of the Innisfallen and Other Stories*)—"Circe." Both Circe and Miss Hattie, the rainmaker, are powerful, magical women who take part in metamorphoses of which they are proud. Circe's transformation of Odysseus's men into pigs is, in Welty's portrayal, less an imposition onto them of some alien form than it is a stripping away of a facade: "It takes phenomenal neatness of housekeeping to put it through the heads of men that they are swine" (CS 531). Miss Hattie, in turn, brings the spring rains that transform Dewey's world from shades of gray, black, and white into one that explodes with vibrant colors (CS 525). She symbolizes the fecundity of spring, for after the rain comes, baby chicks appear at her feet as if hatched there (CS 528) and "small spotty pigs" run to meet her and trot alongside (CS 526). Her repetition of the word "trot," first ordering Blackie and Dewey under her umbrella by commanding them to "Trot under here!" as she meets them in the rain (CS 523) and then sending Dewey home by telling him to "Trot!" (CS 529), echoes Circe's reference to the greed of the men she changed into pigs: "The first were trotting at my heels while the last still reached with their hands" (CS 531). A few days after the first rain in "Ladies in Spring,"

Dewey wanders near the river again and comes upon "a little black dog, his whole self shaking and alive from tip to tip. . . . There was no telling where he might have come from. Yet he had something familiar about him too. He had a look on his little pointed face . . . that reminded Dewey of Miss Hattie Purcell" (CS 530). This little dog seems to be the counterpart of the pigs in Circe's story, for such a dog would almost surely suggest its own name: "Blackie." Dewey's father, Blackie, has been exposed for what he truly is in his treatment of women; the slang term for it is "dog." Just as Circe strips away a facade to reveal ungrateful, greedy pigs, Welty implies that Blackie is, underneath it all, an animal too.

Blackie's grooming of his son in the ways of politeness is a lesson in falsity. To the degree that this fabrication disguises the behavior of men in their relationships with women, the story may be seen as embodying a feminist critique, but the larger corpus of Welty's stories calls such a conclusion into some question by emphasizing that virtually everyone in her communities—male and female alike—is complicitous in creating benign versions of reality. She suggests that it is a *human* need, if also a human frailty, to give our lives meaning and importance by imposing stories on them, whatever the reality may be. Communal fictions allow us to pretend that some things are true and to ignore the existence of others that are disconcerting. This is Freud's repression on a community level. In Welty's story Dewey is only beginning to glimpse the disjunctions between what he observes and the stories he is told. Fifteen years later, when he discovers that Opal has run away, driving Miss Hattie's car, her motives will have become much clearer to him. In Dewey, Welty has created someone still innocent enough to believe the stories.

Another sort of evidence for Welty's fascination with the falsification or distortion possible in surfaces is to be found in her ongoing interest in signs, surfaces on which people self-consciously characterize themselves or others for the sake of public notice. Sideshows, freak shows, movie posters, signs in store windows, cemetery monuments, and the titles of books and prizes appear in nearly all of her stories, inviting—even insisting on—particular readings of what they signify. At times names and titles are used to comic effect, as when (in *The Ponder Heart*) Edna Earle Ponder's plant wins a blue ribbon in the "Best Other Than Named" category at the county fair (PH 21), a reference that in itself reveals Welty's ironic and frequently playful attitude toward naming.

As Suzanne Marrs has noted, Welty's pictures of cemeteries, carnivals, and parades offer "unexpected lines of continuity" for the otherwise varied subjects found in her photographs.[12] What is crucial to note about Welty's interest in these subjects is their function *as surfaces* meant to characterize the self. They constitute interpretations, masks, public personae, and Welty is intrigued at the meanings implicit in various choices and in bystanders' reactions to these artifacts. Because of her many photographs of sideshow barkers, entrances, and posters, she has been asked about her reactions to the pictures of human freaks taken by photographer Diane Arbus; her answer illuminates both her values and her concerns: "I think that [such photographic work] totally violates human privacy, and by intention. My taking the freak *posters*—not the human beings—was because they were a whole school of naive folk art. And, of course, totally unrelated to what you saw inside the tent."[13] Not only is Welty uninterested in either photographing or writing about freaks themselves, she seems positively repelled by the prospect of intruding into the lives of such figures, as she made clear in an interview with Roger Mudd in which he asked her about one of her pictures, "Mule Face Woman." She emphasized that she had not photographed the woman but the poster of her, "somebody's dream, you know. . . . I didn't want to see the real mule face woman. I *dreaded* the real mule face woman."[14]

Her fiction expresses these same values. Her story "Keela, the Outcast Indian Maiden," based on true events, focuses on the psychology of those involved: "Nothing in this world would have induced me to go and look at the show. . . . I was interested in what sort of points of view people could have toward such an atrocious thing" as the kidnapping and abusive exploitation of Little Lee Roy.[15] In "Music from Spain" Eugene MacLain passes a sideshow every day that features a very fat woman named Emma. Because Eugene's own wife is also named "Emma," he makes of this sideshow figure a bizarre travesty of his wife, whom he has slapped (as he tells himself) because he now finds his marriage unfulfilling, because he is in his forties, and "because she was a fat thing" (CS 395), though he quickly admits that this is "absurd." The enlarged photograph of the sideshow Emma, which is all the reader knows of her, reveals "a look; it was accusation, of course. The sight of a person to whom other people have been cruel can be the most formidable of all" (CS 405). Welty's strong sense of personal privacy here extends to her fictive characterization of others, especially when their very vulnerability is what a surface exposes.

In "No Place for You, My Love" Welty explicitly addresses such human exposure in writing of two unnamed characters, strangers who have met at a lunch with mutual friends, who drive south of New Orleans together. Neither of them is a southerner, and the woman's difference from the other women they are with is part of what attracts the man to her. The other women reveal a "Southern look—Southern mask—of life-is-a-dream irony, which could turn to pure challenge at the drop of a hat," whereas the woman from the Middle West has a more pleasant, naive face, "a serious, now-watch-out-everybody face, which orphaned her entirely in the company of these Southerners" (CS 466). Both protagonists have secrets and no intention of revealing them. Welty's narrator observes about them that "of all human moods, deliberate imperviousness may be the most quickly communicated—it may be the most successful, most fatal signal of all" (CS 466).

The story of this man and woman reveals little in the way of plot, yet what does happen discloses in almost purely symbolic form the dilemma the two characters face. As Welty has written, the "vain courting of imperviousness in the face of exposure is this little story's plot. . . . In the end I tried to make the story's inside outside and then leave the shell behind" (ES 113). The shell is also the story's major image. The protagonists move physically through an uncongenial landscape that itself takes on qualities making clear how tenuous and ineffective are their strategies for remaining unknown to one another. Both characters have personal dilemmas that preoccupy them; the woman even has a bruise on her forehead suggesting a troubled relationship that her companion quickly concludes must be an affair with a married man. Their actual problems are never revealed nor is any resolution of them reached. What readers experience with the characters is a trip through heat and glare over roads that vary from pavement to shells, barely covering an unstable, swampy ground that seems only tenuously held at bay. In the primitive world they drive through, they encounter creature after creature with its own shell-like protective covering: crayfish, shrimp, terrapins, turtles, snakes, even an alligator. These "shell creatures . . . little jokes of creation, persisted and sometimes perished [beneath the wheels of their car], the more of them the deeper down the road went. . . . Back there in the margins were worse—crawling hides you could not penetrate with bullets or quite believe, grins that had come down from the primeval mud" (CS 468).

The very river they cross seems "like an exposed vein of ore" (CS 471), as if the earth itself were splitting open. Aware that this entire land is poised on swampy earth beneath which is more water ("There was water under everything" [CS 472]), the woman feels "a panic rise, as sudden as nausea. Just how far below questions and answers, concealment and revelation, they were running now—that was still a new question, with a power of its own, waiting. How dear—how costly—could this ride be?" (CS 472). And as if to emphasize their need to keep running away to avoid exposure, Welty shows her characters as being enveloped by biting mosquitoes and gnats whenever the car slows down or stops.

The couple stops at a roadside shack, "Baba's Place," for beer and a sandwich, and they dance together "like a matched team—like professional, Spanish dancers wearing masks" (CS 478), but their immunity from each other's queries, and the exposure that would result, is only temporary. Poised at the edge of the Mississippi River, which may again serve as a threshold leading to other possibilities (as did bodies of water in the stories of Ran and Eugene MacLain), the couple retreats, joking that they are at a "jumping-off place" (CS 474). They take the car back to the labyrinth of New Orleans (CS 467), driving at a "demoniac" speed, and then separate. The "something that must have been with them all along suddenly, then, was not" (CS 480), for the couple has chosen not to act on the possibility for connection and exposure, for a relationship, that each of them has glimpsed in the other. They part as strangers, masks still in place. Like Welty's other wanderers, they seem free—and lost.

.   .   .

The theme of wandering is at the very center of Welty's collection of stories *The Golden Apples,* which features as a basic duality its characters' concerns with being connected with one another (through family or community) and with the freedom to roam, seeking some more autonomous vision of one's life.[16] Welty's concern with how people use language to fabricate the meanings of their lives is especially evident in this collection of stories permeated with gossip, mistaken identities, and characters pondering the implications of naming. The collective voice of the community of Morgana is itself virtually a character in these stories, filtering each event that takes place through its configuration of possible meanings and, to the detriment of some of its citizens, treating phenomena that do not comfortably fit its preconceptions as nonexistent.

The stories all have as a background figure King MacLain, who (except for rare, brief, and unannounced visits) has abandoned his wife and family to travel around the country rather than stay in Morgana and meet what the community would call his "responsibilities."[17] Welty's shifting points of view in these stories allow the reader to know King almost entirely through the local legends about him, tales that emphasize his sexual prowess and irresistibility to women (he is rumored to have fathered a number of children who are now at the county orphanage), his arrogance, and his indifference to what people think of him. Unverified sightings of King in other towns and misidentifications of him in Morgana establish a pattern of misunderstanding what is seen that recurs throughout the stories. Until the final story, "The Wanderers," King is known to the reader only through his neighbors' eyes. The same is true of a young woman protagonist, Virgie Rainey, who is viewed by the town as a gypsy, a fine pianist wasteful of her talent, a thoroughly reckless and irresponsible teenager, sexually promiscuous and, like King, indifferent to the town's assessment of her. Virgie and King are known as wanderers (although, in fact, Virgie goes away for only a year or so) whose sense of adventure links them to other characters in the book whose desire to experience the larger world makes them seem daring and romantic to those citizens who remain all of their lives in Morgana. These anomalous figures include Easter, the orphan in "Moon Lake"; Ran and Eugene MacLain, whom we have seen struggle against a sense of entrapment; Miss Eckhart, the piano teacher, who hides an unsuspected passion for music in her soul; and Loch Morrison, the lone figure who actually appears to succeed in leaving Morgana behind, rumored in "The Wanderers" to be settled in New York.

This final story forces the reader to reconsider the early communal judgments about a number of characters. King MacLain, returning home after many years away, is revealed as a poignant figure, no longer really needed by his family, somewhat in the way, and facing his final years. Rather like the title character in Tennyson's poem "Ulysses," Welty's "idle king" seems more lost at home than ever, as if he too would prefer to die in some moment of glory or adventure rather than quietly, at home.[18] The most significant revelation, however, concerns Virgie, who is shown to be utterly unlike what the town had assumed: she has been taking care of her mother for more than twenty years, holding down a dull job, milking her mother's cows, and delivering the milk to customers.[19] The enormous disjunction between what Virgie is and what people have come to expect her to be is seen even in her mother's persistent expectations that Virgie will be late, that she will not "mind," that she is unreliable. What becomes evident in this final story is that Virgie is someone her mother has been able to rely on completely. The community's insistence on her recklessness and indifference to people's opinions, moreover, is undermined when, for the first time, Welty's narration admits the reader into Virgie's consciousness and this memory from her childhood is revealed: "Virgie had a sudden recollection of recital night at Miss Eckhart's—the moment when she was to be called out. She was thirteen . . . she remembered it now: an anxiety which brought her to the point of sickness, that back in there they were laughing at her mother's hat" (CS 434). This passage, along with the fact that Welty attributes to Virgie the single meaningful epiphany in the book, demonstrates Welty's intention that the reader understand Virgie's humanity and compassion, unrecognized by those around her. Her neighbors have never seen beyond the categories and labels they have imposed on her, so they sense little about the reality of her experience.

Welty explores the Morgana community's relationship with language—and its consequences for its citizens—most explicitly in the story "June Recital," which is told from the point of view of two young characters who have yet to assimilate fully their town's habitual ways of thinking about reality. The narrative moves back and forth between the perspective of Loch Morrison, a young boy who is supposed to be staying in bed while he recovers from malaria, and that of his sixteen-year-old sister Cassie, who is tie-dyeing a scarf in her nearby bedroom. The limited vision of these (and, by implication, all) characters is emphasized by Welty's focus on what each child can see of the house next door through the window of his or her bedroom. To each of them, parts of some rooms are clearly visible, while others are hidden from view. Together, what they see makes up a fuller yet still only partial view of the "vacant" house next door.

Loch's perspective is limited not only by the position of his bedroom window but by his youthful misunderstanding of some of what he sees.[20] He misidentifies a number of objects, often with humorous results. For example, he observes sixteen-year-old Virgie Rainey and her sailor boyfriend cavorting, possibly naked,[21] in an upstairs bedroom, chasing one another, and (apparently) making love on the bare mattress and thinks not of the scandalous nature of their behavior but of the fact that, lying next to one another, "their legs in an M and their hands joined between them," they look "exactly like the paper dolls his sister used to cut out of folded newspaper and unfold to let him see." Loch speculates that "if Cassie would come in now, he would point out the window and she would remember"

(CS 282). The reader realizes, of course, that Cassie's thoughts, were she to view this scene, would *not* be about paper dolls.

Loch also incorrectly identifies an old woman who enters the house and proceeds to festoon newspaper strips all across a front room downstairs; he thinks it must be the sailor's mother, come to find her son. When he hears its ticking, he mistakes a metronome the woman places in the center of her decorations for "where she has the dynamite" (CS 285). Just as Loch has never seen Miss Eckhart and so does not recognize her as the old woman, he has also never seen King MacLain, so that when King arrives at the house just after Miss Eckhart has tried to set it on fire, Loch believes he is Mr. Voight, who used to rent a room there. Loch's mistakes are straightforward ones, based on his lack of experience. He is not yet old enough to question, as his sister Cassie does, anything adults have told him about reality. Thus, whereas Cassie recognizes the oddity of her mother's insistence on calling the house next door "the vacant house" even though Old Man Holifield, night watchman at the cotton gin, sleeps there most of every day (CS 285), Loch never thinks of questioning its identity as the "vacant house" next door (CS 275).

Cassie is a type of character who recurs in Welty's fiction—a timid girl who has thoroughly internalized the myriad cautionary lessons adults have tried to teach her. In her reactions to the lessons of adults, she represents, perhaps, an extreme, the kind of person who takes herself and the world too seriously ever to act on any adventurous impulse she might feel. She is the opposite of someone like Virgie Rainey, who, though raised in the same social milieu, rebels and goes out to face life and its consequences in her personal insistence not to let life pass her by. Perhaps because she recognizes this contrast, Cassie is fascinated with Virgie. She feels both love and hate for her (CS 292) and thinks of her as being "as exciting as a gypsy would be" (CS 291). Cassie's occupation with tie-dyeing and hay-rides places her far behind Virgie, who behaves much more independently and recklessly than the typical sixteen-year-old in this conservative community. Virgie's greater sophistication, as Cassie sees it, has led her "to skip an interval, some world-in-between where Cassie and Missie and Parnell were, all dyeing scarves" (CS 302–3). Virgie has "gone direct into the world of power and emotion" (CS 303) by holding a job playing a piano at the picture show and by living her personal life just as she wishes. Cassie views her with awe, sensing that her own life will be quite different, her relationship to the unknown much less daring: "She could never go for herself, never creep out on the shimmering bridge of the tree [as Loch has just done], or *reach the dark magnet* there that drew you inside, kept drawing you in. *She could not see herself do an unknown thing.* She was not Loch, she was not Virgie Rainey; she was not her mother. She was Cassie in her room, *seeing the knowledge and torment beyond her reach,* standing at her window singing" (CS 316; emphasis mine).

Cassie exhibits the most diffident of responses to the cautionary socialization imposed on girls early in the twentieth century. Her fearfulness about life leads her to see love entirely in terms of protection, a view that, as we have seen, Welty treats as limited and inhibitory. Even in her own room on a summer afternoon in June, Cassie sees herself as a "small, solemn, unprotected figure . . . standing scared at the window . . . pathetic—homeless-looking" (CS 287). In recognizing that her younger brother already lives a more courageous life than she ever will, she broods about *his* vulnerability, as well. When she sees him in the tree outside his bedroom window, "the sight of his spread-eagled back in the white night drawers seemed as far from her as the morning star. It was gone from her, any way to shield his innocence" (CS 315).

Cassie is far more introspective than her brother about the definitions and interpretations she has learned from adults. Whereas her brother questions only the *fact* of definitions, assuming that words do, indeed, correspond to particular features of the world ("was it an echo—was an echo that?" [CS 278]), Cassie has begun to think about the appropriateness of defining experience and people in particular ways. It is through Cassie's portions of the story that Welty makes clearest how she feels about a community's tendencies to categorize people and insist upon its own interpretations of their experience.[22]

The figure who occasions Welty's severest criticism of such close-mindedness is Lotte Elisabeth Eckhart, the piano teacher, who is ultimately destroyed by the community's failure of imagination and refusal to view her with compassion. Cassie does feel compassion for her, because she took piano lessons with her as a child and experienced firsthand many of the odd behaviors that the town has been unable to acknowledge. Perhaps because she has seen moments of pain and passion in Miss Eckhart, Cassie has never quite accepted her community's hurtful, restrictive definitions of her teacher.

Miss Eckhart is an outsider, too different from anyone else in Morgana to fit into their notions of acceptability. She is ostracized because she is

German in an era that included World War I, a Lutheran (an unheard of religion), unmarried, passionate about the music her pupils play, a stern teacher, rumored to be in love with a shoe salesman who does not return her feelings, and (so the local grocer reports) an eater of cabbage and pigs' brains. She cannot be assimilated because she refuses to succumb to the community's insistence that she offer a basis for doing so: "Missie Spights said that if Miss Eckhart had allowed herself to be called by her first name, then she would have been like other ladies. Or if Miss Eckhart had belonged to a church that had ever been heard of, and the ladies would have had something to invite her to belong to . . . Or if she had been married to anybody at all, just the awfullest man—like Miss Snowdie MacLain, that everybody could feel sorry for" (cs 308).

This is the problem. There are no words to define her, and because social acceptance is of little interest to her, Miss Eckhart does not cooperate to make herself understood in this cultural milieu. The price she pays is a severe one—the harshest imaginable interpretations of her behavior, an utter absence of affection, and final abandonment (except by the town's "saint," Miss Snowdie MacLain).

When Mr. Sissum, the shoe salesman Miss Eckhart was rumored to love, drowned and the town went to his funeral, everyone watched Miss Eckhart in order to judge her behavior. After his coffin was placed in the ground, she "broke out of the circle," went forward, and looked into the grave. She is held back, but the town concludes that "she might have thrown herself upon the coffin if they'd let her," behavior they would hardly consider appropriate from anyone but his mother or wife. The town punishes the teacher for having "a feeling that failed to match the feelings of everybody else" (cs 299) by removing their children from her piano classes: "After the way she cried in the cemetery—for *they decided it must have been crying she did*—some ladies stopped their little girls from learning any more music" (cs 300; emphasis mine). Meanwhile, Cassie has observed something quite different: "Cassie had the impression that Miss Eckhart simply wanted to see—" (cs 299).

The town's conclusion that she must have been crying reflects their blindness to events or emotions they don't have words for. Experience must conform to their categories; if it doesn't, they label it "inappropriate" and thus justify their prejudices and cruelty.[23] Yet Welty is careful to show that not everyone is susceptible to the town's severe judgments. Miss Eckhart is singled out because of her foreignness. Her treatment may be compared to that of Mr. Voight, the sewing machine salesman, another roomer at Snowdie MacLain's boarding house, who protests the piano lessons by coming part way downstairs and flapping his bathrobe (under which he wore "no clothes at all" [CS 294]) at Miss Eckhart and the pupils. Cassie told her parents about it "only to have her father say he didn't believe it; that Mr. Voight represented a large concern and covered seven states" (CS 295). In her bewilderment at her parents' refusal to believe what was happening, Cassie comes to understand that "for what Mr. Voight did there were no ready words" (CS 295) and that "some performances of people stayed partly untold for lack of a name . . . as well as for lack of believers" (CS 296).

One night Miss Eckhart was attacked by "a crazy Negro" who jumped out from behind a hedge. Cassie recalls that "she had been walking by herself after dark; nobody had told her any better" (CS 301). The town responds by blaming the victim and thus rationalizing away its own culpability in being a community in which such a thing could happen. They show surprise "that she and her mother did not move away. They wished she had moved away . . . then they wouldn't always have to remember that a terrible thing once happened to her. But Miss Eckhart stayed, as though she considered one thing not so much more terrifying than another" (CS 301). Refusing to play the role the community has in mind—scapegoat and victim and, thus, deserving of sympathy—Miss Eckhart is denigrated with even fiercer intensity: "Miss Perdita Mayo . . . said Miss Eckhart's *differences* were why shame alone had not killed her and killed her mother too; that differences were reasons" (CS 302). Ultimately vicious in their refusal to accept their role in Miss Eckhart's fate, the town begins to circulate stories of the teacher's "crimes," including the unsubstantiated and wildly implausible accusation that she killed her mother with opium (CS 307).

On the day "June Recital" takes place, Miss Eckhart is apprehended for setting fire to the room (the "studio") where she used to teach piano in the vacant house next to the Morrisons'. Seeing her led away by the marshal and his fishing companion, Cassie is distraught at her appearance in "a gray housedress prophetic of an institution" (CS 324) with a cloth held over her head, and she runs out of her house in her petticoat, calling for her mother to help. Ladies returning from a rook party, the marshal, Miss Eckhart, Virgie and her sailor boyfriend—all converge in front of the house; yet

Cassie, hearing their remarks to one another, realizes that she and Loch are alone in seeing what is happening as extraordinary. Everyone else seems to be taking these events as a matter of course:

> Cassie could only think: we were spies too. And nobody else was surprised at anything—it was only we two. People saw things like this as they saw Mr. MacLain come and go. They only hoped to place them, in their hour or their street or the name of their mothers' people. Then Morgana could hold them, and at last they were this and they were that. And when ruin was predicted all along, even if people had forgotten it was on the way, even if they mightn't have missed it if it hadn't appeared, still they were never surprised when it came. (CS 325)

This passage reveals the degree to which the community's publicly sanctioned view of things enables its citizens to deal readily with local events. Miss Eckhart, already defined as "crazy," would be expected to do something like this and need to be taken away to the Jackson Asylum. The scandalous Virgie Rainey would be expected to act "as if nothing had happened" when she is caught with her half-dressed sailor boyfriend (CS 325). The adults Cassie observes are not startled by what they have seen, as she is, because their categories for thinking about things, their vocabularies for accounting for whatever might happen, are firmly in place. They may have had temporary difficulty in finding language in which to think about the sad fate of Miss Eckhart, but the word "crazy" encompasses any dark future she may have and successfully obscures the town's own role in abandoning her to loneliness and poverty.

Miss Eckhart's experience, however, should not be seen to indicate that Welty considers assimilation into this community and its myths about itself a solution to loneliness. She makes clear in the character of Mrs. Morrison, Cassie's mother, that accepting a community's values and perspectives on life is not necessarily fulfilling. In "The Wanderers" Mrs. Morrison, "after being so gay and flighty always" and appearing to be a happily married mother of two, "went out of the room one morning and killed herself" (CS 449). Yet the reader recalls that in earlier stories she had thoroughly met her community's expectations for a socially respected wife and mother. In "June Recital" she even tells her son with apparent delight about a ladies' rook party she has just attended, which featured such "feminine" delicacies as scooped-out oranges, "sweet peach pickle with flower petals around it of different-colored cream cheese," and the "swan made of a cream puff . . .

[with] whipped cream feathers, a pastry neck, green icing eyes" (CS 328). But then the narrator notes that she sighs "abruptly." Cassie believes she shares small, pleasant secrets with her husband (CS 327), yet there are signs of dispute between them. Mr. Morrison disapproves of hayrides, and Cassie attends them "against [her] father's will, slipped out by [her] mother's connivance" (CS 276), suggesting that at times Mrs. Morrison finds ways around her husband's predominance in the family.

And Mrs. Morrison had other dreams. "Child, I could have *sung*," she announces to Cassie on one occasion, "as though all music might as well now go jump off the bridge" (CS 293). In the context of stories in which several characters are distinguished in terms of their feeling for music (as with Eugene and Randall MacLain), Mrs. Morrison's abandoned desire to sing is particularly significant. Her attitude toward Miss Eckhart, the major artistic figure in the book, is deeply ambivalent; she refers to her on one hand as "the witch" in the Hansel-and-Gretel-like studio (CS 288) next door where she gives piano lessons, and on the other she sends her daughter Cassie to take those lessons after all the other mothers have stopped: "Cassie's instinct told her her mother despised herself for despising [Miss Eckhart]. That was why she kept Cassie taking [lessons]. . . . The child had to make up for her mother's abhorrence, to keep her mother as kind as she really was" (CS 306). Welty may be implying some jealousy on Mrs. Morrison's part about the life Miss Eckhart, with her musical talent, might have led. Or perhaps she sees Miss Eckhart as threatening. Miss Eckhart's life has, after all, turned out so disappointingly—she devotes her energies to teaching music to mostly untalented and unenthusiastic students—and Mrs. Morrison would have wanted so much more out of her own life if she had pursued a musical career. Mrs. Morrison may well fear that her own life would have turned out just as bleakly, a possibility Miss Eckhart's sorrowful presence does not let her forget.

Another, more impressionistic piece of evidence for Mrs. Morrison's discontent is Cassie's belief that her mother repeatedly disappears, that she doesn't stay near enough to her children: "Cassie would try to stay in sight of her mother, but no matter how slightly she strayed . . . when she got back to their place her mother would be gone. She always lost her mother" (CS 298). Even at Mr. Sissum's funeral Cassie looks up to see that "her mother had slipped away" (CS 299). Whether these perceptions are a product of Mrs. Morrison's actual behavior or Cassie's excessive attachment to her,[24] Cassie *is* perpetually concerned with her mother's letting her down.

On the night of the annual piano recital, Cassie always worries that her mother will be late, and when she arrives on time, her daughter thinks of her as "not betraying her, after all" (CS 313). Cassie's disappointment in her mother extends to her answers to Cassie's questions and pleas for help. When she reports Mr. Voight's misbehavior to her parents, her mother doesn't take it seriously: "Her mother's laugh, which followed, was as usual soft and playful but not illuminating" (CS 295). On the other hand, "when she told bad news, she wore a perfectly blank face and her voice was helpless and automatic, as if she repeated a lesson" (CS 295). Cassie broods about her mother's inconsistencies, not realizing that they may themselves be the telling sign of her mother's struggles with the conformity her community wants from her. She *is* repeating a lesson when she projects a benign and "gay" facade, but the blank look and helpless voice she reveals when faced with troubling news suggest despair about the possibility of changing anything. As if to emphasize Mrs. Morrison's complete absorption in her roles of wife and mother, Welty does not reveal her given name—Catherine— until after she has died, at the very end of *The Golden Apples*.

The next story in the collection, "Sir Rabbit," focuses on a country girl, Mattie Will Sojourner, who comes face to face with the two MacLain twins, King's sons, and mistakes them at first for their father, daring "him" to come near her. The boys are not their father, but prompted perhaps by what they know of his reputation, they fulfill Mattie Will's expectations that they could only be up to mischief by tackling her together. This sexual encounter is anything but ominous, for Mattie Will shares in it fully, although she mocks Eugene and Randall as they leave: "I just did it because your mama's a poor albino," she calls to them (CS 333), referring to Snowdie, King's wife and their mother. But if her encounter with his sons failed to substantiate the legend of King's power over women, Mattie Will has an actual opportunity to judge King's prowess when, a short while later, King himself appears and seduces her. By now Mattie Will has become a child bride to the rather dimwitted Junior Holifield, who is out for an afternoon of shooting. When King fires his gun toward Junior, Mattie's husband faints, and Mattie cannot resist seeing what King is really all about. Junior has warned her away, saying "you done heard what he was, all your life, or you ain't a girl" (CS 336), but Mattie Will's curiosity is too strong to deny.

Mattie Will's sexual encounter with King is framed in terms of the legend of Leda and the swan, as Welty explicitly echoes lines from Yeats's famous poem.[25] However, even more than the sexual dimension, Welty emphasizes what Mattie Will "knows" as a result of their meeting: "She had to put on what he knew with what he did—maybe because he was so grand it was a thorn to him. Like submitting to another way to talk, she could answer to his burden now, his whole blithe, smiling, superior, frantic existence" (CS 338). As Mattie Will experiences King acting on what his mythic identity within this community seems to require of him, she senses that his role is, in fact, a burden that he carries, unable somehow to make anything else of himself. Mattie Will realizes, too, that she is now merely part of that myth: "She was Mr. MacLain's Doom, or Mr. MacLain's Weakness, like the rest . . . now she was something she had always heard of" (CS 338). And perhaps because this event has not proved overwhelming, as the myth seemed to promise, King is quickly reduced in stature in her eyes. When she sees him asleep a few minutes later, he seems quite vulnerable, his neck and leg and "all those parts looking no more driven than her man's now, or of any more use than a heap of cane thrown up by the mill and left in the pit to dry" (CS 340). In the song that she recalls about "Sir Rabbit," Mattie Will implicitly undermines whatever glory might have inhered in the myth by seeing King in the image of a rabbit, merely reproducing itself at some feverish pace. This story demonstrates how fragile such myths as the one about King's irresistibility can be, for, if anything, Mattie Will's experience is a disappointment, dispelling illusions she (along with the rest of the community) had enjoyed having. Later, in "The Wanderers," Welty reinforces this lesson by showing how invariably such myths prove to be false.

"Moon Lake" treats the matter of adult naming humorously, with little girls at summer camp persistently encountering the limitations of adult definitions of their experience. From the opening pages in which they are made to sing "Good morning, Mr. Dip, Dip, Dip, with your water just as cold as ice!" as they enter lake water that "is the temperature of a just-cooling biscuit" (CS 343), Nina Carmichael and the other girls exhibit an ironic and patient tolerance toward the adults who insist on initiating them into their own idea of camp life. Even the mosquito oil that their counselors dutifully rub all over them proves to be deceptively named: "Sweet Dreams didn't last" (CS 352). The special circumstance that most affects Nina and the other Morgana girls during their week at camp is that they share the experience with a number of orphans, headed by the orphan Easter, who, as critics have frequently noted, has a relationship to Nina like that of Virgie Rainey to Cassie Morrison in "June Recital." Easter and Virgie are both like gypsies, somewhat reckless and adventurous in a way that Cassie and Nina observe with no little degree of awe and envy. Nina is a particularly sensitive observer of the orphans, trying (as noted in chapter 1) to place herself imaginatively into their experience in order to appreciate it. She also knows that the very word "orphan" is always said with a poignancy that she recognizes should inspire pity in her: "She was going over a thought, a fact: Half the people out here with me are orphans. Orphans. Orphans. She yearned for her heart to twist. But it didn't, not in time" (cs 346). Nina is discerning enough to understand what lies behind the orphans' differences: "The reason orphans were the way they were lay first in nobody's watching them, Nina thought, for she felt obscurely like a trespasser. They, they were not answerable. Even on being watched, Easter remained not answerable to a soul on earth. Nobody cared! And so, in this beatific state, something came out of *her!*" (cs 352).

The orphans are free of that protectiveness that surrounds girls like Nina and able, therefore, to develop an independence of spirit Nina never feels. But as we have seen, to be free in Welty's world also means to be helpless and vulnerable, a fact Welty emphasizes symbolically by having her narrator state that none of the orphans "could or would swim, ever" (cs 344).

One day three of the girls (Easter, Nina, and Jinny Love Stark) find themselves alone near a boat on the edge of a secluded part of the lake. Nina pensively writes her name in the sand: "Nina, Nina, Nina. Writing, she could dream that her self might get away from her—that here in this faraway place she could tell her self, by name, to go or to stay" (cs 355). Thoughtful about what her name means and what its relationship might be to her inner sense of self, Nina is startled a moment later to see Easter "misspelling" her own name, "Esther," when she writes it in the sand. Easter insists that she pronounces her name "Easter" and, at Nina's challenge, announces that no one else named her: "I let myself name myself" (cs 357). Nina and Jinny Love find this notion bewildering and utterly incompatible with the fatefulness and inevitability they have always assumed about names. Jinny Love, named for her maternal grandmother, is convinced her own name "couldn't be anything else" (cs 357). Nina, who still believes in the efficacy of names, tries to show her new friend what her name looks like "spelled right": "Nina lifted the stick from Easter's fingers and began to print, but had to throw herself bodily over the name to keep Easter from it. 'Spell it right and it's real!' she cried" (cs 357). Easter remains unperturbed, but Nina is shaken to see that names, a feature of her world she had considered stable and significant, may, in fact, be more or less randomly chosen.

The two succeeding stories, already considered from other perspectives, deserve additional attention in terms of their concern with naming and communal myths. A good portion of Randall's despair (in "The Whole World Knows") in dealing with his wife's infidelity is because the town of Morgana (which he thinks of narrowly as "the whole world") persists in interpreting his dilemma, so that "well-meaning" neighbors like Miss Perdita Mayo and even his young acquaintance Maideen Sumrall repeatedly tell him his own story. In doing so, they seem to doom him to a particular role in what is happening as they spell out (and implicitly limit) his options. Ran cannot think beyond the town's interpretations. He cannot escape the stories. As Lowry Pei has noted in an excellent essay on *The Golden Apples,* there are very few ways for the characters in these stories to free themselves "from society's inadequate names."[26] Pei argues that "the imposition of names, the observing gaze of community—can become a ruthless imprisonment . . . [yet] the power to withhold one's life from others becomes highly paradoxical" for it leads to "the horror in love . . . the separateness."[27] Pei is correct in concluding that those few characters who achieve a full sense of their selves do so only when—through dream, art, abandonment of the community, or some other form of disengagement from communal definitions (as in the orphans in "Moon Lake," free because they *are* orphans)—they come to terms with the complex interplay of love and separateness necessary in a self-chosen life. Virgie Rainey is such a figure.

"The Wanderers" addresses and seems to offer a final vision of many of the major themes already discussed: legacy; love as protection; how naming preserves and obscures truths about our lives; and the individual's relationship to the community's insistence on particular interpretations of experience. The story features not only the consciousness of Katie Rainey, the protagonist/narrator of the first story, "Shower of Gold," but also that of Virgie Rainey, her daughter, who has been viewed until now only through others' eyes. Katie herself was one of the community voices perpetuating the speculations about King MacLain that gave him increasingly mythic stature in Morgana. Her early monologue with a passing stranger makes it clear that she shares with other women in town a fascination with King that may have left her vulnerable to becoming one of his sexual conquests. It is Katie who explains how the town has come to view Snowdie MacLain, his oft-abandoned wife, as virtually a saint because of her patience and apparent tolerance of his ways.

In "The Wanderers," just before Katie dies, she lies in bed while Virgie fans her and Katie repeats to herself the names of the flowers and quilts she is leaving behind, counting and correcting herself, concerned not to forget any of them or "the places things grew" (CS 431). Katie's list is a particularly feminine one, recording things she had loved, created, and nourished, and constituting at the same time a legacy for her daughter. Her memories of the quilts she is leaving behind become confused with the quilts her own mother had left her, just as she confuses herself with Virgie as their recipient, in a blurring of generations that Welty often attributes to her older characters. Moreover, the text moves directly from Miss Katie's consciousness to Virgie's, where it remains, thus suggesting structurally that the younger woman is now moving into a different stage of her life. Welty has written about such movement as one of the crucial ways in which humans come to understand one another:

> Through learning at my later date things I hadn't known, or had escaped or possibly feared realizing, about my parents—and myself—I glimpse our whole family life as if it were freed of that clock time which spaces us apart so inhibitingly, divides young and old, keeps our living through the same experiences at separate distances.
>
> It is our inward journey that leads us through time—forward or back, seldom in a straight line, most often spiraling. Each of us is moving, changing, with respect to others. (OWB 102)

A book such as *The Golden Apples*, which follows characters through several decades, makes readers especially aware of how characters move through different positions in life, replacing one another as time and circumstance entail. Extensive mythological allusions in this text—for example, references to Virgie cutting cloth and later the grass with her sewing scissors (CS 441) and to other women with needles in their collars or tape measures hung around their necks—evoke images of the three Fates, mythic women who spin, measure, and ultimately cut the thread of life. They also recall the triple nature of the most ancient goddess, whose incarnations express the virgin, mother, and "crone" aspects of a woman's life, defined in terms of her successive sexual roles.[28] Virgie, unmarried, has in a sense remained a maiden, and in her lifelong independence, she has certainly been a "virgin" in the original meaning of that term. Now, however, the death of her mother and her forty and more years suggest her movement into a later stage of autonomy and freedom from family responsibilities. She has never been a mother, as most of her contemporaries are—Jinny Love has two children, and Nina Carmichael Nesbitt is "heavy with child" (CS 433)—but Katie's childlike nature in her last years has made her virtually a child, needing Virgie's care and patience. Thus Katie's death creates a freedom for her daughter quite like that of women whose children are now older and self-sufficient. Throughout this collection, women are seen to grow older and replace one another successively, even in the sorrowful role of laying out the dead.

When the community arrives at Virgie's house after her mother's death, she finds herself caught up in a ritual that moves relentlessly forward, based on Morgana's notions of the ceremonial attentions due one of its respected citizens. People who had never before entered Katie's home appear there now and watch to see that Virgie fulfills their expectations for a bereaved daughter, not allowing her to grieve in her own way. Some of her visitors take Virgie's arms and pull her toward her mother when Katie has been prepared for burial, and when Virgie resists, saying "Don't touch me," they explain her own motives to her: "Honey, you just don't know what you lost, that's all." Welty's narrator notes that "they were all people who had never touched her before who tried now to struggle with her, their faces hurt. She was hurting them all, shocking them. They leaned over her, agonized, pleading with the pull of their hands" (CS 435). Acknowledging Virgie's refusal to cooperate with what they believe is "right" on this occasion, Miss Perdita Mayo pronounces the verdict that seems likely to become part of the town's story about this day: "Your mama was too fine for you, Virgie, too fine. That was always the trouble between you" (CS 435). As she listens to the talk now filling the house, Virgie thinks, "always in a house of death . . . all the stories come evident, show forth from the person, become a part of the public domain. Not the dead's story, but the living's" (CS 433). And when a neighbor characterizes Katie as "a living saint" (CS 436), Virgie realizes how hopeless it is to expect to hear truths from them. The mistake that old King MacLain makes in mixing up Katie with Nellie Loomis in his memory of how she used to set her cotton stockings ablaze (CS 438) is ultimately no more false than what Virgie's other visitors say about her mother. Their stories have little to do with trying to remember Katie clearly. Most of them had thought of the Raineys as being of a different, poorer class than such families as the Starks or Carmichaels, and apparently none of them truly befriended Katie while she was alive. As they tell anecdote after anecdote that fails to say anything accurate or meaningful about Katie or her life, Virgie feels trapped: "She wept because they could not tell it right, and they didn't press her for her reasons" (CS 435). Content now that she has cried, they feel they have done well in "comforting" her.

Virgie's loss of her mother and her release from any further family ties occasions her reconceptualization of her place in the world. Her sudden freedom is experienced first as numbness and then as a peacefulness and reconnection with the things that matter that is powerfully rendered by Welty's description of her swim in the nearby river. Unlike the poor swimmers and nearly drowned figures found in several of the earlier stories, Virgie enjoys a swim that offers a nearly mystical moment of suspension in which she feels herself part of the natural world, both cleansed and poised on the verge of some new transformation of her understanding. What others had experienced as tangible obstacles to their enjoyment of the lake and river (sand, shells, mud) touch her "like suggestions and withdrawals of some bondage that might have been dear, now dismembering and losing itself. . . . She hung suspended in the Big Black River as she would know to hang suspended in felicity" (CS 440). Virgie's capacity for a complete appreciation of the natural world and the present moment is Welty's means of suggesting the human wholeness that is the nearest thing to fulfillment and peace in her fiction. Feeling the ephemerality even of her self ("Virgie had reached the point where in the next moment she might turn into something without feeling it shock her" [CS 440]), she can view her life from a wider, less time-bound perspective. Later in the story, Virgie is comforted when she recalls that on autumn nights at the river, there would be a cone of light between her eyes and the moon, "a long silent horn, of white light. It was a connection visible as the hair is in air, between the self and the moon, to make the self feel the child, a daughter far, far back" (CS 454). Reconnection and the image of feminine fecundity implicit in the image of the moon suggest a genuine rebirth of this woman who renews the "daughter" in herself, fulfilling a promise implicit in her name ("Rainey" having evolved from the French for rebirth, "renée" [CS 442]).

Whereas her contemporary, Cassie Morrison, the town's piano teacher and a spinster, the timid successor to Miss Eckhart, devotes her imagination and energy to spelling out her "Mama's Name" in flowers (CS 456), in what seems a rather pathetic attempt to create in retrospect the illusion of a perfect love between mother and daughter,[29] Virgie's true growth is signaled by her ability to *let go* of merely tangible reminders of the past and venture forward to new experiences. Sitting on a stile (an image of crossroads, of decisions) in the nearby town of MacLain, Virgie reviews her relationships, including those with the men she has known, men she may once have thought of as offering her marriage and a particular type of future. But the distance this particular wanderer has traveled is suggested when she thinks of her current beau: "Mr. Mabry imagined he was coming to her eventually, but was it to him that she had come, *backward to protection?*" (CS 459; emphasis mine). Protection is the least of what she would want from love, for, as Welty's text implies, Virgie has transcended the safe, protected way of life chosen by characters like Cassie.

A final memory recorded in the story is Virgie's recollection of a picture of Medusa and Perseus that Miss Eckhart ("whom Virgie had not, after all, hated—had come near to loving" [CS 460]) had kept on her wall. If, as critics have suggested, this picture represents a kind of paradigmatic mythical moment in which a male figure is triumphant, while a female figure, once an object of love, is transformed into someone to be reviled and duly destroyed,[30] then Welty's treatment of it suggests a new role for the female victim/villain.

> Cutting off the Medusa's head was the heroic act, perhaps, that made visible a horror in life, that was at once the horror in love, Virgie thought —the separateness. . . . she must believe in the Medusa equally with Perseus. . . . [Miss Eckhart] had absorbed the hero and the victim and then, stoutly, could sit down to the piano with all Beethoven ahead of her. With her hate, with her love, and with the small gnawing feelings that ate them, she offered Virgie her Beethoven. She offered, offered, offered— and when Virgie was young, in the strange wisdom of youth that is accepting of more than is given, she had accepted *the* Beethoven. . . . That was the gift. (CS 460)

This excerpt makes clear that Virgie has gone well beyond the limitations of her fellow citizens in Morgana by having accepted the legacy Miss Eckhart had to offer—the vision of a woman's life as one transcending the predictive roles of wife and mother and committing itself to art, whatever the consequence. Few would consider Miss Eckhart's life successful, yet it was particularly significant to Welty because author and teacher shared through their art a passion that few people in Morgana seem even to have glimpsed.[31] In these last moments of the text, then, Virgie has truly learned what her teacher implicitly taught—to identify both with the hero and the victim, to understand both of them through empathy and bring the intensity of the drama between them into art. The separateness brought about by the act of violence at the core of this masculine myth of heroic triumph is absorbed and transmuted into the fusion of hero and victim that Virgie ultimately finds in the memory of Miss Eckhart playing Beethoven: "In Virgie's reach of memory a melody softly lifted, lifted of itself. Every time Perseus struck off the Medusa's head, there was the beat of time, and the melody. Endless the Medusa, and Perseus endless" (CS 460).

Virgie's acceptance of the necessary interplay of separation and connection in the passionate drama of loving other people serves as a final tribute to Miss Eckhart's legacy. Moreover, her imagination of herself as being, once again, a daughter, leads into Virgie's final fantasy, in which she imagines that she can hear through falling rain the music of the spheres, "the magical percussion, the world beating in [her] ears . . . the running of the horse and bear, the stroke of the leopard, the dragon's crusty slither, and the glimmer and the trumpet of the swan" (CS 461). This final convergence of the ideas of daughterhood and legacy, passion, music, and the swan embodies a compensatory beauty that echoes Virgie's newfound integrity.

Parents and children take turns back and forth,
changing places, protecting and protesting each other:
so it seemed to the child.
Welty, The Optimist's Daughter

Vulnerability is a personal and valuable and selfish
possession—perhaps more; perhaps in effect it is the self.
Welty, "Henry Green: Novelist of the Imagination,"
The Eye of the Story

CHAPTER 5

Embracing Vulnerability

Letting Go of Love as Protection

As we have seen, Eudora Welty is particularly fascinated with those moments in children's lives when they glimpse a way of living that centers on beliefs and interpretations other than those of their parents. Sometimes this move toward a more autonomous understanding occurs after disillusionment, when what parents say conflicts with the child's own observations or experience. Perhaps just as often, however, the movement away from the insularity or protectiveness of parental views comes about naturally, with the passage of time and the young person's gradually emerging sense that other possibilities exist.

This latter sort of development is featured in "The Winds," an early story that explores in greater depth than Welty had attempted before the richness and fluidity of a young girl's imagination and her recognition that adults do not share her vision; it also reveals Welty's first conscious attention to the passage of time and to the crucial role memory plays in holding on to experiences she finds both precious and ephemeral.[1] Josie is poised between the self-indulgent pleasures of her imaginative relationship with the world and the next, rapidly approaching stage of her life, adolescence, represented for her by an older girl, Cornella, who lives across the street and embodies, through much of the story, the future that Josie believes awaits her. The storm indicated by the story's title is an equinoctial storm that signifies the end of summer, symbolically the end of Josie's childhood freedom and the beginning of her entrance into a way of living replete with assumptions about gendered behavior.

Until now Josie has been living all of the roles in her fantasies; she is not only the queen waiting in a sand castle, but the suitor calling to her his words of love. Her freedom to ride her bicycle and wander with her best friend throughout the neighborhood, eating freely of the fruits and flowers she encounters, covering herself with transfer pictures, following after the monkey-man, and pulling her shoe-box steamboat along the sidewalks at twilight, greeting other children (pulling their own steamboats) "dreamily" with "Choo-choo!" (CS 218) suggests a blissful state in which there are no limitations to what she might choose to be. Occasionally, however, adults interrupt her, calling her back, as she realizes, "because they had no memory of magic" (CS 212). Josie is beginning to sense that the special moments in her life are all too brief; plunged into time, she has begun self-consciously to attempt to hold on to the drifting, dreamy life of sensations that has constituted her summer experience until now. "Summer was turning into the past. The long ago . . ." (CS 211): "For the first time in her life she thought, might the same wonders never come again? Was each wonder original and alone like the falling star, and when it fell did it bury itself beyond where you hunted it?" (CS 219).

Sensing a different future, Josie longs for more of the past:

All that she ran after in the whole summer world came to life in departure before Josie's eyes and covered her vision with wings. It kept her from eating her dinner to think of all that she had caught or meant to catch before the time was gone—June-bugs in the banana plants to fly before breakfast on a thread, lightning-bugs that left a bitter odor in the palms of the hands, butterflies with their fierce and haughty faces, bees in a jar. A great tempest of droning and flying seemed to have surrounded her as she ran, and she seemed not to have moved without putting her hand out after something that flew ahead. . . . (CS 214)

The objects that Josie tries to capture and hold (fireflies, bees, butterflies) include images noted earlier as signifying phenomena readily at hand that we tend to assume constitute knowledge we can catch hold of and keep. Like so many of Welty's younger protagonists, Josie seems deeply compelled to understand everything she can. Her impulse to hold things long enough to make them into knowledge "she would allow to enter her heart, for which she had been keeping room" (CS 218) reflects a stage Welty believes many people go through as they face the potential for loss implicit in the passage of time—they would like to stop time in order not to miss anything. Josie, in hoping to postpone her own inevitable movement into a new stage of life, is facing the poignancy of mortality and its inevitable limitation of her opportunities for knowledge.

Josie's future seems foreshadowed in Cornella, who spends all of her time "making ready" for the moment when love will enter her life and give it meaning. Josie observes that, in contrast to her own nearly ceaseless activity, big girls "are usually idle"; Cornella differs only slightly in that she washes, brushes, and suns her hair frequently, while always "looking out, steadily out, over the street." Josie compares her to the fairy-tale Rapunzel ("Cornella, Cornella, let down thy hair, and the King's son will come climbing up" [CS 214]), who, like so many fairy-tale maidens, seems only to come to life when a prince arrives on the scene. Yet despite the romantic possibilities Cornella's waiting implies, Josie's compassion leads her to recognize the poignancy of her neighbor's situation. With a ribbon in her hair and a sash "in pale bows" hanging from the back of her dress, Cornella moves back and forth between her house and the front yard; for Josie, observing the older girl's repeatedly deferred hopes, "the pity for ribbons drove her to a wild capering" (CS 217).

At the Chautauqua Josie attends with her family on the evening before the storm, they watch a trio of women musicians, among them a cornetist whose music and beauty are so compelling to Josie that she glimpses another way of thinking of the future. "If morning-glories had come out of the horn instead of those sounds, Josie would not have felt a more astonished delight" (CS 220). What this woman conveys is the possibility of living one's life as an artist. Her life clearly embodies a far greater creativity and richness than Cornella's waiting can promise. "Josie listened in mounting care and suspense, as if the performance led in some direction away—as if a destination were being shown her" (CS 220). Welty is implicitly offering Josie a choice: to become like Cornella, waiting for someone else to invest her life with (apparently) the only meaning she can imagine it having, or like the cornetist, creating beauty and passion of her own. Cornella's waiting is cast into a sad and frustrating light. In a note Josie finds the morning after the storm, Cornella has written to some unnamed (perhaps imaginary) suitor: "O my darling I have waited so long when are you coming for me? Never a day or a night goes by that I do not ask When? When? When? . . ." (CS 221). Implicitly, her postponement of living is shown to be a waste, the antithesis of Josie's conscious appreciation of each moment she experiences, a way of living that Josie does not ever want to give up. Cornella's face seems "all wild" (CS 220) at the Chautauqua as she observes the cornetist, betraying, perhaps, despair and fear that her waiting may end in nothing. Josie, however, after hearing the musician play, concludes "that after that there would be no more waiting and no more time left for the one who did not take heed and follow. . . ." (CS 220).

Josie's powerful desire to hold in her memory everything that occurs— "if they would bring the time around once more, she would lose nothing that was given, she would hoard the nuts like a squirrel" (CS 219)— characterizes memory as, above all, preserving experience and something of its original wonder. But this conception of memory was gradually supplanted by Welty's emerging understanding that memory, like language itself, does not simply record but actually *structures* experience.[2] It generates for people, much as a final vocabulary does, a way of thinking about their lives that corresponds to their general assumptions about the way things are. Welty recognizes that even in thinking about such distant phenomena as the stars, one's consciousness structures and imposes meaning on what might have seemed featureless objects: "After all, the constellations, patterns, we are used to seeing in the sky are purely subjective; it is because our combining things, our heroes, existed in the world almost as soon as we did that made us long ago see Perseus up there, and not a random scattering of little lights."[3]

In her novel *The Optimist's Daughter* (1972), Welty offers her most focused consideration of how memory functions in preserving the past. With

Laurel McKelva Hand, Welty's protagonist, the reader becomes aware of how memory, so precious because it preserves the most meaningful moments in people's lives, also manipulates, delimits, and even distorts what it preserves.

Welty's close friend, novelist Elizabeth Bowen, had written about memory in her novel *The Death of the Heart,* and Welty would probably have been intrigued to encounter this passage in which St. Quentin Miller urges a teenage girl, Portia Quayne, *not* to keep a diary:

> "It is madness to write things down. . . . I should never write what had happened down. One's nature is to forget, and one ought to go by that. Memory is quite unbearable enough, but even so it leaves out quite a lot. It wouldn't let one down as gently, even, as that if it weren't more than half a fake—*we remember to suit ourselves.* No, really, er, Portia, believe me: if one didn't let oneself swallow some few lies, I don't know how one would ever carry the past. Thank God, except at its one moment there's never any such thing as a bare fact. Ten minutes later, half an hour later, one's begun to gloze the fact over with a deposit of some sort. The hours I spent with thee dear love are like a string of pearls to me. But a diary (if one did keep it up to date) would come much too near the mark. One ought to secrete for some time before one begins to look back at anything. Look how reconciled to everything reminiscences are . . ."[4]

St. Quentin's advice is permeated, of course, by his cynicism and his own motives for urging Portia not to write down what happens, but Welty would have been especially interested in the metaphors through which Bowen characterizes memory. The idea of memory as a string of pearls mirrors Welty's own tendency to speak of threads as moving through one's experience and memories, giving them direction. If everyday life is often labyrinthine (ES 20), then memory is like Ariadne, finding a way for us through the chaotic complexity of what the mind has noted. The thread of continuity and meaning generated by memory is very close in Welty's imagination to the thread of significance writers create in guiding their readers through a text: "No two stories ever go the same way, although in different hands one story might possibly go any one of a thousand ways; and though the woods may look the same from outside, it is a new and different labyrinth every time" (ES 120–21). The frequency of Welty's reliance on the image of thread—as well as her persistent references to sewing and weaving and to the three Fates who control the thread of life—seems ultimately to more than offset her references to autonomy; Welty nearly always emphasizes the continuity of things, and when she speaks of separation, it is typically to add the idea of something (like a thread) bridging the distance.[5] She is very fond of E. M. Forster's well-known epigraph to *Howards End*: "Only connect . . ." For Welty, writing differs from memory in being a more conscious functioning of the imagination as it works to find the forms of continuity in experience. Her fascination with memory may well reflect a belief that memory and art function toward the same ends: "Writing fiction has developed in me an abiding respect for the unknown in a human lifetime and a sense of *where to look for the threads,* how to follow, how to connect, find *in the thick of the tangle what clear line persists. The strands are all there:* to the memory nothing is ever really lost" (OWB 90; emphasis mine).

The Optimist's Daughter features dialectic patterns apparent, as well, in Welty's other work. The novel as a whole is structured through a tension between order and disorder, as an interplay between Apollonian and Dionysian forces.[6] Her fascination with words also leads Welty to pair the activities of "protecting" and "protesting" as she focuses on Laurel Hand's desire to preserve the remembered perfection of her family's life together. How these dualities and related ones, such as speech and silence, work within the novel will become clearer as we proceed.

The story of Laurel McKelva Hand's loss of her father and her struggle to come to terms with her memories of all the loved ones she has lost seems on one level to reflect a personal meditation such as Welty herself may have undergone. When she wrote it, she had recently lost both her mother and her brother Edward within just a few days of one another, a crisis that left her, like Laurel, without parents or siblings. In framing Laurel's story, however, Welty has gone well beyond this compelling personal situation. Through the creation of Judge McKelva's young second wife, Wanda Fay, in particular, she has transformed the outlines of Laurel's story into a vivid drama. In the figure of the exasperating Fay,[7] Laurel recognizes and confronts forces of disruption and chaos that threaten the ordered serenity of her long-held memories, both of her parents' relationship and of her own brief marriage with Philip Hand. Her father had placed a wedding photograph of Laurel and Philip Hand in a silver frame (OD 121), and Welty's narrator emphasizes that Laurel had done this, too, in remembering her marriage as "the old perfection undisturbed and undisturbing" (OD 154). Fay, in contrast, is the first of several figures in the book who bring a primal, destructive Dionysian energy into Laurel's life through their un-checked self-centeredness and crass oblivion to the sensitivities of anyone but themselves: they include the Dalzell family, whom Laurel encounters in the hospital the night her father dies; the audacious handyman, Mr. Cheek; and Fay's own relatives, the Chisoms, who (appropriately) run a wrecking concern back in Texas. Fay is explicitly linked to subversive forces in her passionate desire to be part of the Mardi Gras festivities in New Orleans.[8] Such a carnival, of course, has as a basic purpose the reversal and mockery of normal hierarchies of order in a culture, and Fay, representing these ele-mental disruptive forces, regularly leaves confusion in her wake (as Laurel discovers in finding the trail of nail polish on her father's desk and the gouges in her mother's breadboard).

It is through her efforts to account for the disturbing presence of Fay and to understand how her father could have chosen to marry such a per-son that Laurel is led to grapple with the limitations of memories she has long accepted as accurate. For Laurel, Fay becomes an emblem of the ter-rible disjunctions and violations, the things that don't fit and can never make sense, that enter one's life seemingly at random and destroy one's peace of mind. Laurel is much like her father, who calls himself an opti-mist (OD 10) and who has chosen in both of his marriages to avoid any deep acknowledgment of the existence of hurtfulness and pain.[9] When her father calls Laurel by her childhood name, "Polly" (OD 15), he evokes that excessive optimism associated with a "Pollyanna's" view of the world, but the adult Laurel's epistemological task in the novel is to understand the distortions of her own former thinking, to recognize the failure of mere optimism to do justice to the complexity of experience.

Laurel learns through the course of the story that her memories of her parents and husband have failed to reflect the reality of their lives because she has insisted on remembering them only at their best. The nature of this selective restructuring of what is saved is a central concern in this novel, in which Welty also returns to other familiar themes: the value of love con-ceived of as protection; our search for understanding of one another and ourselves; and how we use language to create patterns of thought that keep us from knowledge as often as they guide us toward it.

Laurel's new understanding of herself results from events surrounding the death and funeral of her father, Clint McKelva. Having returned home with his body to Mount Salus, Mississippi, Laurel undergoes the same dis-may and frustration that Welty attributed to Virgie Rainey in *The Golden*

Apples, when, at the death of her mother, she was forced to listen to anecdotes and characterizations about her mother that bore little relation to the truth. Serving as a paradigmatic occasion on which people tell stories about themselves and others, the funeral (and elsewhere in Welty's stories, such gatherings as weddings and family reunions) provides an important focus for allowing Welty to explore such fabrications in the making. These occasions expose the dynamics through which, as Welty has phrased it, "relationships run the whole gamut of love and oppression" (Con 221).

In her efforts to "protect" her father and his memory, Laurel vigorously "protests" when Fay flings herself histrionically across his body in its open casket (which Laurel had wanted closed to preserve his privacy), and she repeatedly objects to her father's friends as they tell stories that misrepresent both his character and his values. Like the sewing woman Verna Longmeier, who was "out of her mind, yet even she was not being kept back from Judge McKelva's coffin," the judge's friends talk, repeat, and get "everything crooked" (OD 71–72). They attribute to him a flamboyant fearlessness in facing the "White Caps" (OD 79) that Laurel disputes: "He hadn't any use for what he called theatrics. . . . He had no patience for show" (OD 80). But when she protests, her friends urge her to let people say what they wish. Laurel concludes that "what's happening isn't real" and thinks of her father now as "helpless in his own house . . . to have reached at this moment the danger point of his life" (OD 82). She appeals to her family's oldest friend, Adele Courtland:

> "This is still his house. After all, they're still his guests. They're misrepresenting him—falsifying, that's what Mother would call it." Laurel might have been trying to testify now for her father's sake, as though he were in process of being put on trial in here instead of being viewed in his casket. "He never would have stood for lies being told about him. Not at any time. Not ever. . . . I'm his daughter. I want what people say now to be the truth. . . . The least anybody can do for him is *remember* right." (OD 83)

But Laurel, like Virgie, is forced to continue witnessing her neighbors' and friends' recitations of their stories about the judge's life—as well as the vulgarity of Wanda Fay and her family, with their own ideas of how to behave when paying respect to someone who has died. Wanda Fay's mother, Mrs. Chisom, suggests on the day the judge is buried that his home, now Fay's, would make a fine boarding house (OD 96). At Fay's wishes, the judge is buried in the new part of the cemetery, "dotted uniformly with indestructible plastic Christmas poinsettias" (OD 90–91). The travesty of what her father would have wished leaves Laurel numb, yet the very shock opens the way for her soul-searching and recognition that her own beliefs and memories, too, however benign and lovingly motivated they may be, preserve false (because perfect) versions of her life with her family and with her husband, Philip. Her evolving understanding constitutes the central momentum of the novel.

The style and structure of Welty's novel make it strikingly different from her earlier texts. The complex allusiveness and lyrical intensity of *The Golden Apples* (1949) and the garrulous charm of *Losing Battles* (1970) do not prepare the reader for the spareness and apparent simplicity of *The Optimist's Daughter*. Moreover, a number of factors have led to critical readings of the later novel that are far different from those prompted by such works as *The Golden Apples*.[10] Numerous biographical correspondences between Welty's life and the details of her story and her explicit articulation of her theme at the novel's end—having to do with the fragility of memory and its role in understanding—have led to explications of the novel that nearly always emphasize theme and content.[11] And although the novel's critics have also to varying degrees discussed one or more of its pervasive images, no full understanding of the nature of the coherence underlying their presence has yet been achieved.[12] *The Optimist's Daughter,* as much as anything Welty has written, deserves the close, attentive reading Ruth Vande Kieft recommends, "the kind of patient and loving scrutiny we apply to poems."[13]

The narrative strategies that inform Welty's novel especially deserve examination because of their subtlety and complexity and because they directly contribute to the implications of her themes. Welty uses allusive and imagistic devices in at least three ways: through her exploitation of the etymological meanings of single words, through her syntactical juxtaposition or pairing of images themselves, and through her oblique references to various mythic substructures. By creating an explicit structure of relationships *between* images, Welty generates an intricate network of meanings in which no single image stands alone, because each is modified by the simultaneous presence of others. Her strategies for insisting on the interdependence of her images and their meanings enable Welty to express more fully the complexity of her view of how understanding itself takes place and of how we—ostensible seekers of knowledge—manage so often to evade it.

Welty's objectives are carried forward in large part by the special cogency of her dominant images, vision and blindness. On the surface Welty seems merely to exploit their traditional meanings, using them as expressions of the broader symbolism of light and darkness—as emblems of human understanding. But as with her use of imagery throughout this novel, she evokes the full range of meanings implied by each symbol, from the most positive to the most negative. Light connotes illumination, comprehension, and clarity, yet its excess leads to just the opposite. With Emily Dickinson, Welty believes "The Truth must dazzle gradually / Or every man be blind—."[14] Thus she gives an especially appropriate name to the vulgar family Laurel meets at the hospital, who incarnate an ugliness she needs to come to terms with; they are homonymously named the "Dalzells." Similarly, the darkness that normally signifies obscurity, ignorance, or an inability or unwillingness to understand can also imply a restfulness that makes introspection and later "vision" possible. The window *blind* in Judge McKelva's hospital room serves this function, darkening the room and protecting his eyes while they recover; twice, it is torn down by disruptive figures in the novel, the blind patient (Mr. Dalzell) in the next bed and later (apparently) by Wanda Fay (OD 20, 34). On the first occasion, Laurel, the nurse, and the judge's doctor put it back in place to protect his vulnerable eyes from the light. The second time there is no point in replacing it. The blind falls at the judge's final crisis, as if signaling his death.

Welty's narrative methods often involve exploring a range of words signifying particular concepts, as she does to pursue the myriad linguistic connections between eyesight and insight. Words like "eye," "see," "watch," and "look" pervade Welty's novel, but so do terms that reflect limitations of vision brought about by factors both internal and external to the perceiving self.[15] The ultimately blinding light (conveyed by such terms as "glare," "blaze," "dazzle," and "brightness") is intimated throughout the novel by yet other words that express the intermittent, ambiguous light of objects themselves ("twinkling," "shimmering," "flickering," and "flashing") and, in doing so, suggest the indeterminacy and tenuousness of the objects toward which people look for understanding. Welty suggests, too, that perceivers allow their own preoccupations to interfere with seeing clearly through her use of images of "mirrors" or "reflections" that cause them to see themselves instead—a kind of narcissistic blindness. And finally, she shows that vision fails when one looks at the wrong object; a major example of this is her use of the word "slipping," which, evoking the idea of an eclipse or a veneer, suggests that an object is hidden by something in front of it that one sees instead. Recurrent references to curtains and screens enhance this motif. Judge McKelva has a "slipped retina," and his larger problem in the novel is that he has mistaken one wife (the young Fay) for his beloved late wife, Becky.[16] This last device is part and parcel, of course, of Welty's assumption that surfaces often serve as disguises for deeper "truths" that they hide, a perceptual pattern discussed in chapter 4.

In one of her most fascinating narrative strategies, Welty creates linkages between the sustained motif of blindness and sight and other motifs by using key terms that serve as pivots between them. Thus, she enables the connotations of one set of images to enhance or modify those of a second group. This technique becomes evident when we consider another major motif in the novel, that of rushing water. With the word "cataract," Welty connects the eye disease leading potentially to blindness with the waterfall to suggest a particular obstacle to clarity of vision. In its destructive aspect, rushing water represents the overwhelming emotions or thoughts that can blind us to what is happening; in its more benign form, it signifies a cleansing of the eyes that frees us to see better, as in the tears that fill Laurel's eyes at the moment of her fullest understanding in the novel (OD 154). In both instances, the power of rushing water is an image for a compelling influx of memories, an experience attributed to a number of characters in Welty's stories, among them Cassie Morrison in *The Golden Apples:* "Like a wave, the gathering past came right up to her. Next time it would be too high. . . . Then the wave moved up, towered, and came drowning down over her stuck-up head" (CS 287). In that collection of stories the characters' ability to swim—to withstand the force of the waters, the implications of their memories—is one reflection of their heroic potential (or its absence).

The judge, his first wife Becky, and Laurel are all specifically associated with the linkages between vision and rushing water. Before she died, Becky, after several eye operations for cataracts, lay on her sickbed sightless and recaptured a sense of her longed-for childhood world of order and peace by reciting Southey's "Cataract of Lodore," which in its very rhythms and momentum mimics the experience of rushing water (OD 147). Years later, when Judge McKelva is recovering from his eye operation, he is told to rest his eyes in the dark and, above all, that there are to be no tears. Laurel sees him just before his death and fights back her own tears, to keep *him* from crying. The judge dies just after Laurel finds Wanda Fay shaking him to demand that he get up out of bed and take her to the Mardi Gras. Since the novel makes clear that his eye operation is not the cause of his death, the reader is urged narratively to recognize that he has "seen" too much—Fay's cruelty and his mistake in believing she is like his first, gentler wife Becky—and that in his despair at seeing, he has just given up. At the moment just before his death, his "whole, pillowless head went dusky, as if he laid it under the surface of dark, pouring water and held it there" (OD 33). It remains for Laurel to come to terms with what they both have seen.

Images of water are especially significant in connection with Judge McKelva, because his basic emotional failure in the novel is shown to be his refusal to acknowledge Becky's despair when, in her last days, she experienced a horrible fear that her optimist husband would not face. In his belief that his love for her would make everything all right (OD 146), he left her feeling that she was facing alone the worst crisis of her soul. Indeed, this sense of abandonment severely exacerbated Becky's pain as she struggled with her fear of death. In view of his wife's suffering and his inability to acknowledge it, there is both irony and poignancy in the fact that formerly, as mayor of the town, the judge had been in charge of flood control for his community. In a letter written to his daughter, Laurel, shortly before he became engaged to Fay, the judge's particular blindness, which would eventuate in this second marriage, is foreshadowed when he says, "there was never anything wrong with keeping up a little optimism over the Flood" (OD 121). Flood control, in these terms, is precisely what optimism is about.[17] Thus, at the moment of Laurel's fullest epiphany, when she transcends the comfort of optimism, Welty writes: "A flood of feeling descended on [her]. She . . . put her head down on the open lid of the desk and wept in grief for love and for the dead. . . . Now all she had found had found her. The deepest spring in her heart had uncovered itself, and it began to flow again" (OD 154). The waters here are to be seen as emblems of life itself.

Just as the presence of water signifies emotion or life, its absence suggests the lack or diminishment of these qualities. In the scenes with both the Dalzell and Chisom families, conversations take place about family members who have died or nearly died "wanting water" (OD 39–40, 71). The final deprivation of water is associated with the last of one's living, a sort of final betrayal. This variation on the theme becomes especially provocative in thinking about the characterization of Becky, to whom Welty gives the maiden name "Thurston," as if suggesting some absence there, as well. Becky is in many respects the most problematic and mysterious character in Welty's novel, and it is intriguing to speculate about the nature of what might be missing.

A third image pattern emphasized in the novel involves hands and their functions; how they create, give, manipulate, hold and withhold, touch, restrain, and express. Although numerous instances of this pervasive motif (prominent, for example, in the name and the talents of Laurel's deceased husband, Philip Hand) occur, its *presence* is in some ways less interesting than how Welty incorporates it into her larger concern with the nature of knowledge. She links the hand imagery of this novel to the blindness motif through the notion of hands that can see, through *braille*. Although the word itself is not used, this pivotal concept is recurrently enacted, as when Welty writes that the sensitive hands of Dr. Courtland, the eye specialist, "had always looked, to Laurel, as if their mere touch on the crystal of a watch would convey to their skin exactly what time it was" (OD 4), or when Laurel, in exploring her mother's writing desk, discovers the little stone boat carved by the judge when he was courting Becky, "her fingers remembering it before she held it under her eyes" (OD 135).[18] By repeatedly describing the motions of her characters' hands (both sensitive and insensitive ones), Welty pursues nearly every imaginable variation on the image to show the strategies people use in experiencing and responding to new knowledge by accepting, modifying, denying, or using it. Ineptitude with one's hands is depicted as a type of blindness to the nuances of things, as when Laurel admits late in the novel that—unlike Philip Hand— she, her father, and her mother, Becky, "were a family of comparatively helpless people" (OD 176). Moreover, with the word "blunder," used several times (in association with the Mardi Gras crowds, the men who carry Judge McKelva's coffin, the trapped bird, and the offensive Mr. Cheek), Welty merges hands and blindness once more: to blunder is to stumble or be clumsy as if one cannot see. Thus, Welty connects blundering (a word that at times she herself italicizes) with the chaotic and disturbing world of darkness and disorder that Laurel and her optimist father have struggled to deny. As for the remembered perfection of her marriage with Philip, Laurel believes "there had not happened a single blunder in their short life together" (OD 162).

A fourth motif in Welty's novel involves her use of birds. They serve several imagistic functions at different points in the novel and ultimately point, even more directly than Welty's other images do, to her explicitly articulated thematic concern with memory. Birds not only pull together the issues represented by the other images but also become at crucial moments images of memory itself.

A review of their more traditional uses in the novel helps us to understand the significance of Welty's later amplification of the image and its incorporation into her allusions to mythic stories. At times, for example, birds are used rather straightforwardly to represent nature commenting on the actions of humans. A mockingbird sings throughout a conversation among four elderly women, Judge McKelva's contemporaries, when, after his funeral and in Laurel's presence, they discuss his two marriages; here birds serve as a kind of chorus to the Greek chorus constituted by the women themselves vis-à-vis Laurel, who is working quietly among the flowers. The flowers also reflect her struggle to see: they are irises.[19] The mockingbird, meanwhile, "let fall a *cascade* of song" (OD 108; emphasis mine).

At other times birds mirror what Laurel fears: the pigeons that feed out of one another's craws and whose pecking as they ate out of her hands when she was a girl terrified her (OD 140) seem to represent Laurel's avoidance of the complicating entanglements of human love in the nearly twenty years since Philip died in World War II. She experiences the apparently painful interdependence of these birds ("sticking their beaks down each other's throats, gagging each other") as an entrapment: "They convinced her that they could not escape each other and could not themselves be escaped from" (OD 140). The scene Welty creates is closely reminiscent of one in D. H. Lawrence's *Lady Chatterley's Lover* in which Connie Chatterley's fear of life and sexuality is expressed in her timidity in handling baby chickens.[20]

Birds serve as images of Laurel's own aspiring soul. The chimney swift trapped in her house on her last night there echoes her panic and feelings of entrapment within anachronistic thoughts and feelings that no longer "fit." During the long, stormy night, she and the bird alike struggle toward "light" (OD 129). And in the morning, when she frees the bird, the reader feels that she is freeing herself as well (OD 168). Birds also reflect the souls of Laurel and Philip Hand on a happier occasion. On their train trip to Mount Salus to be married, the young couple saw a flock of birds "flying in a V of their own, following the same course" south that the lovers were taking (OD 160), mirroring, in fact, the convergence of the Ohio and Mississippi rivers beneath them all. This redoubled image of convergence seemed to Laurel and Philip like a reflection of the joy of their coming together.

Finally, birds are used to suggest a more complex meaning within the novel. Welty enhances her consideration of how memory works and of "the danger of caging memory in" by using birds as images of memory itself.[21] They are present on nearly every occasion when Laurel thinks about the past, at every one of her moments of revelation. When the funeral procession arrives at the cemetery, Welty writes that "as they proceeded there, black wings thudded in sudden unison, and a flock of birds flew up as they might from a ploughed field, still shaped like it, like an old map that still served new territory, and wrinkled away in the air" (OD 91). These birds, and the shape they retain as they fly upward, express Welty's vision of how memory continues to pattern one's thoughts "like an old map" that may or may not fit new territory. Laurel's memories about her parents and husband, perfect and therefore necessarily distorted, constitute an old map that fails to account for Wanda Fay, fails to accept the reality of the difficult, painful moments in her parents' lives together, and fails as well to acknowledge the implications of Philip's loss of his own life. (In a later vision Laurel sees Philip looking "at her out of eyes wild with the craving for his unlived life" as his voice rises to a "roar" of despair [OD 154–55].) Laurel's growth in the novel involves learning to allow her memories to remain vulnerable to the changes in her own understanding. She must, to begin with, stop denying the fact of Fay's existence in her father's life and so come to terms with *his* needs and vulnerabilities. Welty is explicit about the lesson Laurel is to learn, and when she has finally learned it, Welty depicts her as, first, freeing the trapped bird and, then, withstanding waves of emotion in her final confrontation with Fay. In this penultimate scene in the novel, Laurel raises a breadboard Philip had made for her mother "above her head, but for a moment it seemed to be what supported her, a raft in the waters, to keep her from slipping down deep, where the others had gone before her" (OD 177).

Examples alone cannot convey a sense of how intricately Welty structures her motifs in this novel. Blindness and sight, hands, birds, and rushing water—as well as a number of analogous motifs, such as fire, time, and bridges[22]—are linked in a variety of ways through individual words that cross etymological paths (as with "cataract" and "iris") and through their juxtaposition in various contexts (as in the mockingbird's "cascade of song"). Welty rarely fails to pursue the thematic suggestiveness of words' synonyms and homonyms. She seems vividly aware of the multiplicity of meanings inherent in single words, and her linguistic playfulness creates echoes on various levels as she moves among etymological realms. These explorations, in fact, account for a number of otherwise bewildering details. One decidedly lighthearted example involves the images associated with braille, a concept that serves as a link between the motifs of blindness/ sight and hands. Welty introduces a minor character in the novel, atypically, without her last name. The judge's former secretary, who "to everyone in town . . . was known simply as Dot" (OD 64), had years ago bought herself an expensive mah-jongg set. The palpable (raised) dots of braille are recalled in Dot's name itself; in the palpable (recessed) dots on the dominolike tiles, the small sticks, and the dice of the mah-jongg set (used as graphic signs in themselves or to count points); in expressions like "on the dot," which (like "the blink of an eye") appear recurrently in the text to signify time; and in the fact that Welty has her narrator call attention to the word characterizing the sentimental feelings Dot had for the judge and the judge's excessive fondness for his young wife Fay (again, disclosing a type of blindness): "He doted on her," Miss Adele Courtland declares. "'Doted. You've hit on it. That's the word,' said Miss Tennyson" (OD 107). "Mah-jongg" itself is Chinese for "house sparrow," a bird pictured on one of the tiles and a reminder of the bird that disrupts Laurel's home late in the novel, leaving spots everywhere it touches. Much of this may simply be playfulness, an expression of Welty's exuberant, even sensuous, pleasure in the resonances of language. And while placing too much interpretive importance on such passages would be a mistake, they are consistent with Welty's overall narrative strategies, which so often involve encouraging her readers to let their imaginations roam among the network of meanings implied by her linked motifs.

. . .

The linkages we have seen at the level of language take the reader repeatedly back to the surface message of Welty's story, a message about how understanding is jeopardized by our own habits of perception. Welty reinforces the ironies and complexities of her subject at a deeper level, moreover, through allusions—some straightforward and others more oblique —to mythological stories that themselves have to do with evading and searching for truth. Unlike *The Golden Apples,* in which Welty overtly signals each mythic motif she offers as a way of understanding the patterns of meaning she intends, in *The Optimist's Daughter* she has used—but left submerged—mythic substructures that add coherence and nuance to her depiction of the problematics of understanding. Early in the novel, for example, she mirrors the story of Daphne (whose name is Greek for "laurel"), who eluded Apollo's pursuit of her by being transformed into a laurel tree.[23] Laurel confuses her own image in a window with that of a beech tree as she dozes on the train trip to Mount Salus (OD 45). This brief allusion serves as a foreshadowing of Laurel's problem; Daphne's avoidance of sexual encounter serves as a synecdoche for Laurel's avoidance not only of sexuality but of entangling human relationships as a whole and suggests the nature of her failure to acknowledge fully the complexities of her memory of her parents and her husband.

There are suggestions, too, that the mountain in West Virginia where Laurel's grandmother lived is a type of magic mountain, perhaps one of the Venusberg mountains believed in medieval legend to be where the goddess Venus held court, enticing travelers who were then reluctant to leave. A high priestess served the goddess under the name of Queen Sibyl (Welty calls the river at the foot of the mountain "Queen's Shoals"), and because of her prophecies the mountain came to be seen as a place of wisdom. The novel places such emphasis on the bliss that Becky experienced when she was there that the mountain seems to be the prototype of the lost paradise Becky thought of when she decided to keep her "diagrams of *Paradise Lost* and Milton's Universe" (OD 153), and so the mountain, like the figure of Daphne, serves as an image of escape.[24] Becky, remembering that longed-for sanctuary in West Virginia, expressed scorn for the word "Mount" in Mount Salus's name (OD 142); and now Becky's daughter, Laurel, recalling her experiences on that mountain, undergoes her fullest epiphany, after which she dons her "*Sibyl* Connolly" suit for the flight back to Chicago (OD 170; emphasis mine). Among the objects sacred to the goddess Venus were the dove/pigeon (recalling Laurel's crucial childhood encounter with pigeons), bread (Becky's breadboard in the final scenes of the novel), and figs (OD 153)—all associated with Laurel's mother. Welty is drawing from the mythological tradition in which mountains represent the Great Mother, a place of nurturance and wisdom.

The relationship between Becky in Mount Salus and her mother (Laurel's grandmother) in West Virginia, moreover, clearly echoes the mythic story of Demeter and her daughter by Zeus, Persephone.[25] Persephone's abduction into the underworld by Hades led Demeter to search everywhere for her daughter, inconsolable at her loss. Because Persephone had eaten some pomegranate seeds, she could not return to her mother permanently but was able to visit her for part of each year. The times when Persephone was with her mother became the spring and summer seasons, as Demeter in her joy made the earth fertile; when Persephone returned to the underworld, however, Demeter let barrenness return to the earth, as fall turned into winter. The loneliness of Becky's mother is powerfully rendered in Welty's novel, as is her association with the changing of the seasons, because Becky returns every summer to visit "up home." The judge travels north to pick up Rebecca and Laurel each year, as if reenacting the original capture of Persephone, and Laurel speculates that "they might have stayed always. Her father had not appeared to realize it" (OD 141–42). When Becky is back in Mount Salus, the reader is told of her mother's sorrow at her absence as well as of her associations, now, with winter, as in the episode when her hands are bleeding from trying to cut through the ice (OD 150–51).

On her sickbed Becky recalls—with apparent bitterness because she is not there—the white strawberries on the hillside near her mother's home in West Virginia. She says that the strawberries must be eaten the moment they are picked, that they spoil immediately and cannot be carried elsewhere. This bit of folklore corresponds precisely to a story told of the mountain laurel, which is said to die if picked. Both stories, of course, reflect Becky's severe homesickness, the sense in which she longs to be in West Virginia, however much she loves her home and family in Mississippi. Again, her maiden name, "Thurston," is reminiscent of this longing. The very tenacity and fervor of her passion to be "up home" rather than "down South" suggests a permanent sadness in Becky that poignantly recalls the sad compromise that ends the story of Persephone, who, in being taken from her home, enters the world of the dead. This sadness seems a central factor in the perpetual mystery and elusiveness of the character of Becky, who will not travel except to West Virginia, declining even to visit her daughter in Chicago.

A quite different but extremely important mythological substructure for the novel consists of the Oedipus/Teiresias story, especially as reflected in Sophocles' *Oedipus the King*.[26] By alluding to the complex, ironic echoes of Oedipus's story, Welty is able to build on Sophocles' intricate depiction of the relationship between vision/blindness and memory. The paradoxical ways in which memory can both know and yet not know are central to Sophocles' themes, as they are to Welty's, for they explain how our own predilections and motives obscure our ability to see what would otherwise be evident. Oedipus in one sense knew that he had killed a man and married a woman, but his memory failed to grasp the connection with the prophecies about his fate. Laurel, similarly, knows of the complex hurtfulness that existed between her parents at the end of Becky's life, but she has needed or preferred to remember only their love and harmony. Judge McKelva, in turn, refused to see his dying wife's pain, preferring to trust in love to make things right. Laurel, the judge, and Oedipus alike have all been optimists and have blinded themselves to some ugly realities. Fay, in fact, accuses Laurel (as she had the judge) of "putting your eyes out, too" (OD 25) by reading too much, recalling Oedipus's deliberate blinding of himself. And Laurel, like Oedipus, has failed to know who her parents are, so that her enlightenment at the end of her story, like his, constitutes the overcoming of an otherwise fatal flaw.

Welty has followed through even to minor details with her mirroring of this important mythic source. The incident in which the judge as a boy cut his foot open and had to be carried home by his friend (OD 74) reminds us of Oedipus's name, which means "swollen foot." Young Clint, on that occasion, would necessarily have walked, as Oedipus does, with a limp, and both would have had scarred feet as a legacy of their childhood experiences. Moreover, the riddle given to Oedipus by the Sphinx—what "has sometimes two feet, sometimes three, sometimes four, and is weakest when it has the most?"[27]—itself acted out in Oedipus's story as, blind, he walks with a cane or leaning on others, is also mirrored by various characters in Welty's novel. Tom Farris, the town's "blind man," comes to Judge McKelva's funeral tapping his cane "from side to side in a lordly way" (OD 78), a phrasing that closely echoes the language of *Oedipus the King*.[28] And Sam, Becky's youngest brother, had attended her funeral some dozen years ago on two canes and was thus, in a sense, four-footed (OD 152).

The cogency of a number of details in Welty's novel consists in their reference to intertextual sources. Euripides' play *Ion* serves as one minor echo, reinforcing the more prominent Oedipal story. Welty names the place where the judge and Fay ate Sunday dinner the "Iona Hotel," and the judge's old friends describe their going there as a "saddening exhibition" of the old man's blindness in choosing a wife who could not cook (OD 108). *Ion* closely resembles *Oedipus the King* in that both stories chronicle a protagonist's discovery of the true identities of his mother and father. Interestingly, the first scene of the play shows Ion, a servant in the temple of Phoebus Apollo at Delphi, sweeping out the temple with a broom and threatening to use a bow and arrow to shoot the birds that are defiling the temple. This scene mirrors Laurel and her housekeeper Missouri's pursuit (with a broom) of the chimney swift that has entered and left its sooty mark upon so many things in the McKelva home. The bird "*shot* out of the dining room and now went *arrowing* up the stairwell in front of her eyes" (OD 129; emphasis mine). When the bird is gone and the curtains have all been pulled down and cleaned, the house resembles the temple of the sun god: "All the windows . . . let in the full volume of spring light. There was nothing she was leaving in the whole shining and quiet house" (OD 170).

Just as significant as the associations with Oedipus are those with Teiresias, the blind old Theban prophet who became a seer by virtue of understanding "the tongue of birds" ("The Winds," CS 212). Just as Sophocles mirrored the ambiguities of blindness and understanding in Oedipus through the parallel blindness and "vision" of Teiresias, so Welty projects the paradox implicit in the figure of a blind seer onto several figures in her novel. A number of her characters, major and minor, are either blind or threatened by blindness: the judge with his slipped retina; Becky, Laurel's mother, who was blind during the last few years of her life; the blind Mr. Dalzell in the judge's hospital room; and "Mount Salus's blind man," Tom Farris. Moreover, scenes of precognition are attributed to all three of Welty's central characters. This happens first when Laurel, unbeckoned but sensing that something is very wrong, returns to her father's hospital room the night he dies and discovers Fay abusing him (OD 30–32). The judge foresaw the future twice: although he had only been going to have his eyes examined in New Orleans, he left complete instructions with a friend about how to get in touch with Fay's family should anything happen to him (OD 84), and years earlier, he had made his only trip to Chicago to see Philip during what was to be his "last leave" before dying in the Pacific in World War II (OD 162). Becky, too, Laurel concludes, had "predicted" Fay (OD 173); part of her anger and sense of betrayal as she lay near death had been her recognition of that aspect of her husband's personality that would make such a choice as Fay possible. As a figure both male and female, then, who both sees and does not see, Teiresias is embodied in Laurel, Becky, and the judge. Just as Teiresias was blinded as a result of his poor judgment—in one version of the myth because he had declared that women have more sexual pleasure than men—so too the judge is blinded for failing to judge a woman rightly. Laurel, a judge's daughter, spends time in the novel introspectively holding a trial and marshaling evidence to help her reach a verdict about Fay; the courtroom language is explicit (OD 130–31). Even the mystically potent number seven, associated in a variety of ways with Teiresias, is reflected in the judge, who at seventy has blindly married the self-absorbed young Fay.[29] Teiresias, moreover, is linked with the judge in a more subtle way; Robert Graves notes that he had a daughter named Daphne.[30]

Most central to Welty's purposes, however, is the fact that Teiresias is associated with being able to interpret, or read, the language of birds, a gift he received in compensation for having been blinded. The judge's eye troubles began when he saw "flashes" from "bird-frighteners" on the family's fig tree (OD 4), suggesting perhaps that in the implicit effort to keep birds away, the judge was leaving himself open to "blinding" (because unanticipated) flashes of understanding. As I have emphasized, birds are persistently connected with Laurel's moments of understanding, as if the lessons of birds will free her spirit.

These mythic allusions illuminate Welty's novel by foregrounding the emotional and epistemological issues at stake for Laurel. As we have seen, Laurel's tendency to withdraw from life since Philip's death and her evasion of the truth about her memories is suggested by the analogy with Daphne. The idea of blindness as somehow a self-inflicted willfulness not to see the truth, a tendency that Welty sees in many of us, is echoed in the Oedipus story and by the storytelling at Judge McKelva's funeral. Combining two of her favorite resources—the etymological origins of words and mythic tales—Welty offers at least one other important myth, that of Philomela. In doing so, she is able to suggest that Laurel's very *silence* through much of the novel may reflect her implicit participation in the sorts of false versions of reality she recognizes and protests in others.

One of the most unfortunate young women in mythology, Philomela was abducted, raped, and brutalized by her brother-in-law Tereus when he had promised to bring her safely from the kingdom of her father, Pandion, to visit her sister Procne. Provoked by his lust, Tereus imprisoned his victim in a tower to keep her from revealing her story to Procne, telling Procne she had been lost at sea. To secure her silence, Tereus cut out Philomela's tongue, but she wove her tale into a tapestry and was thus able to convey her story to Procne. When Procne realized her sister's fate, she inflicted a terrible revenge, destroying her and Tereus's son, Itys, and feeding him to his father. At the end of this horrific tale, the gods changed all three major figures into birds: Tereus became a bird of prey, Procne a nightingale, and Philomela a swallow.[31]

Philomela's fate as a swallow, whose legend is that it has no tongue, is linked to a pivotal memory brought to Laurel's consciousness on the last night in her family's home, just before her epiphanic revelation of the depth of her loss. At the end of her night of soul-searching, Laurel discovers a letter written by Becky's mother to her daughter in which she mentions her wish that she could send her granddaughter Laurel one of her pigeons. The grandmother's pigeons had frightened the child Laurel when she visited her mother's family in West Virginia, but the family had not realized this and had persisted in referring to the birds as if they were Laurel's pets. Invited to feed them, Laurel stood "panic-stricken," for she had "already seen a pair of them sticking their beaks down each other's throats, gagging each other, eating out of each other's craws, swallowing down all over again what had been swallowed before: they were taking turns. The first time, she hoped that they might never do it again, but they did it again next day while the other pigeons copied them. They convinced her that they could not escape each other and could not themselves be escaped from" (OD 140).

This repeated swallowing and taking of food out of one another's mouths by the birds is a reflection of Welty's concern with the tales we tell one another, "swallowing" one another's fictions, accepting them— issues Laurel struggles with throughout the novel. Bringing to consciousness the dual meanings of the word "swallow" as both a verb and a noun is just one way in which Welty exploits the etymological histories of favorite words, uncovering the cultural memories that words bring with them. The word "swallow," in fact, plays a rather consistent role throughout her fiction in suggesting how people force their ideas, values, and authority on one another.[32] One thinks of the startling scene in *Losing Battles,* in which Gloria Renfro's female relatives force her to swallow chunks of watermelon, while simultaneously insisting that she agree with them that she is the daughter of Sam Dale Beecham, her husband's uncle (LB 259). In this scene, as in *The Optimist's Daughter,* Welty explicitly shows how human relationships, however desirable they usually are, may also become oppressive as others try to enforce conformity (Con 221). Loch Morrison's youth and susceptibility to parental authority (in "June Recital") are visualized in his dutiful (if enraged) swallowing of the medicine his mother gives him (CS 275). And in Welty's "A Worn Path," Phoenix's grandson suffers from having "swallowed lye" (CS 148) in a story that seems to invite our recognition of the lie that white society tries to force Phoenix and other blacks of her time to accept—a formalized charity that doesn't begin to hide the condescension of those who administer it. Welty's phrasing as she speaks of the cold water she would drink at her grandmother's mountain home in West Virginia makes clear that swallowing signifies an acceptance of something foreign into one's very nature: "The coldness, the far, un-seen, unheard springs . . . the iron strength of its flavor . . . its fern-laced smell, all said mountain mountain mountain as I swallowed. Every swal-low was making me a part of being here, sealing me in place" (OWB 57). In *The Optimist's Daughter,* Welty signals the final decline of Judge McKelva's will to live in his indifference to what even his beloved daughter Laurel can do for him, a response she finds dismaying as she begins to understand its implications: "He opened his mouth and swallowed what she offered him with the obedience of an old man—obedience!" (OD 22).

In view of the emphasis in Welty's novel on the stories the mourners tell at Judge McKelva's funeral, many of which Laurel refuses to "swallow," her memory of the pigeons may be interpreted as an allegory of the com-plexity, difficulty, and even messiness of human beings' dependence on one another and of the lack of perfection, ease, or order in human relationships. The pigeons "take turns," just as humans do, protecting and protesting one another. Laurel is silent through much of the novel except when she is protesting Wanda Fay's histrionics, the open casket, the false stories, and her friends' recollections about her parents—trying to protect her memo-ries. The swallow, then, a poetically appropriate image for Philomela, who was silenced as part of her victimization, serves equally well for Laurel, a remarkably silent protagonist, who chooses silence as a way of preserv-ing *her* stories, her versions of past realities. Even her friends observe her reticence, one of them concluding that a "cat's got her tongue" (OD 112). Laurel speaks nearly always to protect her memories and to protest others' threats to them.

This interpretation of Welty's use of the term "swallow" is reinforced by Christian and pagan mythology, in which the acceptance of new truths is so often imaged as the incorporation of food by swallowing. When the goddess of wisdom, Metis, was pregnant with Athena, Zeus appropriated her powers by swallowing her whole and then giving birth to Athena himself, through his forehead. As Philip Gallagher has argued, this "detail in [Hesiod's] *Theogony* about Zeus's attainment of wisdom by *swallowing* Metis has as its prototype the *eating* of the forbidden Fruit" in the Garden of Eden.[33] At various times in her stories, Welty hints at precisely this meaning; the girl in "A Visit of Charity" bites into an apple at the end of her adventure at the old ladies' home in an act that signals the end of her innocence, and among the many myths and meanings alluded to by Welty's title *The Golden Apples* is the persistent association of apples with knowledge.

Some remarkable details early in *The Optimist's Daughter* deserve further attention in terms of this focus on swallows. The following passage from Hesiod's *Works and Days* is intriguing in relation to Judge McKelva's first awareness of his eye problems. Hesiod's text is a basic source for the continuing association of the swallow with the coming of spring: "Now, when Zeus has brought to completion sixty more winter days, after the sun has turned in his course, the star Arcturus, leaving behind the sacred stream of the ocean, first begins to rise and shine at the edges of evening. After him, the *treblecrying swallow, Pandion's daughter,* comes into the sight of men when spring's just at the beginning. *Be there before her. Prune your vines.* That way it is better."[34]

The judge was pruning rose bushes on George Washington's birthday (22 February) when he first noted the vision problems that led him to seek medical assistance. As Dr. Courtland, a former resident of Mount Salus, recalls, "George Washington's Birthday is the time-honored day to prune roses back home" (OD 6). When Laurel responds to her father's phone call about his trouble with his eyes, she, like the migrating bird in Hesiod's text, becomes a harbinger of spring. Welty writes that Laurel "had come flying" (OD 7). That the coming of spring is important is also emphasized by the Mardi Gras festivities that have begun as Laurel, Fay, and the judge arrive in New Orleans to see the doctor. This timing of events early in the novel, moreover, corresponds closely to that of the migration of swallows that arrived in Italy "about February 24 according to Ovid."[35] An ancient Athenian festival featuring the swallow, the nightingale, and the figure of Pandion took place "at or near the Vernal Equinox," around 21 March— which often falls at the time of Mardi Gras, the last day before Lent. This final day of merrymaking, Mardi Gras itself, is both the night the judge dies in New Orleans and Wanda Fay's birthday. Their stay in New Orleans corresponds exactly to the duration of the festivities, a time of upheaval.[36] In featuring the word "swallow" in her novel, Welty evokes still other mythic connections: Thompson's *Glossary of Greek Birds* tells us that the swallow-stone, or "eyestone," is so named because it is assumed to be a cure for early blindness in baby swallows; moreover, swallows were believed to restrain the annual spring flooding of the Nile.[37] These persistent associations among the images of birds, blindness, floods, spring, and memory suggest mythic connections that Welty has deeply assimilated.

Philomela's silence is often seen by feminist scholars as a *silencing*, as part of her victimization by a patriarchal culture that does not want her to tell the truth and, consequently, inflicts a condition upon her that makes her appear to sanction its lies. There seems little reason to view Laurel Hand's silence as a reflection on patriarchy per se, but it does seem justified to view it, in part at least, as a response to *society's* lies, its official versions (however benevolent or misguided) of truth. Like Philomela, Laurel finds a way out of her silence in order to tell herself the truth. She does this by learning that, like the stories others tell that distress her so, her own silence has protected and preserved, in effect, a family mythology, a distorted view of the past.

Laurel's evolving understanding shows her that old patterns of thought cannot do justice to new experience. It is important that she not merely accept Fay or assimilate her into her worldview, because that would be to fail to recognize Fay's role as an emblem of the *fact* of disjuncture or chaos in life. If Laurel is to eschew the comforts of her old ways of seeing things, then she must come to tolerate ambiguity, complexity, and even horror in the world around her. She thus frees herself of her inclination to hate Fay, because hating Fay is only an expression of her need for things to cohere. Accepting the fact of Fay, Laurel is ready to look at her own memories in a much more fruitful way, not simply as comforting stories about those she has loved but as living and changing with her own evolving experience. Memory, Welty insists, needs to remain vulnerable, open to revision, even to hurtful new insights. Moreover, because holding onto objects such as Becky's breadboard constitutes clinging to particular stories about her life, Laurel is able to leave behind mere artifacts as she returns home to Chicago. Unlike Josie in "The Winds," Laurel no longer reaches for objects that embody her memories of past experience. As Welty's narrator observes in a line frequently cited by the novel's critics, "memory lived not in initial possession but in the freed hands, pardoned and freed, and in the heart that can empty but fill again, in the patterns restored by dreams" (OD 179). With Laurel we learn that love that insists on protecting its memories ends by obscuring their truth and that to the degree we do this as adults, we perpetuate the sort of benign fabrications with which love protected us when we were children—thus keeping ourselves from deeper understanding.

Welty ultimately views memory much as T. S. Eliot does literary tradition. In "Tradition and the Individual Talent," Eliot argues that when a genuinely new piece of literary art is created, it causes the preexisting body of literature to be, "if ever so slightly, altered" as "the relations, proportions, values of each work of art toward the whole are readjusted."[38] Eliot's "historical sense" is very similar to Welty's idea of memory as something that needs to remain open to new perspectives, "vulnerable to the living moment" (OD 179). Welty is explicit in saying that the memory is *not* meant to freeze the past into something impervious to new experience. Instead, it repeatedly redefines the patterns of our lives as we reach fuller understanding; the body of all we know alters slightly with each new addition as memory works its magic.

Welty's narrative decisions reinforce her thematic message by refusing to offer clear-cut and definitive readings of her story. Her images modify the reading of other images as she exploits the multiple meanings of single words ("watch," "pupil," "iris," "cataract") and juxtaposes them in various ways (birds and hands, water and eyes). By recovering some of the lost metaphorical dimensions of our everyday language and evoking mythic tales such as those of Oedipus and Philomela, she suggests ever wider realms of meaning. The subtle nature of these linkages enables Welty's readers to experience her story at a variety of depths depending upon their awareness of these linguistic and literary/mythic associations. Her strategies to revive our cultural memories of stories embodying the subjects of knowledge and blindness, silence and communication, are meant to enact in her readers' memories the lessons *about* memory implicit in Laurel's story. Just as Laurel is urged to allow her memory to glimpse correspondences and new implications, so the reader is urged to recognize the connections implicit in Welty's intertextual and etymological allusions. We make sense of Welty's novel only to the degree that our cultural memories enable these connections to take place. *The Optimist's Daughter* asserts the truth of Welty's statement that memory is her greatest treasure: "during its moment, all that is remembered joins, and lives" (OWB 104).

.   .   .

This book began with the consideration of a paradigm for thinking about how people perceive and experience relationships. This theme has always been central to Welty's writing, most obviously in her alternating focus on isolated, lonely, and often inarticulate characters (especially in her early stories) and on the dynamics of family and community. Being included within a circle of loved ones may carry with it affection and protectiveness, but it may also entail inhibitory expectations, even prohibitions, about a variety of autonomous choices one might make about one's life—a sense of oppression that has been seen at times to affect both male and female characters in Welty's stories. As if intuitively understanding what Nancy Chodorow's and Carol Gilligan's studies have revealed about men and women, however, Welty has shown with special force how males (the MacLains, her traveling salesmen, Odysseus, Howard in "Flowers for Marjorie," Lorenzo Dow, James Murrell) choose wandering or otherwise struggle against a relationship that has come to feel like entrapment. Her women characters—for whom the private sphere has so often been seen as their "proper" realm—face especially harsh public scrutiny when they too move beyond the family toward some broader goal of adventure or art. Miss Eckhart in "June Recital" and Virgie Rainey in both that story and "The Wanderers" are relentlessly judged. The loyalty implicit in Virgie's caring for her mother for well over twenty years is quite lost on her community, for although she was away for only about a year when she was sixteen, they expect her to abandon Katie again at any moment. As one Morgana citizen smugly puts it: "Left once, will again" (CS 429).

Perhaps because Welty felt a troubling guilt whenever she traveled away from her family and because she too had gone away (to college) for several years and seemed likely to make a career in New York, she recurrently addresses the issue of a woman's responsibility to her family—not only caring for them but *being there* with them—in her stories. Daughters, for the most part, are *not* free to become wanderers, as is seen in the sad fates of the protagonists of "Why I Live at the P.O." and "Clytie." And while an especially severe judgment is reserved for women who choose to leave, men are just as likely to be mythologized (as King MacLain was) or elected mayor (as Ran MacLain was) for their wandering from family responsibility and marital fidelity. Laurel Hand faces repeated charges from friends and foes alike about how she has let her father down by choosing to make her career as a fabric designer in Chicago: "'Why track back up to the North Pole?' asked Miss Tennyson. 'Who's going to kill you if you don't draw those pictures?'" (OD 112–13). It is easy to imagine that Welty herself may have met with such queries from friends and neighbors early in her career.

Thus the question of how to maintain an optimum balance between the requirements of familial love and the pleasures of adventurous new experience remains unresolved, a matter—for women, at least—of balancing equally compelling values. Welty has chosen to maintain this balance in her own life, while always emphasizing through her fiction the importance of art. Her artist figures pay a price for their choices—more of a price than Welty feels she has had to pay, for she considers her own life to be very full of love (OWB 101)—yet she knows very well that art takes place apart from other people, that to the degree you place your passion there, you are turning (if only momentarily) away from others. This may be why Welty so closely allies her definitions of love, knowledge, and art itself, insisting implicitly that the choice an artist must make is *not* between love and art, but between two *kinds* of love. If the love in her relationships fills much of her life, the art that she also devotes herself to is an act of love, as well: "Love of art," she writes, "is love accomplished without help or need of help from another" (ES 55).

Welty's use of Dionysian images and energies as a compelling counterpart to Apollonian form and order is a way of reflecting not only the dynamic through which art itself comes into being but the larger question of how an orderly, well-behaved life such as her own can (and, in Welty's view, should) be enlivened by a Dionysian courageousness that is enacted in a decision to embrace art itself, and the unknown to which it gives you access, with passion. Perhaps this is the reason the unknown is so positively viewed in Welty's world: one might so easily have missed it all.[39] Welty's fascination with Dionysus allows her to introduce into her fiction a place for all of those factors her well-protected life might have precluded: adventure itself; a courageous, even joyful approach to the unknown; and an awareness and acceptance of the disjuncture and chaos in life that allows us to free ourselves of anachronistic beliefs in the harmony and perfect orderliness of the universe.

The final line of *The Optimist's Daughter* returns to the image of schoolchildren: "The last thing Laurel saw, before they whirled into speed, was the twinkling of their hands, the many small and unknown hands, wishing her goodbye" (OD 180). As Yeats had done in "Among School Children," Welty has her protagonist, newly arrived at a stage of fuller maturity and understanding, observe schoolchildren just setting out on their own search for understanding. And although their search may only lead to a knowledge of how limited their knowledge finally must be, Welty believes the quest itself is the source of the greatest pleasure they are ever likely to know. As she has done throughout her fiction, she turns finally to children to offer an image for the openness and wonder that alone make any such knowledge possible.

Introduction. The Paradoxical Interplay of Love and Knowledge

1 Psychoanalytic theory has contributed significantly to the prevalence of such "explanations" of artistic achievement. André Green is among many theorists who believe that writing "presupposes a wound and a loss, a work of mourning." See "The Double and the Absent," trans. Jacques F. Houis, in *Psychoanalysis, Creativity, and Literature,* ed. Alan Roland (New York: Columbia University Press, 1978), 283.

   As examples of such studies as they pertain to one writer, Faulkner, we might note that works linking his early sense of loss and betrayal directly to his evolving vision of his art include Michel Gresset's "Faulkner's Self-Portraits," *Faulkner Journal* 2 (Fall 1986): 2–13; and Panthea Reid Broughton's essay "The Economy of Desire: Faulkner's Poetics, from Eroticism to Post-Impressionism," *Faulkner Journal* 4 (Fall 1988/Spring 1989): 159–77. Broughton argues that partly as a result of his early abandonment by Estelle Oldham, Faulkner developed a sense that art could result only from sublimating his longing for an unattainable woman. Although his fiction shows that he later achieved a more empathetic vision of women, Faulkner continued to view art as somehow compensatory; he contrived "to keep himself all his life sufficiently frustrated so that longing for something better could continue to drive his writing self" (Broughton, "Economy of Desire," 169). As its title makes clear, André Bleikasten's study *The Ink of Melancholy: Faulkner's Novels from "The Sound and the Fury" to "Light in August"* (Bloomington: Indiana University Press, 1990) assumes such a background of loss; Bleikasten believes that "any great work of fiction . . . carries inscribed in it the paradox of a life betrayed and recaptured" (vii).

2 In an interview with Charles T. Bunting in 1972, for example, she answered the question "What have been some of your more distressing moments as a writer?" by saying, "I can't think of any, really. I love to write. I'm never happier than when I'm working. . . . I'm utterly happy when I'm revising. Throwing away gives me a great elation sometimes. So I haven't had any distressing moments, and I've had good luck in my writing life with good friends as editors and agents, and I've had a very happy time as a writer. . . . The fact that I never made much money doesn't have anything to do with it because the writing itself is the deepest pleasure to me" (Con 60).

3 Carolyn G. Heilbrun, *Writing a Woman's Life* (New York: W. W. Norton, 1988), 13–15. Heilbrun writes, "I do not believe in the bittersweet quality of *One Writer's Beginnings,* nor do I suppose that the Eudora Welty there evoked could have written the stories and novels we have learned to celebrate" (14).

4 Her father, hearing of her desire to become a writer, was concerned about her ability to achieve financial security and urged her to prepare herself to earn a living "some other way" (OWB 81), even if she wrote, too. In an interview with Hermione Lee published in 1988, Welty appears to admit to some disagreement, only to back away, acknowledging the good sense of her father's cautions: "For a while I thought my father couldn't be supporting me because—oh, he was against fiction, because he thought it wasn't true. He said, it's not the truth about life. And he thought I might be wasting my time, because he thought I was going to write the sort of things that came out in the *Saturday Evening Post,* and if I *didn't* write those things I couldn't earn a living. . . . And how did I know what I *could* do? But he did support me. All he wanted to do was to make sure that I could survive, make my living. And that was good advice. I was rather scornful at the time—'Live for art', you know." In answer to the interviewer's next question, "He never said, 'Don't do it'?" Welty responds, "No, he never did" (Hermione Lee, interview with Eudora Welty in *Writing Lives: Conversations between Women Writers,* ed. Mary Chamberlain [London: Virago Press, 1988], 252–53).

5 In the interview with Charles Bunting cited earlier, Welty said, "All that talk of women's lib doesn't apply *at all* to women writers. We've always been able to do what we've wished. I couldn't feel less deprived as a woman to be writing" (Con 54). For a very different view of the situation facing American women writers in the 1920s and 1930s, see Elaine Showalter, *Sister's Choice: Tradition and Change in American Women's Writing* (New York: Oxford University Press, 1991), especially chapter 6, "The Other Lost Generation," 104–26. Peter Schmidt offers a fascinating account of Welty's relationship to earlier women's writing in America in *The Heart of the Story: Eudora Welty's Short Fiction* (Jackson: University Press of Mississippi, 1991), 204–65.

6 On the significance of the oral tradition throughout Welty's fiction, see Carol S. Manning, *With Ears Opening Like Morning Glories: Eudora Welty and the Love of Storytelling* (Westport, Conn.: Greenwood, 1985).

7 Heilbrun, *Writing,* 14.

8 See Gail L. Mortimer, "'The Way to Get There': Journeys and Destinations in the Stories of Eudora Welty," *Southern Literary Journal* 19 (Spring 1987): 61–69.

9 Welty has used the expression "from away" in speaking of her parents' origins, as she did at a reading on 7 December 1991 in Tulsa, Oklahoma.

10 G. Wilson Knight's *Starlit Dome: Studies in the Poetry of Vision* (New York: Oxford University Press, 1971) is particularly helpful for understanding the image clusters used by these "poets of vision."

11 See Michael Kreyling, *Eudora Welty's Achievement of Order* (Baton Rouge: Louisiana State University Press, 1980), which assumes as a basic premise in Welty's fiction the conflict between order and disorder, at times appearing embodied in Apollonian and Dionysian figures.

12 The best general introduction to Welty's work remains Ruth M. Vande Kieft's

Eudora Welty, rev. ed. (Boston: Twayne, 1987), which explores themes and ideas that have characterized her stories from the beginning.

13 The correspondence collected by Kreyling in *Author and Agent: Eudora Welty and Diarmuid Russell* (New York: Farrar, Straus, Giroux, 1991) is especially illuminating in suggesting the issues that led Welty to try out different styles and textures in various works.

14 Welty's admiration for Yeats is well recognized among critics. Her recurrent use of excerpts from "The Song of Wandering Aengus" in "June Recital" and her playful re-visioning of "Leda and the Swan" in her story "Sir Rabbit" are only the most obvious of her textual allusions to his work. On the latter story, see Patricia S. Yaeger, "'Because a Fire Was in My Head': Eudora Welty and the Dialogic Imagination," *PMLA* 99 (October 1984): 955–73.

15 In my discussion of "A Still Moment" in chapter 2 I argue that Welty and Yeats also use the heron for similar purposes.

16 William Butler Yeats, "Nineteen Hundred and Nineteen," *The Collected Poems of W. B. Yeats* (London: Macmillan, 1950), 234–35.

17 Yeats, "Nineteen Hundred," 235.

18 Yeats, "Leda and the Swan," 241.

19 Barbara Harrell Carson argues that wholeness is always the result of a harmony of opposites in Welty's fiction (*Eudora Welty: Two Pictures at Once in Her Frame* [Troy, N.Y.: Whitston, 1992]).

20 Yeats, "Among School Children," 244.

21 Yeats, "Among School Children," 243.

22 The Persephone motif has been recognized by a number of Welty's critics in stories such as "At the Landing" and "Livvie." Guy Davenport considers the Persephone myth to be a basic theme, whose variations appear throughout Welty's work, beginning with *Delta Wedding.* See "That Faire Field of Enna" in *The Geography of the Imagination* (San Francisco: North Point, 1981), 250–71. Louise Westling explores the figures of Persephone and of Dionysus, also in *Delta Wedding,* in *Eudora Welty* (Totowa, N.J.: Barnes and Noble, 1989), 98–120, and in *Sacred Groves and Ravaged Gardens: The Fiction of Eudora Welty, Carson McCullers, and Flannery O'Connor* (Athens: University of Georgia Press, 1985), 65–93.

23 Ebenezer Cobham Brewer, *Brewer's Dictionary of Phrase and Fable,* rev. and enlarged (New York: Harper and Brothers, 1953), 876.

24 Brewer, *Dictionary,* 876.

25 Yeats, "Coole Park and Ballylee, 1931," 275, 276.

Chapter 1. Love and Separateness

1 Robert Penn Warren's essay "The Love and the Separateness in Miss Welty" appeared originally in the *Kenyon Review* 6 (1944): 246–59. It was revised and

expanded as "Love and Separateness in Eudora Welty" in Warren's *Selected Essays* (New York: Random House, 1958), 156–69, the version from which I quote.

2 Warren, "Love and Separateness in Eudora Welty," 160.

3 Thus far in Welty's stories, love had appeared, for the most part, as the *implicit* alternative to her characters' loneliness, as a road not taken by protagonists such as R. J. Bowman in "Death of a Traveling Salesman" (CS 119–30). The few exceptions, including "First Love," are discussed later in this book.

4 Nancy Chodorow, *The Reproduction of Mothering: Psychoanalysis and the Sociology of Gender* (Berkeley: University of California Press, 1978), 7. Chodorow's more recent work on these issues appears in *Feminism and Psychoanalytic Theory* (New Haven: Yale University Press, 1989); see in particular chapter 5, "Gender, Relation, and Difference in Psychoanalytic Perspective," pp. 99–113.

5 The psychoanalytic term for this achievement of a coherent sense of self is "individuation." Jane Flax provides succinct definitions: "Separation means establishing a firm sense of differentiation from the mother, of being a me/self different from but in relation to an other. . . . Individuation entails establishing a range of characteristics, bodily experiences, skills, personality traits, and an inner world that are uniquely one's own 'true self' or a creative core of being and aliveness" (*Thinking Fragments: Psychoanalysis, Feminism, and Postmodernism in the Contemporary West* [Berkeley: University of California Press, 1990], 112). See also Margaret S. Mahler, *On Human Symbiosis and the Vicissitudes of Individuation* (New York: International Universities Press, 1968). For an insightful discussion of the premises of object-relations theory, see D. W. Winnicott's *Maturational Processes and the Facilitating Environment* (New York: International Universities Press, 1965) and *Playing and Reality* (New York: Basic Books, 1971).

6 Chodorow, *Reproduction*, 97.

7 This characteristic, combined with its corollary, a greater tendency to define one's identity in terms of others, appears to account to some degree for various psychological problems that are much more common among women than among men, such as the difficulty battered women face in attempting to extricate themselves from destructive relationships, and women's fear of success, which appears to be linked to the belief that success has severe social costs.

8 Chodorow, *Feminism*, 109.

9 Chodorow, *Reproduction*, 185.

10 Chodorow, *Feminism*, 110, and *Reproduction*, 174.

11 Chodorow, *Reproduction*, 181, 184.

12 Active, ongoing debates about this theory focus, for example, on whether or not it entails an *essentialist* view of the differences between males and females in our culture. Nothing, however, in the work of Chodorow or Gilligan seems to require such a conclusion; the traits and inclinations they have sought to explain seem fully accounted for when one realizes how completely and decisively our culture has tended to socialize its infants. Other dimensions of the debate—such as the question of how it contributes to the preoccupation in our cul-

ture with "blaming the mother" for how children "turn out," a habit feminists rightly deplore—do not apply to my application of these ideas. First of all, the theorists who have attempted to illuminate the nature of these felt differences between the genders are writing of what they observe, what has been done to our children to make them into the kinds of adults we are; they are not prescribing in any sense what *ought* to be differences between men and women and, in fact, advocate dual parenting as a means of ameliorating the impact on a child of having a single parent (during the pre-oedipal period) who is perceived as omnipotent. These cultural phenomena were largely unquestioned at the time Welty and Faulkner grew up, and it would be quite natural for their fiction to reflect their awareness, at whatever level of consciousness, of the gender dynamics of their society. To some degree, they directly address and even deconstruct these dynamics, but their stories also, necessarily, reflect them insofar as they accurately depict social reality.

13 Erik H. Erikson's most famous model appears in *Childhood and Society,* 2d ed. (New York: W. W. Norton, 1963), in chapters 2 ("The Theory of Infantile Sexuality") and 7 ("Eight Ages of Man").

14 Carol Gilligan, *In a Different Voice: Psychological Theory and Women's Development* (Cambridge: Harvard University Press, 1982), esp. 5–23. Gilligan discusses Erikson's developmental stages on pp. 11–13.

15 In *Women's Ways of Knowing: The Development of Self, Voice, and Mind* (New York: Basic Books, 1986), Mary Field Belenky et al. explore specific features in women's cognitive development that may result from females' distinctive socialization.

Among the most provocative feminist anthologies reflecting a wide range of disciplines are *The Future of Difference,* ed. Hester Eisenstein and Alice Jardine (New Brunswick, N.J.: Rutgers University Press, 1985); *Theoretical Perspectives on Sexual Difference,* ed. Deborah L. Rhode (New Haven: Yale University Press, 1990); and *Gender/Body/Knowledge: Feminist Reconstructions of Being and Knowing,* ed. Alison M. Jaggar and Susan R. Bordo (New Brunswick, N.J.: Rutgers University Press, 1989).

16 Evelyn Fox Keller, "Feminism and Science," *Signs: Journal of Women in Culture and Society* 7 (Spring 1982): 589–602; Carroll Smith-Rosenberg, "The Female World of Love and Ritual: Relations between Women in Nineteenth-Century America," *Signs: Journal of Women in Culture and Society* 1 (Autumn 1975): 1–29; rpt. in *Disorderly Conduct: Visions of Gender in Victorian America* (New York: Oxford University Press, 1986), 53–76; Elizabeth Abel, "(E)Merging Identities: The Dynamics of Female Friendship in Contemporary Fiction by Women," *Signs: Journal of Women in Culture and Society* 6 (Spring 1981): 413–35; Judith Kegan Gardiner, "On Female Identity and Writing by Women," in *Writing and Sexual Difference,* ed. Elizabeth Abel (Chicago: University of Chicago Press, 1982), 177–91, and *Rhys, Stead, Lessing, and the Politics of Empathy* (Bloomington: Indiana University Press, 1989).

17 Nancy K. Miller, ed., *The Poetics of Gender* (New York: Columbia University

Press, 1986); and Elizabeth A. Flynn and Patrocinio P. Schweickart, eds., *Gender and Reading: Essays on Readers, Texts, and Contexts* (Baltimore: Johns Hopkins University Press, 1986).

18 The very definitions of key terms such as "pride," "prejudice," "sensibility," and "sense" may prove to be negotiated between characters based on their gendered understandings of those terms, as Carol Gilligan suggested during a conference ("Reconstructing Individualism") held at the Stanford Humanities Center, 18–20 February 1984. On the same basis, the works of Henry James and Joseph Conrad appear to invite such analysis.

19 Gail L. Mortimer, *Faulkner's Rhetoric of Loss: A Study in Perception and Meaning* (Austin: University of Texas Press, 1983).

20 See Sandra M. Gilbert and Susan Gubar, *No Man's Land: The Place of the Woman Writer in the Twentieth Century,* vol. 1, *The War of the Words* (New Haven: Yale University Press, 1988) and vol. 2, *Sexchanges* (1989), for extended discussions locating Woolf, Wharton, Cather, and others within the context of the (male) modernist imagination.

21 Virginia Woolf, *Mrs. Dalloway* (New York: Harcourt, Brace and World, Harvest, 1925), 185, 181.

22 Susan Bordo, "The Cartesian Masculinization of Thought," *Signs: Journal of Women in Culture and Society* 11 (Spring 1986): 439–56. Jane Flax was among the first feminists to consider the implications of dichotomous thought in Western philosophy and political theory. The mind-body "problem," the debate over the universal and the particular, and other instances of either/or thinking may, she argues, be as much the products of particular, dualistic ways of viewing reality as they are fundamental philosophic dilemmas ("Mother-Daughter Relationships: Psychodynamics, Politics, and Philosophy," in *The Future of Difference,* ed. Eisenstein and Jardine, 20–40, and "Political Philosophy and the Patriarchal Unconscious: A Psychoanalytic Perspective on Epistemology and Metaphysics," in *Discovering Reality: Feminist Perspectives on Epistemology, Metaphysics, Methodology, and Philosophy of Science,* ed. Sandra Harding and Merrill B. Hintikka [Boston: D. Reidel, 1983], 245–81).

23 Bordo, "Cartesian," 441.

24 Bordo, "Cartesian," 442. This epistemological view is quite consistent with the modernist experimentation of writers like James Joyce and Faulkner, the content of whose interior monologues seems to bear such a tenuous relationship with "external" fictional events.

25 Mortimer, *Faulkner's Rhetoric,* 23–26.

26 William Faulkner, *Light in August. The Corrected Text* (New York: Random House, Vintage, 1987), 172–73 and 247–48.

27 Bordo, "Cartesian," 444.

28 Below are a few of the more notorious of such passages from Faulkner: "*Women are like that they dont acquire knowledge of people we are for that they are just born with a practical fertility of suspicion that makes a crop every so often and usually right they have an affinity for evil for supplying whatever the evil lacks in itself for drawing*

it about them instinctively as you do bed-clothing in slumber" (*The Sound and the Fury. The Corrected Text* [New York: Random House, Vintage, 1987], 110).

"Because women so delicate so mysterious Father said. Delicate equilibrium of periodical filth between two moons balanced. . . . With all that inside of them shapes an outward suavity waiting for a touch to. Liquid putrefaction like drowned things floating like pale rubber flabbily filled getting the odor of honeysuckle all mixed up" (*Sound and the Fury,* 147).

"On all sides, even within him, the bodiless fecundmellow voices of negro women murmured. It was as though he and all other manshaped life about him had been returned to the lightless hot wet primogenitive Female" (*Light in August,* 126).

"It was as though with the corruption which she seemed to gather from the air itself, she began to corrupt him. He began to be afraid. He could not have said of what. But he began to see himself as from a distance, like a man being sucked down into a bottomless morass" (*Light in August,* 285).

29   Bordo, "Cartesian," 451. In an article on Faulkner's *Sound and the Fury* Philip Cohen and Doreen Fowler argue that in one of the discarded drafts of his introduction to the novel, Faulkner had "momentarily dropped his guard . . . and revealed that he had projected on the three brothers [Benjy, Quentin, and Jason] his own attachment to the mother, an attachment that he himself described as incestuous, possessively paternal, and regressively childlike" ("Faulkner's Introduction to *The Sound and the Fury,*" *American Literature* 62 [June 1990]: 270). This, Faulkner's own interpretation of one dimension of his psyche, may well be played out in those Faulknerian protagonists who recurrently struggle to deny loss and assert their self-sufficiency and control of their lives. For important readings of the implications of loss in Faulkner's fictive world, see John T. Irwin, *Doubling and Incest/Repetition and Revenge: A Speculative Reading of Faulkner* (Baltimore: Johns Hopkins University Press, 1975); John T. Matthews, *The Play of Faulkner's Language* (Ithaca: Cornell University Press, 1982); and David Minter, *William Faulkner: His Life and Work* (Baltimore: Johns Hopkins University Press, 1980).

30   William Faulkner, *Go Down, Moses* (New York: Random House, Vintage, 1973), 111.

31   Faulkner, *Go Down, Moses,* 112.

32   Faulkner, *Go Down, Moses,* 112.

33   Charles Mallison in *Intruder in the Dust* commits a similar act when he tries to pay for the help and food Lucas and Molly Beauchamp have given him after he falls through the ice into a creek. Charles holds out the coins "and in the same second in which he knew she would have taken them he knew that only by that one irrevocable second was he forever now too late, forever beyond recall." Shame and chagrin haunt him throughout the novel, entangling him in Lucas's fate (William Faulkner, *Intruder in the Dust* [New York: Random House, 1948], 15).

34   Faulkner, *Go Down, Moses,* 110, 117.

35 Faulkner, *Light in August,* 172.

36 Bordo, "Cartesian," 449.

37 This is not an isolated passage. Cassie Morrison in "June Recital" is one among many of Welty's characters who find that knowledge comes through imagining yourself in another's place. Thinking of the belligerent sewing machine sales-man, Mr. Voight, Cassie "could not now, any more than then, really describe Mr. Voight, but without thinking she could *be* Mr. Voight, which was more frightening still" (CS 296). And elsewhere, seeing Miss Eckhart, "Cassie felt that the teacher was filled with terror, perhaps with pain. She found it so easy . . . to feel terror and pain in an outsider" (CS 298).

38 Faulkner, *Go Down, Moses,* 154–59.

39 This contrast in relational styles between Faulkner and Welty is echoed quite specifically in two essays by Peter Elbow: "The Doubting Game and the Be-lieving Game—An Analysis of the Intellectual Enterprise," in *Writing without Teachers* (New York: Oxford University Press, 1973), 147–91, and "Method-ological Doubting and Believing: Contraries in Inquiry," in *Embracing Con-traries: Explorations in Learning and Teaching* (New York: Oxford University Press, 1986), 254–300. Elbow contrasts what he perceives as two opposing intellectual styles of encountering the new and the unknown and of coping with and assimilating new knowledge. One is a methodology of believing in the stance of the other (which Elbow sees as a somewhat more "feminine" way of responding), and the other a more "masculine" methodological doubt. Elbow's characterization of the traits involved in adopting either stance vis-à-vis new knowledge reflects experiential differences characteristic of the two ends of the continuum listed in figure 1: "To doubt well we learn to extricate or detach ourselves. . . . Doubting asks us to heighten our sensitivity to dissonance. . . . Doubting is the act of separating or differentiating and thus correlates with individualism: it permits the loner to hold out against the crowd." Conversely, "to believe well we learn to invest or insert ourselves. . . . Believing asks us to learn to accept and integrate foreign bodies and put up with dissonance in the process. . . . Belief involves merging and participating in a community" ("Methodological Doubting," 264). Faulkner's "doubting" characters, affirm-ing the differences between themselves and others, tend to experience the gaps, the distances, the isolation that is so much assumed in twentieth-century, male, modernist experience. Welty's characters tend to experience and appreciate the similarities they share with others and to make the imaginative, empathic leap rather readily.

40 Faulkner, *Light in August,* 339. Compare Faulkner's letter to Joan Williams, 8 September 1951, quoted in Joseph Blotner, *Faulkner: A Biography* (New York: Random House, 1974), 2:1395: "I am too old to have to miss a girl of twenty-three years old. By now, I should have earned the right to be free of that."

41 William Faulkner, *The Hamlet* (New York: Random House, 1964), 218–58; Faulkner, *The Wild Palms* (New York: Random House, Vintage, 1966).

42 Mortimer, *Faulkner's Rhetoric*, 37–38, 48.

43 Evelyn Fox Keller and Christine R. Grontkowski, "The Mind's Eye," in *Discovering Reality,* ed. Harding and Hintikka, 207.

44 Welty sees herself as having "the most common type of mind, the visual" (ES 31), but there are essential differences between her characters' experiences of the visual and Faulkner's. His characters use vision as part of an attempt to control and keep their distance from aspects of the external world; Welty's characters use it as one of several senses (especially touch, sound, and smell) that lead them into a fuller experience and appreciation of the sensual world they inhabit. Welty's direct allusions to the senses are almost always permeated with the notion of pleasure. Later in this chapter I discuss the role of vision in her perception of the artist's proper distance from her subject.

45 William Faulkner, *Absalom, Absalom! The Corrected Text* (New York: Random House, 1986), 111–12.

46 Faulkner, *Go Down, Moses,* 107–8.

47 The last two ellipses in the quotation (those within the quotation marks) are Welty's.

48 Faulkner participates in a long tradition of seeing the world in terms of dichotomized categories: black/white, male/female, good/evil, Yankee/southerner. There is an ongoing discussion among Faulkner scholars about whether, in depicting them, Faulkner is simply *reflecting* the mindset of his patriarchal, turn-of-the-century southern culture or, rather, *deconstructing* these categories to reveal their inherent distortions.

See Mary Douglas's *Purity and Danger: An Analysis of Concepts of Pollution and Taboo* (New York: Frederick Praeger, 1966) for an extended consideration, at the cultural level, of how order and separation serve to keep disorder, evil, and chaos away. For particular societies these issues are far more urgent than for others; that is, societies themselves appear to have different styles of perceiving and interacting with the unknown.

49 Faulkner, *Wild Palms,* 87.

50 Meta Carpenter Wilde and Orin Borsten, *A Loving Gentleman: The Love Story of William Faulkner and Meta Carpenter* (New York: Simon and Schuster, 1976), 77.

51 Faulkner, *Wild Palms,* 57.

52 Chodorow, *Reproduction,* 93, 169.

53 Faulkner, *Light in August,* 230–31, 301; Faulkner, *Collected Stories of William Faulkner* (New York: Random House, Vintage, 1977), 6, 8; Faulkner, *The Hamlet,* 221.

54 Gilligan, *In a Different Voice,* 39–45.

55 Gilligan, *In a Different Voice,* 42, 41.

56 Welty has written: "Of all my strong emotions, anger is the one least responsible for any of my work. I don't write out of anger. For one thing, simply as a fiction writer, I am minus an adversary—except, of course, that of time—and

for another thing, the act of writing in itself brings me happiness" (OWB 38). She admits that anger "lit the fuse" of her decision to write "Where Is the Voice Coming From?" just after the murder of civil rights leader Medgar Evers, but the story itself is a chillingly precise chronicle of a racial bigot's state of mind.

Carolyn Heilbrun, as well as other feminist critics, has noted that anger is the emotion women in our culture are least permitted to express (*Writing*, 15). She believes, as noted earlier, that Welty "has camouflaged herself" (14) and that the sort of nostalgia found in Welty's work, "particularly for childhood, is likely to be a mask for unrecognized anger" (15). Heilbrun, in other words, would see the lack of anger in Welty's writing as a result of its nearly perfect repression rather than its absence.

57 See Peter Schmidt, *The Heart of the Story: Eudora Welty's Short Fiction* (Jackson: University Press of Mississippi, 1991), 123–28, for a darker reading of these stories in which the two protagonists are seen as merely exchanging one form of "thralldom" for another when they choose to follow new men who, like the old, seem likely to circumscribe their lives.

58 Consider, for example, Faulkner's description of Emily Grierson in "A Rose for Emily" as having "cold, haughty black eyes in a face the flesh of which was strained across the temples and about the eye-sockets as you imagine a lighthouse-keeper's face ought to look" (*Collected Stories*, 125).

59 In comparing the novelist Henry Green with Jane Austen, Welty discusses their differing perceptions of the unknown in life in precisely such terms. Considering the apparent sources of their comic visions, Welty notes that despite Green's "at-homeness" in a much wider world than the one Austen writes of, "it would be he who finds human behavior extraordinary and she who finds it not too different from what she'd expected" ("Henry Green: Novelist of the Imagination," ES 15).

60 The major exception—"Where Is the Voice Coming From?"—is Welty's fictional attempt to re-create the mindset of the man who shot civil rights leader Medgar Evers (CS 603–7). In this story she depicts the murderer's hatred as based in that racist-separatist mentality that has proved so devastating in American cultural history. Obviously, such a man feels that distinctions must be maintained, that something very basic to his concept of himself is threatened by racial integration.

61 There is a passage in Virginia Woolf's *Mrs. Dalloway* in which her protagonist, Clarissa, reaches a similar conclusion about the privacy of one's soul. Clarissa notes that she had been right to marry Richard Dalloway rather than Peter Walsh, for whereas Richard gave her the "little independence there must be between people living together day in day out in the same house . . . with Peter everything had to be shared; everything gone into. And it was intolerable" (10). Peter, reflecting their culture's beliefs about what a woman should want in a relationship, declares her "cold, heartless, a prude" (10). Welty is well aware that no woman can make a choice of this sort without being susceptible to such judgments, as is clear in *The Optimist's Daughter*, where Laurel must listen to

her neighbors' opinion that her selfishness in choosing to live in Chicago is the reason her father made an unfortunate marriage (OD 115).

62 Lillian B. Rubin, *Intimate Strangers: Men and Women Together* (New York: Harper Colophon, 1984), esp. 75–77.

63 See also Noel Polk, "Water, Wanderings, and Weddings: Love in Eudora Welty," in *Eudora Welty: A Form of Thanks*, ed. Louis Dollarhide and Ann J. Abadie (Jackson: University Press of Mississippi, 1979), 95–122.

64 One of Carol Gilligan's findings seems pertinent here. After analyzing the responses of men and women in one of several studies consistently leading to the same results, Gilligan observes: "The interplay between these responses is clear in that she [the female subject], assuming connection, begins to explore the parameters of separation, while he [the male subject], assuming separation, begins to explore the parameters of connection. But the primacy of separation or connection leads to different images of self and of relationships" (*In a Different Voice*, 38).

Chapter 2. Fireflies and Constellations

1 Although we should always be cautious about attributing fictional experiences to an author, Welty has repeatedly confirmed how much of her family life is explicitly recalled in *The Optimist's Daughter*, a fact evident to any reader of both the novel and *One Writer's Beginnings*. More to the point, she has insisted that writers can only work out of their own feelings, that quite apart from the experiences and scenes generated to convey the ideas they have in mind, the feelings must already be known if they are to be effectively conveyed. A brief but important passage about the novelist from one of her essays on writing, cited in the Introduction, bears repeating here: "his novel, whatever its subject, is the history itself of his life's experience in feeling" (ES 142). Especially in passages as richly evocative as this one about falling to sleep under a "cloak of words," we are justified in assuming that Welty has indeed drawn from her own vivid memories.

2 In another context Welty writes, "Revolt itself is a reference and tribute to the potency of what is left behind" ("Place in Fiction," ES 131). She is speaking of writers (Katherine Mansfield, James Joyce) who leave their places of origin, yet continue to write about them almost obsessively, but her comment may be equally pertinent to the reaction she had to being free of restrictions in childhood.

3 Patti Carr Black confirmed in a telephone conversation on 23 July 1993 that Welty originally planned to attend Randolph-Macon College in Virginia (nearer her mother's family) after leaving Mississippi State College for Women. However, their decision not to accept a number of her credits led Welty to contact her family; her father traveled to Chicago, met Welty there, and together they went to Madison, where she enrolled at the University of Wisconsin.

4 In writing about her first meeting with her future editor, John Woodburn, Welty employs this same image: "Eventually, without stirring a mile from home, I fell into the safest possible hands" (OWB 96).

5 In *The Eye of the Story* Welty says that "the writing of each story is sure to open up a different prospect and pose a new problem; and . . . no past story bears recognizably on a new one or gives any promise of help" (107).

6 Richard N. Coe, *When the Grass Was Taller: Autobiography and the Experience of Childhood* (New Haven: Yale University Press, 1984), 27. Conversely, Coe argues that the unhappy childhood may cause an impoverishment of these very imaginative possibilities: "Its unhappiness is caused by the fact that the child, in pure self-defense, is forced to develop its rationalizing faculties earlier than need be, thus losing, perhaps forever, the possibility of bypassing rational language and of communicating directly with the world of pure phenomena" (260). If creativity is born in part from pain and loss, then the artist would seem to be someone who manages to retain the imaginative richness of childhood experience *despite* the pressures to relinquish it.

7 *Our Wonder World: A Library of Knowledge* (Chicago: George L. Shuman, 1930), 1:46. Previous copyright dates on the 1930 edition—1914, 1918, 1926, 1927— suggest that it is essentially the same text Welty was given as a birthday gift when she was six or seven (OWB 8); she would have received the 1914 edition. The only obvious difference is that Welty's set included ten volumes; the 1930 edition includes an additional eleventh volume. The two books most relevant to a study of Welty, volume 1, *The World and Its Peoples*, and volume 5, *Every Child's Story Book*, appear to be identical in the two editions.

8 *Our Wonder World* 1:26. Welty's knowledge of this is confirmed in an interview with Jo Brans in 1980 (Con 307).

9 Kreyling, *Eudora Welty's Achievement*, 23–28 passim.

10 Davenport, "That Faire Field," 264.

11 Madelon Sprengnether, "*Delta Wedding* and the Kore Complex," *Southern Quarterly* 25 (Winter 1987): 128.

12 See also Cheryll Burgess, "From Metaphor to Manifestation: The Artist in Eudora Welty's *A Curtain of Green*," in *Eudora Welty: Eye of the Storyteller*, ed. Dawn Trouard (Kent, Ohio: Kent State University Press, 1989), 133–41; and Gary Carson, "Versions of the Artist in *A Curtain of Green*: The Unifying Imagination in Eudora Welty's Early Fiction," *Studies in Short Fiction* 15 (1978): 421–28.

13 Friedrich Nietzsche, *The Birth of Tragedy Out of the Spirit of Music*, in *Basic Writings of Nietzsche*, trans. and ed. Walter Kaufmann (New York: Random House, Modern Library, 1968), 31–144.

14 Cheryll Burgess cogently argues that Mrs. Larkin's garden, "rather than representing a completed story or even a story in progress, seems to be a metaphor for a story's unconscious origin." The chaotic plenitude from within which Mrs. Larkin must begin to make choices is bewildering, and she will need to select and shape her material into something corresponding to an artistic

vision, just as the artist may begin by attending to the impulses, intuitions, and images emerging from his or her unconsciousness (Burgess, "From Metaphor to Manifestation," 137).

15 The reader may find in these descriptive patterns echoes of the idea of order discussed by E. M. W. Tillyard in his classic work *The Elizabethan World Picture* (New York: Random House, Vintage, n.d.). The plenitude of Welty's natural world and her images of correspondence among different realms do suggest a world teeming with life and possibility. Her vision, however, seems intended to encourage an appreciation of the richness of our physical universe, *not* to persuade us of any theological or teleological significance. Nor does Welty's use of such imagery imply anything like the Elizabethans' insistence that every link in the great chain of being must be accounted for by one of God's creations or that every creature has an assigned position within the chain. It is worth noting, however, that Tillyard attributes his Elizabethan subject to the "main outlines of the medieval world picture as modified by the Tudor regime" (108). In other words, the impression of harmony and orderliness we sometimes note in reading Welty is part of a tradition going far back in Western intellectual history. Moreover, the medieval worldview is one already noted (in chap. 1, where it was contrasted with Cartesian thought) as revealing a sense of continuity and organic interrelatedness between the self and the world that is fully compatible with the sense of being-in-the-world reflected in Welty's fiction.

16 Welty's imaginative insistence on similarity and relationship contrasts with many occasions in Faulkner's writing when a character's anxiety about the autonomy of the self leads to a palpable, even anguished confusion of boundaries between the self and others. For a fuller discussion, see Mortimer, *Faulkner's Rhetoric*, 15, 17–20 passim.

17 There are a few exceptions, to be sure. Welty has created alienated figures, nearly all males, in characters such as Howard in "Flowers for Marjorie," Eugene MacLain in "Music from Spain," Ran MacLain in "The Whole World Knows," and the traveling salesmen in "The Hitch-hikers" and "Death of a Traveling Salesman."

18 The fact that Welty's narrators and characters are likely to view the unknown as benign is addressed in chapter 1.

19 Consider these typical situations in Faulkner's stories. In *Light in August* Joe Christmas delays for days reading a note that Joanna Burden has left on his cot, believing that it will entrap him, and then, ironically, is caught in her schemes for his future by the fact that he has *not* read it: "He should have seen that he was bound just as tightly by that small square of still undivulging paper as though it were a lock and chain" (*Light in August*, 299). In *Go Down, Moses* sixteen-year-old Ike McCaslin discovers in his family's ledgers evidence of their involvement in miscegenation, rape, incest, and suicide so shameful (and yet anticipated by him) that he locks himself into the commissary in order to read them (*Go Down, Moses*, 268). And in *The Hamlet* sacks of what V. K. Ratliff, Odum Bookwright, and Henry Armstid believe to be money buried before the Civil War lead them

into a Snopesian trap to fleece them of their money and property. Ratliff, who understands what the Snopeses are like well enough to have known better, is appalled at his own folly, but Armstid undergoes a worse fate; he has, at the end of the story, gone completely mad (*The Hamlet*, 334–66).

20 In *The Optimist's Daughter* Welty offers a vivid example of this in seven-year-old Wendell Chisom's family, which either completely ignores his questions or gives him abrupt and unsatisfactory answers (OD 70, 74).

21 In "Katherine Anne Porter: The Eye of the Story" (ES 30–40), Welty discusses how Miranda, Porter's most frequently invoked protagonist, fights "back [in "Old Mortality"] at the cheat she has discovered in all that's been handed down to her as gospel truth." Welty concludes that "seeing what is not there, putting trust in a false picture of life" is among the "worst nightmares that assail [Porter's] characters" (ES 35). When at the end of the story Miranda insists to herself that "at least I can know the truth about what happens to me," Porter's narrator has the final word, noting that Miranda has made this promise to herself "in her hopefulness, her ignorance." Quoted by Welty (ES 37). Porter's vision is considerably darker than Welty's: whereas love usually ends in betrayal in Porter's stories, in Welty's, love (even if it is only a broader love for life itself) often returns to heal a character's pain. See also Manning, *With Ears Opening*, 33 passim.

22 In an interview with Jean Todd Freeman in 1977, Welty clarifies her distinction between "obscurity" and "mystery" (Con 172–99). Responding to a question about reviewers who had accused her of being obscure, Welty said, "I think it would be the worst sin I could commit, if I were. I certainly don't do such a thing on purpose. If I'm obscure, it's where I've made a mistake somewhere in trying to be clear, because I abominate deliberate obscurity" (Con 189–90). On the other hand, in response to a follow-up question in which Freeman used the word "mysterious," Welty replied, "well, mysterious is something else; I don't mind being mysterious. I think life is mysterious. But to be obscure would be a fault in the teller of the story; and that is something I would have avoided, or overcome, as far as I'm able" (Con 190).

23 "A Sketching Trip" is discussed in chapter 4.

24 Students sometimes conclude that one or even both of Mr. Marblehall's marriages are also fantasized, a reading suggested by the detachment with which he contemplates (and seems to interact with) his families.

25 Little Lee Roy was kidnapped and placed in a sideshow, where he was advertised as a freak and forced to eat live chickens. A question that is never addressed in the story is why Steve should have been so appalled at his participation in the torture of a black man, when apparently he wouldn't have been as bothered if Little Lee Roy *had* been what he was claimed to be, an Indian maiden. Steve seems more preoccupied with his dismay at discovering who Little Lee Roy is than at the inhumanity of the treatment itself.

26 For an intriguing reading of this story that explores Ruby and Clyde's marriage

in terms of their respective relationships to language, see Patricia S. Yaeger, *Honey-Mad Women: Emancipatory Strategies in Women's Writing* (New York: Columbia University Press, 1988), 114–23.

27 Gilligan, *In a Different Voice,* 42, 43.

28 Emily Dickinson, *Final Harvest: Emily Dickinson's Poems,* ed. Thomas H. Johnson (Boston: Little, Brown, 1961), 29.

29 See, for example, Warren, "Love and Separateness in Eudora Welty," 162, who argues that Audubon "loves the bird, innocently, in its fullness of being. But he must subject this love to knowledge; he must kill the bird if he is to commemorate its beauty, if he is to establish his communion with other men in terms of the bird's beauty. There is in the situation an irony of limit and contamination." Danièle Pitavy-Souques sees the killing of the bird as symbolizing "some form of severance . . . [an] inevitable fracture" that is a necessary step in the creative process ("A Blazing Butterfly: The Modernity of Eudora Welty," in *Welty: A Life in Literature,* ed. Albert J. Devlin [Jackson: University Press of Mississippi, 1987], 125).

30 For useful discussions of the historical accuracy of this story, see Pearl Amelia McHaney, "Historical Perspectives in 'A Still Moment'," in *Critical Essays on Eudora Welty,* ed. W. Craig Turner and Lee Emling Harding (Boston: G. K. Hall, 1989), 52–69; and Albert J. Devlin, *Eudora Welty's Chronicle: A Story of Mississippi Life* (Jackson: University Press of Mississippi, 1983), 49–62.

31 Northrop Frye, "Yeats and the Language of Symbolism," in *Fables of Identity: Studies in Poetic Mythology* (New York: Harcourt, Brace and World, Harbinger, 1963), 225.

32 J. Hillis Miller, "Yeats: The Linguistic Moment," in *William Butler Yeats,* ed. Harold Bloom (New York: Chelsea House, 1986), 206; emphasis mine.

33 Helen Hennessy Vendler, *Yeats's Vision and the Later Plays* (Cambridge: Harvard University Press, 1963), 173.

34 Harold Bloom writes that "the subject of the poem, as is so frequent in Yeats and throughout Romantic tradition, is a single moment" (*Yeats* [New York: Oxford University Press, 1972], 365).

35 Gilligan, *In a Different Voice,* 48.

36 Sigmund Freud, *Civilization and Its Discontents,* trans. and ed. James Strachey (1930; New York: W. W. Norton, 1962), 60.

37 Gilligan, *In a Different Voice,* 46–48.

38 The relationship between human (that is, mortal) and immortal views of time is addressed in chapter 3 in the discussion of Welty's "Circe."

Chapter 3. Circles and Labyrinths

1 See, for example, John Edward Hardy, "Marrying Down in Eudora Welty's Novels," in *Eudora Welty: Critical Essays,* ed. Peggy Whitman Prenshaw (Jack-

son: University Press of Mississippi, 1979), 93–119; and Jane L. Hinton, "The Role of Family in *Delta Wedding, Losing Battles,* and *The Optimist's Daughter,*" in the same volume, 120–31.

2 See Victor Turner, *Dramas, Fields, and Metaphors: Symbolic Action in Human Society* (Ithaca: Cornell University Press, 1974) and *The Ritual Process: Structure and Anti-structure* (Ithaca: Cornell University Press, 1977). I am indebted to Carey Wall, who first brought to my attention the value of Victor Turner's ideas in thinking about Welty's texts. See Wall's essay, "Eudora Welty's *Delta Wedding* and Victor Turner's 'Liminality'," *Southern Studies* 25 (Fall 1986): 220–34.

3 Manning, *With Ears Opening,* 12–13. See also Peggy W. Prenshaw, "Woman's World, Man's Place: The Fiction of Eudora Welty," in *Eudora Welty,* ed. Dollarhide and Abadie, 46–77, for a reading of this novel emphasizing women's relationship to the earth and to nature and its rhythms of fertility and renewal; and Sprengnether, *"Delta Wedding,"* 120–30, for an insightful consideration of the novel's "patterns of loss and recovery" in the context of its theme of "maternal protectiveness" (125, 124).

4 Westling, *Sacred Groves,* 96.

5 Welty clarifies these two reasons for making Joel a deaf character in an interview with Linda Kuehl in 1972 (Con 84).

6 This scene is specifically reminiscent of Welty's childhood illness when she was allowed to fall asleep while her parents sat under a lamp nearby, talking. As Welty recalls, "What was thus dramatically made a present of to me was the secure sense of the hidden observer" (OWB 20).

7 The stories and novels of Faulkner reveal persistent and sometimes obsessive concern with the passing of time. Faulkner's Quentin Compson in *The Sound and the Fury* is perhaps the most obvious example; he spends the entire day of his interior monologue (the last day of his life) trying to remain unaware of what time it is, and his obsessional thoughts all revolve around his inability to stop time from passing (86–205). John Irwin focuses on the imaginative consequences of this preoccupation with time in his important study *Doubling and Incest.*

8 Julia Kristeva, "Women's Time," trans. Alice Jardine and Harry Blake, *Signs: Journal of Women in Culture and Society* 7 (Autumn 1981): 17.

9 Kristeva, "Women's Time," 17.

10 Kristeva, "Women's Time," 16. As a footnote to this passage explains, *jouissance* is a "word for pleasure which defies translation." Kristeva goes on to note that these two experiences of time are far from being exclusive to women but are also found in "numerous civilizations and experiences, particularly mystical ones" (17).

11 See Devlin and Prenshaw, "A Conversation with Eudora Welty," held in Jackson on 22 September 1986, in *Welty: A Life in Literature,* ed. Devlin, 19.

12 See also Schmidt, *Heart of the Story,* 53–58.

13 Penelope Reed Doob, *The Idea of the Labyrinth from Classical Antiquity through the Middle Ages* (Ithaca: Cornell University Press, 1990), 39.

14 See Wendy B. Faris, *Labyrinths of Language: Symbolic Landscape and Narrative Design in Modern Fiction* (Baltimore: Johns Hopkins University Press, 1988).

15 Doob, *Idea of the Labyrinth*, 30, 50.

16 In the discussion on pages 94 and 95, I am indebted to three critical studies: Knight, *Starlit Dome*; Peter Elbow, *Oppositions in Chaucer* (Middletown, Conn.: Wesleyan University Press, 1975), especially the chapter entitled "Boethius' *The Consolation of Philosophy*," 19–48; and Angus Fletcher, "'Positive Negation': Threshold, Sequence, and Personification in Coleridge," in *New Perspectives on Coleridge and Wordsworth: Selected Papers from the English Institute*, ed. Geoffrey H. Hartman (New York: Columbia University Press, 1972), 133–64.

17 William Butler Yeats, "Byzantium," *The Collected Poems of W. B. Yeats* (London: Macmillan, 1950), 280.

18 Knight, *Starlit Dome*, 203; Knight quotes these lines from Shelley.

19 Elbow, *Oppositions*, 30, 37.

20 Fletcher, "'Positive Negation'," 135.

21 See Rebecca Mark, *The Dragon's Blood: Feminist Intertextuality in Eudora Welty's "The Golden Apples"* (Jackson: University Press of Mississippi, 1994); Elizabeth M. Kerr, "The World of Eudora Welty's Women," in *Eudora Welty*, ed. Prenshaw, 132–48; and Ann Romines, *The Home Plot: Women, Writing, and Domestic Ritual* (Amherst: University of Massachusetts Press, 1992), esp. 230–46. For a consideration of this theme in other Welty novels, see Margaret Jones Bolsterli, "Woman's Vision: The Worlds of Women in *Delta Wedding, Losing Battles,* and *The Optimist's Daughter*," in *Eudora Welty*, ed. Prenshaw, 149–56.

22 This is an image Welty shares with Yeats, who wrote lines that might well be applied to the MacLain twins: "A man in his own secret meditation / Is lost amid the labyrinth that he has made" (Yeats, "Nineteen Hundred," 235).

23 In "The Whole World Knows" Maideen says to Ran, "You don't ever dance, do you" (CS 389), and in "Music from Spain" Emma accuses Eugene of not appreciating music (CS 401).

24 In an interview with John Griffin Jones in 1981 Welty commented that in writing Eugene's story, "I wanted to show somebody from Morgana who'd gone outside the local circle; and yet he was no better outside than he would've been inside" (Con 332). See discussion earlier in this chapter of how inclusion within circles can alter one's perspective.

25 The dormitory where Welty lived at Mississippi State College for Women featured a fire escape that the young women used "to go to class, and at night to slip outside for a few minutes before going to bed" (OWB 78). Welty's description seems relevant to this passage from "Music from Spain" in suggesting a particular experience she had of what is involved in reaching freedom (see also LB 237): "It was the iron standpipe kind of fire escape, with a tin chute running down through it—*all corkscrew turns from top to bottom*, with holes along its passage where girls at fire drill could pour out of the different floors, and a hole at the bottom to pitch you out onto the ground, head still whirling" (OWB 78; emphasis mine).

26 Numerous examples might be cited: in "Going to Naples," when the passengers aboard the *Pomona* arrive there, they hear a cacophony of city noises, including "the cry of a child from somewhere deep in the golden labyrinth" (CS 593); Circe, in the story named for her, retrieves Odysseus's companions from "their muddy labyrinth" (CS 534); Phoenix in "A Worn Path" traverses the maze of a field of dead corn (CS 144); and various other characters have gardens with actual or implicit labyrinthine features—the title character in "Old Mr. Marblehall" has a back garden with a "box maze . . . there on the edge like a trap, to confound the Mississippi River" (CS 92), and in "A Curtain of Green" there is Mrs. Larkin's tangled garden with its border of hedge (CS 107).

27 Mark, *Dragon's Blood*. I am indebted to Mark for sharing with me an early version of a portion of her book concerned with allusions in Welty's "The Whole World Knows" to Faulkner's *Sound and the Fury*. Her insightful work and the contributions of my students in our classroom discussions of intertextual relationships between Welty's work and Faulkner's have significantly clarified my understanding.

28 Kreyling finds echoes of T. S. Eliot's "Love Song of J. Alfred Prufrock" throughout Eugene's story, "Music from Spain" (*Eudora Welty's Achievement*, 94–100). I would add that *both* MacLain brothers suffer the same self-doubt, bewilderment, and ineffectuality found in Prufrock—and in Quentin Compson. Introspective brooding and persistent malaise link all of these twentieth-century antiheroes.

29 Rebecca Mark's book *The Dragon's Blood* features discussion of the idea of heroism for both male and female characters in Welty's *Golden Apples*.

30 Even when she is a baby, her mother comments, "there she runs" (CS 269). See also CS 277, 282, and 297, which tells of Virgie's running that "nobody, even her brother, could catch her."

31 When Bellerophon's arrogance causes him to defy the gods by attempting to fly to heaven on Pegasus, he is thrown from the horse, lamed and blinded, and spends the remainder of his life miserably, as a wanderer. Thus, paradoxically, Eugene shares at least some of the same fate.

32 Kreyling sees George Fairchild in *Delta Wedding* as a type of male in Welty's fiction whose family insists that he play a "dual role of the clan's hero—savior and scapegoat" in their lives as in their stories about themselves (*Eudora Welty's Achievement*, 57). See also DW 63. Eugene MacLain is different from George Fairchild, of course, in his inability to rescue himself, let alone his family, but Welty's evocation of this specific duality in the earlier novel adds credence to this assessment of the choices Eugene faces in his meeting with the Spaniard.

  I am indebted to Frederick Martin, who, while a student of mine at the University of Texas at El Paso, wrote a fine paper on the mythic background that seems to confirm this interpretation of Eugene's plight in "Music from Spain."

33 Euripides, *The Bacchae*, trans. William Arrowsmith, in *Greek Tragedies*, ed. David Grene and Richmond Lattimore (Chicago: University of Chicago Press, Phoenix Books, 1960), 3 : 195.

34 In the play *The Bacchae,* Dionysus speaks of two great blessings that the gods have given to mankind, the "nourishment of grain" from Demeter and the gift of wine from Dionysus: "filled with that good gift, / suffering mankind forgets its grief" (Euripides, *The Bacchae,* 3:204). The name "Eudora" means "good gift."

 Dionysus has been linked in some versions of his myth with the god Pan, who is able to create panic even in the brave: "Thus, at times, you see an army mustered under arms / stricken with panic before it lifts a spear. / This panic comes from Dionysus" (Euripides, *The Bacchae,* 3:205). This aspect of Pan is incarnated in the character Don McInnis in Welty's story "Asphodel" (CS 200–208). Welty's mention in that story of the "little beards" of the billy goats and nanny goats that blow as they pursue the protagonists (just after "Pan" has appeared) is echoed in "Music from Spain" in the Spaniard's suspenders, which are "trimmed in silver with little bearded animal faces on the buckles" (CS 415), one of innumerable details that invite the reader to think of Dionysian possibilities in Eugene's story.

35 Robert Graves, *The Greek Myths* (New York: Penguin, 1960), 1:297; emphases and ellipses are mine.

36 As Robert Graves's many stories about ancient heroes make clear, struggling—and in particular, wrestling—with antagonists is a basic feature of heroic life. The details recorded about Eugene's struggle with the Spaniard all point to these ancient tales. At one point in their encounter on the bluff Eugene "felt himself lifted up in the strong arms of the Spaniard, up above the bare head of the other man" (CS 422) and realized how easily he might be tossed over into the sea. "He was brought over and held by the knees *in the posture of a bird,* his body almost upright and his forearms gently spread" (CS 423; emphasis mine). Graves writes that "the Leucadians used every year to fling a man, provided with wings to break his fall, and even with live birds corded to his body, over the cliff into the sea. The victim [was] a *pharmacos,* or scapegoat, whose removal freed the island from guilt." Moreover, there is evidence that "the winged *pharmacos* flung to his death was originally the king" (*Greek Myths,* 1:303). See also Graves 1:331, where he links the stories of the hero Theseus to such struggles, noting that an icon depicts "Theseus's wrestling with Cercyon" and "shows him being lifted off his feet by his successor . . . a common mythological situation."

37 Freud, *Civilization,* 16–19. Freud ultimately abandons the image as inadequate, but he continues to believe it is "rather the rule than the exception for the past to be preserved in mental life" (p. 19).

Chapter 4. Fictions, Names, Masks

 1 See Wendy Barker, *Lunacy of Light: Emily Dickinson and the Experience of Metaphor* (Carbondale: Southern Illinois University Press, 1987), in which Barker

argues that Emily Dickinson and such writers as Charlotte Brontë in *Villette* and George Eliot in *Middlemarch* often invert the conventional associations of day and night, light and dark. For Dickinson this may have been in part because during the day she was committed to domestic responsibilities and might be interrupted at any moment, whereas at night she could find time and privacy for her work. Because sunlight is classically associated with masculine knowledge, health, potency, and creativity, and women have been placed—as Other—in the realms of darkness, mystery, and the unknown, "it is no wonder," Barker writes, "that in the imagery of many women writers we find the darkness paradoxically offering relief" from the harsh attitudes toward women that are often implicit in masculine valorization of the sun (25). Moreover, in the nineteenth- and early twentieth-century South girls were often kept out of the sun or provided with parasols because the sun was viewed as dangerous. Barker also reminds the reader that in legends we find the idea of the sun impregnating women (7), as in the myth of Danae—featured by Welty in her story "Shower of Gold"—where Zeus appears to Danae disguised as a shower of gold, leaving her pregnant.

2 "I still had my secret childhood feeling that if you hunted long enough in a book's pages, you could find what you were looking for" ("A Sweet Devouring," ES 282).

3 Richard Rorty, *Contingency, Irony, and Solidarity* (New York: Cambridge University Press, 1989), 3.

4 Rorty, *Contingency,* 73.

5 Rorty elaborates on the ironist's beliefs at length in chapter 4, "Private Irony and Liberal Hope," of *Contingency,* 73–95. Rorty's book is itself built on an attempt to explore a specific duality of values. He wants to treat "the demands of self-creation and of human solidarity as equally valid [objectives of human existence], yet forever incommensurable" (xv). This is simply an alternative vocabulary—in philosophic and political terms—for addressing the psychological dilemma of separateness (autonomy, private fulfillment, "self-creation") and connection (a sense of community, responsibility to others, "human solidarity") with which I began this book. Rorty contextualizes his discussion by placing it within the broader debate about the relationship between the public and the private that has been part of Western thought at least since Plato (xiii–xvi).

6 I find no evidence in Welty's writing that she shares Rorty's conviction that "nothing has an intrinsic nature, a real essence" (*Contingency,* 74). She does understand, however, that language fails to get us closer to whatever such "truths" may exist.

7 For a different interpretation of the significance of houses in one of Welty's novels, see Dorothy G. Griffin, "The House as Container: Architecture and Myth in *Delta Wedding,*" in *Welty: A Life in Literature,* ed. Devlin, 96–112.

8 In *"Delta Wedding,"* 123, Madelon Sprengnether finds a similar "shadow relationship between Marmion and Shellmound," two of the Fairchilds' houses.

Welty uses houses to indicate her characters' personalities and fates in much the same way that Faulkner does in such stories as "A Rose for Emily" and *Absalom, Absalom!*.

9 Patricia Meyer Spacks, *Gossip* (New York: Alfred A. Knopf, 1985), 252. Spacks discusses "Asphodel" on pp. 253–56.

10 Spacks, *Gossip,* 255.

11 What Katie Rainey says about King MacLain in "Shower of Gold" is equally true of Blackie: "Beware of a man with manners" (CS 264).

12 Suzanne Marrs, *The Welty Collection: A Guide to the Eudora Welty Manuscripts and Documents at the Mississippi Department of Archives and History* (Jackson: University Press of Mississippi, 1988), 79.

13 Hunter Cole and Seetha Srinivasan, "Introduction—Eudora Welty and Photography: An Interview," *Photographs* (Jackson: University Press of Mississippi, 1989), xix.

14 Roger Mudd, interview with Eudora Welty, "MacNeil/Lehrer Newshour." PBS. WNET, New York. Show no. 3613. 29 November 1989.

15 Cole and Srinivasan, "Introduction," xix.

16 Eugene MacLain in "Music from Spain" sees the lives of artists, foreigners, and wanderers as "all the same thing" (CS 409). Together with heroes (Odysseus, Perseus), evangelists (Lorenzo Dow), traveling salesmen, and acrobatic troupes, they all find a place in Welty's fiction as characters who are removed to some degree from society's pressures to conform, yet they share a palpable vulnerability and isolation. Artists like the Spaniard in "Music from Spain" and Miss Eckhart in "June Recital," however, share a passion for their art that is fully compensatory. Welty, too, feels this joy in art, and in her discussion of "what is deepest and realest in [Willa Cather's] work," she notes that "love of art . . . is love accomplished without help or need of help from another" (ES 55).

The theme of wandering is as basic to Yeats's imagination as it is to Welty's. Explicit allusions to his poem "The Song of Wandering Aengus" permeate *The Golden Apples,* and Yeats, in addition to writing such works as "The Wanderings of Oisin," frequently featured shepherds, heroes, beggars, and wandering lovers as protagonists in his poems. Welty, of course, recognizes that "the errand of search" is basic to literature: "An idea this pervasive simply pervades life" (ES 88).

17 Manning argues that Welty and Anne Tyler share a concern with dismantling the romantic aura with which male texts tend to surround the figure of the wanderer or adventurer: "Both writers undermine the male fantasy of the free-spirited hero by focusing on what the fantasy ignores. As viewed by these clear-eyed realists, the wandering hero is not single but married, and it is the home world he in effect deserts that the authors take as their focus" ("Welty, Tyler, and Traveling Salesmen: The Wandering Hero Unhorsed," in *The Fiction of Anne Tyler,* ed. C. Ralph Stephens [Jackson: University Press of Mississippi, 1990], 112).

18 Alfred Tennyson, "Ulysses," *The Poems and Plays of Alfred, Lord Tennyson* (New York: Random House, Modern Library, 1938), 166.

19 Sandra M. Gilbert notes that "the Anglo-Saxon word 'daughter' can be traced back to the Indo-European root *dhugh,* meaning 'to milk.' . . . [She is] not only milkmaid but milk giver, she who nurtures as well as she who is nurtured" ("Life's Empty Pack: Notes toward a Literary Daughteronomy," *Critical Inquiry* 11 [March 1985]: 362).

20 In "Watchers and Watching: Point of View in Eudora Welty's 'June Recital'," trans. Margaret Tomarchio, *Southern Review* 19 (1983): 483–509, Danièle Pitavy-Souques argues that Loch's perceptions are distorted not only by his malaria but also because his imagination is "basically narcissistic and subversive" (485). Although clearly Loch's perceptions *are* interlaced with episodes of fantasy and he mistakenly identifies several things he sees, I find no grounds for concluding, as Pitavy-Souques does, that his "regard" of events in the house next door is too distorted to constitute a "realist vision" of what is taking place. Otherwise, I find Pitavy-Souques's analysis provocative.

21 The text itself is amusingly ambiguous: "There on a mattress delightfully bare— where [Loch] would love, himself, to lie, on a slant and naked . . . the sailor and the piano player lay" (cs 281–82).

22 Susan V. Donaldson writes that "telling stories from the perspective of Morgana offers a means of setting boundaries between the proper and the improper, the orderly and the anarchic, so that the chaotic possibilities represented by King MacLain and other outsiders are readily defused, catalogued, and eventually contained" ("Recovering Otherness in *The Golden Apples,*" *American Literature* 63 [September 1991]: 492).

23 Pitavy-Souques rightly argues that prejudice is the "central subject" of "June Recital" ("Watchers and Watching," 496).

24 In "The Wanderers," Cassie, after her mother's death, devotes a good deal of time and energy to the monument at her mother's grave (cs 449) and to planting her front garden so that it spells out "Mama's Name" in various types of flowers year-round. Virgie's wry comment is, "I guess it takes a lot of narcissus to spell Catherine" (cs 457).

25 For a rather different reading of this story, which assumes that Mattie Will imagines her encounter with King MacLain, see Yaeger, "'Because a Fire,'" 960–62.

26 Lowry Pei, "Dreaming the Other in *The Golden Apples,*" *Modern Fiction Studies* 28 (Autumn 1982): 421. Pei's essay is particularly helpful on the issue of how communication rarely takes place through language in this book.

27 Pei, "Dreaming the Other," 423. Pei quotes from cs 460.

28 From Welty's earliest stories, such as "Lily Daw and the Three Ladies," women often appear in threes, sometimes to constitute a Greek chorus for the protagonist and at others to recall the Fates. In terms of the lives they affect, the Fates' roles are successively those of creator, preserver, and destroyer.

29 Cassie, as a child, often felt disappointed in her mother. There are signs, too,

that Cassie was envious of the devotion Miss Eckhart showered on Virgie Rainey; she especially noticed the gifts Miss Eckhart gave to Virgie, including a butterfly pin "like silver lace" that "Cassie for many days could close her eyes and see" (CS 306). Cassie would have loved to be the focus of so much attention and admiration, and her devotion to her mother's memory appears to deny the fact that she never received it.

30 For an extended consideration of the Perseus-Medusa myth as it functions throughout *The Golden Apples,* see Mark, *Dragon's Blood.*

31 Welty writes: "As I looked longer and longer for the origins of this passionate and strange character, at last I realized that Miss Eckhart came from me. There wasn't any resemblance in her outward identity: I am not musical, not a teacher, nor foreign in birth. . . . But none of that counts. What counts is only what lies at the solitary core. . . . Exposing yourself to risk is a truth Miss Eckhart and I had in common. What animates and possesses me is what drives Miss Eckhart, the love of her art and the love of giving it, the desire to give it until there is no more left. . . . In the making of her character out of my most inward and most deeply feeling self, I would say I have found my voice in my fiction" (OWB 101).

Chapter 5. Embracing Vulnerability

1 In *Author and Agent* Kreyling writes that this early story, "The Winds," occasioned a good deal of discussion between Welty, her agent, and various editors before its eventual publication in August 1942. Male readers, including Russell himself, found it powerful, but somewhat obscure and bewildering, whereas Mary Louise Aswell, the fiction editor at *Harper's Bazaar,* "discerned a latent female psychology and inner experience that Russell sensed but could not identify" (69). Aswell's influence seems to have been important in encouraging Welty to continue exploring the type of subjective vision first elaborated in this story.

2 See Richard Gray, *Writing the South: Ideas of an American Region* (Cambridge: Cambridge University Press, 1986), 243: "The past, [Welty] suggests, may be something that we do not merely remember but reinvent . . . [through] the power, the shaping presence, of the mind."

3 Eudora Welty, *Short Stories* (New York: Harcourt, Brace, 1950), 11.

4 Elizabeth Bowen, *The Death of the Heart* (London: Jonathan Cape, 1938), 300. The final set of ellipses is in Bowen's text; emphasis is mine. Later in this chapter I discuss Welty's own use of the idea of "swallow[ing] some few lies."

5 The thread image appears as often in her nonfiction essays as in her stories. For example, in describing Ida M'Toy, an old woman who had been for a long time a midwife and was now "a dealer in secondhand clothes," Welty turned naturally to some of her favorite images, including the sky ("she is a kind of meteor") and thread: "Ida's life has been divided in two . . . but there is a thread that runs from one part into the other" (ES 336–37). Welty has spoken in similar

terms of how short stories differ from novels: "It's a different pace, a different timing. In the case of the short story, you can't ever let the tautness of line relax. It has to be all strung very tight upon its single thread" (Con 45).

6 See Introduction, note 11.

7 To interpret Wanda Fay in positive terms seems possible only if she is seen as an explicit foil for the passivity and apparent aloofness of Laurel in the early parts of the novel. Fay's desire to be part of Mardi Gras, then, becomes a reflection of her desire to live intensely. It is necessary, in this reading, to believe that Welty finds truth in Fay's opinion of herself as standing for life ("I was trying to scare him into living!" [OD 175]) and the future ("I belong to the future, didn't you know that?" [OD 179]). But Welty herself has said that she hates what Fay stands for, that Fay's obliviousness to the meaning of experience is "horrifying and even evil, almost sinful" (Gayle Graham Yates, "An Interview with Eudora Welty," *Frontiers* 9 [1987]: 104). Thus, although readers may feel momentary compassion for Fay as they realize the ugliness of the world she has tried to escape in marrying the judge, her persistent self-centeredness and insensitivity make a favorable reading of her virtually impossible to sustain.

8 For a helpful reading of how New Orleans and the carnival festivities imply a vitality that Laurel Hand needs to get in touch with, see Robert H. Brinkmeyer, Jr., "New Orleans, Mardi Gras, and Eudora Welty's *The Optimist's Daughter*," *Mississippi Quarterly* 44 (Fall 1991): 429–41.

9 The word "optimism" refers not only to a generally hopeful view of things but to a belief that everything is *ordered* for the best, a signification that implies, if obliquely, an Apollonian perspective. The judge is also Apollonian by virtue of his profession as one who serves law and order.

10 Welty's specific evocation in *The Golden Apples* of the myths of Danae, Leda and the swan, Perseus and Medusa, and Atalanta have led to insightful commentary on how mythology embodies meaning in that novel. See especially Pitavy-Souques, "Technique as Myth: The Structure of *The Golden Apples*," in *Eudora Welty,* ed. Prenshaw, 258–68; Thomas L. McHaney, "Eudora Welty and the Multitudinous Golden Apples," in *Critical Essays,* ed. Turner and Harding, 113–41; and Mark, *Dragon's Blood.*

11 A number of Laurel's recollections closely echo situations that occurred within Welty's own family history. See especially *One Writer's Beginnings.*

12 Among the critics who have focused on image patterns in *The Optimist's Daughter* are Marilyn Arnold, "Images of Memory in Eudora Welty's *The Optimist's Daughter*," *Southern Literary Journal* 14 (Spring 1982): 28–38; Bev Byrne, "A Return to the Source: Eudora Welty's *The Robber Bridegroom* and *The Optimist's Daughter*," *Southern Quarterly* 24 (1986): 74–85; John F. Desmond, who lists a broad range of images in "Pattern and Vision in *The Optimist's Daughter*," in *A Still Moment: Essays on the Art of Eudora Welty,* ed. Desmond (Metuchen, N.J.: Scarecrow, 1978), 118–38; Robert L. Phillips, "Patterns of Vision in Welty's *The Optimist's Daughter*," *Southern Literary Journal* 14 (Fall 1981): 10–23; Reynolds Price, "The Onlooker, Smiling: An Early Reading of *The Opti-*

mist's Daughter," in *Eudora Welty,* ed. Bloom, 75–88; Jennifer Lynn Randisi, *A Tissue of Lies: Eudora Welty and the Southern Romance* (Washington, D.C.: University Press of America, 1982), 125–50; William Jay Smith, "Precision and Reticence: Eudora Welty's Poetic Vision," in *Eudora Welty,* ed. Dollarhide and Abadie, 78–94; Helen Hurt Tiegreen, "Mothers, Daughters, and One Writer's Revisions," in *Welty: A Life in Literature,* ed. Devlin, 188–211; and Vande Kieft, *Eudora Welty,* 165–85.

13 Vande Kieft, "Preface to the Revised Edition," n.p.

14 Dickinson, *Final Harvest,* 249.

15 Reynolds Price appears to have been first among the critics who have seen "vision, the forms of blindness" as the "central metaphor" of *The Optimist's Daughter;* he writes, "the story is as troubled by eyes as *King Lear*" (Price, "The Onlooker," 79).

16 Among the things that are said to "slip" in the novel are the judge's memory (OD 5), the nurse's "veneer" of Mrs. Martello (OD 32), and the judge's eyesight when he first met Fay (OD 76).

17 A minor mythic echo adds to the irony of the judge's associations with water. Through a variety of details, Welty recalls the myth of Deucalion and Pyrrha, ancient counterparts of Noah and his wife, who survive a flood sent by Zeus and live to found a renewed human race. Pyrrha means "fiery red," a reminder of the scarlet blouse that Becky (Laurel's mother) had made for herself, calling it the "most beautiful blouse I ever owned in my life" (OD 136). The judge is associated with Deucalion not only because of his optimism about the flood but also because of the small stone boat he carved for Becky when he was courting her. After the flood, Deucalion and Pyrrha were left to reproduce humanity (as the gods instructed them) by throwing stones over their shoulders; each stone formed a human being. In the judge's gift to his fiancée, Welty has conflated the boat in which Deucalion and his wife survive the flood with the stones they later use to create new human beings.

18 The relationship is reciprocal. Just as hands can function as eyes, eyes can move and touch people. Lying in his hospital bed, uncharacteristically passive, the judge "didn't try any more to *hold* [Laurel] in his good eye" (OD 24; emphasis mine).

19 The iris controls the amount of light that enters the eye.

20 D. H. Lawrence, *Lady Chatterley's Lover* (1928; New York: New American Library, Signet, 1962), 107.

21 Arnold's discussion of bird imagery in her essay "Images of Memory in Eudora Welty's *The Optimist's Daughter*" is especially noteworthy. I am also indebted to the members of my spring 1989 seminar on Welty for helpful discussions of these matters. In particular Jay Monath (whose phrasing I have borrowed here), Jacqueline Keller, and Fred Martin offered insightful commentary.

22 See, for example, the chapter on *The Optimist's Daughter,* "Learning to See Bridges," in Carson, *Eudora Welty,* 135–55.

23 Graves, *Greek Myths,* 1:78.

24 Just after Laurel freed the trapped bird from her house, she "burned Milton's Universe" (OD 169), her mother's girlhood diagrams. In freeing herself of "perfect" memories, Laurel is acknowledging that she no longer needs to believe in perfection, in paradise. Unlike her mother, Laurel can let go of these illusions left over from childhood.

25 See Introduction, note 22. For an illuminating discussion of the implications and the appeal of the Demeter-Persephone myth for women writers, see Susan Gubar, "Mother, Maiden, and the Marriage of Death: Women Writers and an Ancient Myth," *Women's Studies* 6 (1979): 301–15.

26 Randisi notes—but does not pursue—the fact that the blindness and insight motif in *The Optimist's Daughter* "echoes the Oedipal myth" (*Tissue of Lies*, 126).

27 Graves, *Greek Myths*, 2:10.

28 Teiresias, in a speech to Oedipus, foretells the fate of the murderer of Laius: ". . . blindness for sight / and beggary for riches his exchange, / he shall go journeying to a foreign country / tapping his way before him with a stick" (Sophocles, *Oedipus the King,* trans. David Grene, in *Greek Tragedies,* ed. David Grene and Richmond Lattimore [Chicago: University of Chicago Press, Phoenix Books, 1960], 1:130).

   A rereading of *Oedipus the King* alongside *The Optimist's Daughter* reveals that Welty has tapped deeply into the cluster of symbols Sophocles uses: blindness and (in)sight, the auguries of birds (as in the beating of dark wings suggesting foreboding), the darkness of ignorance, the drowning waves of misery that crash over Oedipus when he finally "sees," and even, perhaps, the idea of a blind man whose daughter (Antigone, Laurel) sees for both of them.

29 Teiresias is said to have lived for seven generations. In one of several stories of his blindness, he came upon two snakes mating; killing the female, he became a woman for seven years. Then he again saw two snakes mating, killed the male, and became male once more. After this he became involved in an argument between Zeus and Hera about which gender found more pleasure in sex, a debate that ended in his being blinded by Hera.

   With Welty's high valorization of memory both in her personal life and her art, she would be drawn to that feature of Teiresias's story that tells of how he alone, of all those in the world of the dead, was allowed to retain his memory and intellect unimpaired.

30 Graves writes that she "remained a virgin and became a Sibyl," but he does not indicate whether she is the same Daphne who was transformed into a tree and who is said to have had a different father, the Thessalian river-god Peneius. Both Daphne figures are associated with the laurel, which was sacred to the god Apollo, and directly or indirectly with the god himself (Graves, *Greek Myths,* 2:24).

31 D'Arcy Wentworth Thompson, *A Glossary of Greek Birds* (London: Oxford University Press, 1936), 22, 314–25. In Greek mythology Philomela is changed into a swallow and her sister Procne into a nightingale. In the Roman version, Philomela is a nightingale and Procne a swallow. In both mythologies neither bird

is assumed to have a tongue. Welty chose the Greek version, using the word "swallow" as both a noun and a verb.

32 Ruth D. Weston writes that "the old folks focus on Laurel throughout the novel, intent on what they will or will not 'make' her do; for the underside of the female support group is its power to intimidate and control. . . . The coercive word, often masquerading as the comforting word, attempts to order society in many informal ways, especially through the perpetuation of cultural codes that are so ingrained that they are accepted as 'normal' " ("The Feminine and Feminist Texts of Eudora Welty's *The Optimist's Daughter*," *South Central Review* 4 [Winter 1987]: 80). This is equally true of Virgie Rainey in *The Golden Apples*.

33 Philip J. Gallagher, " 'Real or Allegoric': The Ontology of Sin and Death in *Paradise Lost*," *English Literary Renaissance* 6 (Spring 1976): 333.

34 Hesiod, *Hesiod: The Works and Days; Theogony; The Shield of Herakles*, trans. Richmond Lattimore (Ann Arbor: University of Michigan Press, 1959), 85, 87; emphasis mine.

35 Thompson, *Glossary*, 318.

36 In keeping with the idea of Apollonian serenity and order confronting Dionysian forces in this novel, it is noteworthy that the chaos of Mardi Gras ends at the very time the judge's turmoil ceases, at his death, and that a storm rages outside and a bird flies frantically through Laurel's home during her ultimate battle with her own memories. Calm comes with the end of the storm, the freeing of the bird, and Laurel's acceptance of the import of her past.

37 Thompson, *Glossary*, 322, 323.

38 T. S. Eliot, "Tradition and the Individual Talent," in *Critical Theory since Plato*, ed. Hazard Adams (New York: Harcourt Brace, 1971), 785.

39 The final line in Welty's story "The Bride of the Innisfallen" depicts a young woman who feels the pure joy of life as she enters a pub in Ireland. Welty's wording reveals a pleasure and anticipation quite rare in twentieth-century fiction: "The girl . . . opening the door walked *without protection* into the *lovely room full of strangers*" (CS 518; emphasis mine).

Abel, Elizabeth. "(E)Merging Identities: The Dynamics of Female Friendship in Contemporary Fiction by Women." *Signs: Journal of Women in Culture and Society* 6 (Spring 1981): 413–35.

Appel, Alfred, Jr. *A Season of Dreams: The Fiction of Eudora Welty.* Baton Rouge: Louisiana State University Press, 1965.

Arnold, Marilyn. "Images of Memory in Eudora Welty's *The Optimist's Daughter.*" *Southern Literary Journal* 14 (Spring 1982): 28–38.

———. "'The Magical Percussion': Eudora Welty's Human Recital on Art and Time." *Southern Humanities Review* 23 (Spring 1989): 101–18.

Barker, Wendy. *Lunacy of Light: Emily Dickinson and the Experience of Metaphor.* Carbondale: Southern Illinois University Press, 1987.

Belenky, Mary Field et al. *Women's Ways of Knowing: The Development of Self, Voice, and Mind.* New York: Basic Books, 1986.

Black, Patti Carr. Telephone conversation with author, 23 July 1993.

Blau DuPlessis, Rachel. *Writing beyond the Ending: Narrative Strategies of Twentieth-Century Women Writers.* Bloomington: Indiana University Press, 1985.

Bleikasten, André. *The Ink of Melancholy: Faulkner's Novels from "The Sound and the Fury" to "Light in August".* Bloomington: Indiana University Press, 1990.

Bloom, Harold. *Yeats.* New York: Oxford University Press, 1972.

———, ed. *Eudora Welty.* New York: Chelsea House, 1986.

Blotner, Joseph. *Faulkner: A Biography.* 2 vols. New York: Random House, 1974.

Bolsterli, Margaret Jones. "Woman's Vision: The Worlds of Women in *Delta Wedding, Losing Battles,* and *The Optimist's Daughter.*" In *Eudora Welty: Critical Essays,* edited by Peggy Whitman Prenshaw, 149–56. Jackson: University Press of Mississippi, 1979.

Bordo, Susan. "The Cartesian Masculinization of Thought." *Signs: Journal of Women in Culture and Society* 11 (Spring 1986): 439–56.

Bowen, Elizabeth. *The Death of the Heart.* London: Jonathan Cape, 1938.

Brewer, Ebenezer Cobham. *Brewer's Dictionary of Phrase and Fable.* Revised and enlarged. New York: Harper and Brothers, 1953.

Brinkmeyer, Robert H., Jr. "New Orleans, Mardi Gras, and Eudora Welty's *The Optimist's Daughter.*" *Mississippi Quarterly* 44 (Fall 1991): 429–41.

Broughton, Panthea Reid. "The Economy of Desire: Faulkner's Poetics, from Eroticism to Post-Impressionism." *Faulkner Journal* 4 (Fall 1988/Spring 1989): 159–77.

Burgess, Cheryll. "From Metaphor to Manifestation: The Artist in Eudora Welty's *A Curtain of Green.*" In *Eudora Welty: Eye of the Storyteller,* edited by Dawn Trouard, 133–41. Kent, Ohio: Kent State University Press, 1989.

Byrne, Bev. "A Return to the Source: Eudora Welty's *The Robber Bridegroom* and *The Optimist's Daughter*." *Southern Quarterly* 24 (Spring 1986): 74–85.

Carson, Barbara Harrell. *Eudora Welty: Two Pictures at Once in Her Frame*. Troy, N.Y.: Whitston, 1992.

Carson, Gary. "Versions of the Artist in *A Curtain of Green:* The Unifying Imagination in Eudora Welty's Early Fiction." *Studies in Short Fiction* 15 (1978): 421–28.

Chodorow, Nancy. *Feminism and Psychoanalytic Theory*. New Haven: Yale University Press, 1989.

———. *The Reproduction of Mothering: Psychoanalysis and the Sociology of Gender*. Berkeley: University of California Press, 1978.

Coe, Richard N. *When the Grass Was Taller: Autobiography and the Experience of Childhood*. New Haven: Yale University Press, 1984.

Cohen, Philip, and Doreen Fowler. "Faulkner's Introduction to *The Sound and the Fury*." *American Literature* 62 (June 1990): 262–83.

Cole, Hunter, and Seetha Srinivasan. "Introduction—Eudora Welty and Photography: An Interview." *Photographs*, xiii–xxviii. Jackson: University Press of Mississippi, 1989.

Davenport, Guy. "That Faire Field of Enna." In *The Geography of the Imagination*, 250–71. San Francisco: North Point, 1981.

Desmond, John F. "Pattern and Vision in *The Optimist's Daughter*." In *A Still Moment: Essays on the Art of Eudora Welty,* edited by John F. Desmond, 118–38. Metuchen, N.J.: Scarecrow, 1978.

Devlin, Albert J. *Eudora Welty's Chronicle: A Story of Mississippi Life*. Jackson: University Press of Mississippi, 1983.

———, ed. *Welty: A Life in Literature*. Jackson: University Press of Mississippi, 1987.

Devlin, Albert J., and Peggy Whitman Prenshaw. "A Conversation with Eudora Welty." In *Welty: A Life in Literature,* edited by Albert J. Devlin, 3–26. Jackson: University Press of Mississippi, 1987.

Dickinson, Emily. *Final Harvest: Emily Dickinson's Poems*. Edited by Thomas H. Johnson. Boston: Little, Brown, 1961.

Dollarhide, Louis, and Ann J. Abadie, eds. *Eudora Welty: A Form of Thanks*. Jackson: University Press of Mississippi, 1979.

Donaldson, Susan V. "Recovering Otherness in *The Golden Apples*." *American Literature* 63 (September 1991): 489–506.

Doob, Penelope Reed. *The Idea of the Labyrinth from Classical Antiquity through the Middle Ages*. Ithaca: Cornell University Press, 1990.

Douglas, Mary. *Purity and Danger: An Analysis of Concepts of Pollution and Taboo*. New York: Frederick Praeger, 1966.

Eisenstein, Hester, and Alice Jardine, eds. *The Future of Difference*. New Brunswick, N.J.: Rutgers University Press, 1985.

Elbow, Peter. "The Doubting Game and the Believing Game—An Analysis of the

Intellectual Enterprise." In *Writing without Teachers,* 147–91. New York:
Oxford University Press, 1973.

———. "Methodological Doubting and Believing: Contraries in Inquiry." In
Embracing Contraries: Explorations in Learning and Teaching, 254–300. New
York: Oxford University Press, 1986.

———. *Oppositions in Chaucer.* Middletown, Conn.: Wesleyan University
Press, 1975.

Eliot, T. S. "Tradition and the Individual Talent." In *Critical Theory since Plato,*
edited by Hazard Adams, 784–87. New York: Harcourt Brace, 1971.

Erikson, Erik H. *Childhood and Society.* 2d ed. New York: W. W. Norton, 1963.

Euripides. *The Bacchae.* Translated by William Arrowsmith. In vol. 3 of *Greek
Tragedies,* edited by David Grene and Richmond Lattimore, 189–260. Chicago:
University of Chicago Press, Phoenix Books, 1960.

Faris, Wendy B. *Labyrinths of Language: Symbolic Landscape and Narrative Design in
Modern Fiction.* Baltimore: Johns Hopkins University Press, 1988.

Faulkner, William. *Absalom, Absalom! The Corrected Text.* New York: Random
House, 1986.

———. *Collected Stories of William Faulkner.* New York: Random House,
Vintage, 1977.

———. *Go Down, Moses.* New York: Random House, Vintage, 1973.

———. *The Hamlet.* New York: Random House, 1964.

———. *Intruder in the Dust.* New York: Random House, 1948.

———. *Light in August. The Corrected Text.* New York: Random House,
Vintage, 1987.

———. *The Sound and the Fury. The Corrected Text.* New York: Random House,
Vintage, 1987.

———. *The Wild Palms.* New York: Random House, Vintage, 1966.

Flax, Jane. "Mother-Daughter Relationships: Psychodynamics, Politics, and
Philosophy." In *The Future of Difference,* edited by Hester Eisenstein and Alice
Jardine, 20–40. New Brunswick, N.J.: Rutgers University Press, 1985.

———. "Political Philosophy and the Patriarchal Unconscious: A Psychoanalytic
Perspective on Epistemology and Metaphysics." In *Discovering Reality: Feminist
Perspectives on Epistemology, Metaphysics, Methodology, and Philosophy of Science,*
edited by Sandra Harding and Merrill B. Hintikka, 245–81. Boston:
D. Reidel, 1983.

———. *Thinking Fragments: Psychoanalysis, Feminism, and Postmodernism in the
Contemporary West.* Berkeley: University of California Press, 1990.

Fletcher, Angus. " 'Positive Negation': Threshold, Sequence, and Personification
in Coleridge." In *New Perspectives on Coleridge and Wordsworth: Selected Papers
from the English Institute,* edited by Geoffrey H. Hartman, 133–64. New York:
Columbia University Press, 1972.

Flynn, Elizabeth A., and Patrocinio P. Schweickart, eds. *Gender and Reading:
Essays on Readers, Texts, and Contexts.* Baltimore: Johns Hopkins University
Press, 1986.

Freud, Sigmund. *Civilization and Its Discontents*. 1930. Reprint. Translated and edited by James Strachey. New York: W. W. Norton, 1962.

Frye, Northrop. "Yeats and the Language of Symbolism." *University of Toronto Quarterly* 17 (October 1947): 1–17. Reprinted in *Fables of Identity: Studies in Poetic Mythology*, 218–37. New York: Harcourt, Brace and World, Harbinger, 1963.

Gallagher, Philip J. " 'Real or Allegoric': The Ontology of Sin and Death in *Paradise Lost*." *English Literary Renaissance* 6 (Spring 1976): 317–35.

Gardiner, Judith Kegan. "On Female Identity and Writing by Women." In *Writing and Sexual Difference*, edited by Elizabeth Abel, 177–91. Chicago: University of Chicago Press, 1982.

———. *Rhys, Stead, Lessing, and the Politics of Empathy*. Bloomington: Indiana University Press, 1989.

Gilbert, Sandra M. "Life's Empty Pack: Notes toward a Literary Daughteronomy." *Critical Inquiry* 11 (March 1985): 355–84.

Gilbert, Sandra M., and Susan Gubar. *No Man's Land: The Place of the Woman Writer in the Twentieth Century*. Vol. 1, *The War of the Words* and vol. 2, *Sexchanges*. New Haven: Yale University Press, 1988 and 1989.

Gilligan, Carol. *In a Different Voice: Psychological Theory and Women's Development*. Cambridge: Harvard University Press, 1982.

Goldenberg, Naomi R. *Returning Words to Flesh: Feminism, Psychoanalysis, and the Resurrection of the Body*. Boston: Beacon Press, 1990.

Graves, Robert. *The Greek Myths*. 2 vols. New York: Penguin, 1960.

Gray, Richard. *Writing the South: Ideas of an American Region*. Cambridge: Cambridge University Press, 1986.

Green, André. "The Double and the Absent." Translated by Jacques F. Houis. In *Psychoanalysis, Creativity, and Literature*, edited by Alan Roland, 271–92. New York: Columbia University Press, 1978.

Gresset, Michel. "Faulkner's Self-Portraits." *Faulkner Journal* 2 (Fall 1986): 2–13.

Griffin, Dorothy G. "The House as Container: Architecture and Myth in *Delta Wedding*." In *Welty: A Life in Literature*, edited by Albert J. Devlin, 96–112. Jackson: University Press of Mississippi, 1987.

Gubar, Susan. "Mother, Maiden, and the Marriage of Death: Women Writers and an Ancient Myth." *Women's Studies* 6 (1979): 301–15.

Gygax, Franziska. *Serious Daring from Within: Female Narrative Strategies in Eudora Welty's Novels*. Westport, Conn.: Greenwood, 1990.

Hardy, John Edward. "Marrying Down in Eudora Welty's Novels." In *Eudora Welty: Critical Essays*, edited by Peggy Whitman Prenshaw, 93–119. Jackson: University Press of Mississippi, 1979.

Heilbrun, Carolyn G. *Writing a Woman's Life*. New York: W. W. Norton, 1988.

Hesiod. *Hesiod: The Works and Days; Theogony; The Shield of Herakles*. Translated by Richmond Lattimore. Ann Arbor: University of Michigan Press, 1959.

Hinton, Jane L. "The Role of Family in *Delta Wedding, Losing Battles*, and *The*

Optimist's Daughter." In *Eudora Welty: Critical Essays,* edited by Peggy Whitman Prenshaw, 120–31. Jackson: University Press of Mississippi, 1979.

Irwin, John T. *Doubling and Incest/Repetition and Revenge: A Speculative Reading of Faulkner.* Baltimore: Johns Hopkins University Press, 1975.

Jaggar, Alison M., and Susan R. Bordo, eds. *Gender/Body/Knowledge: Feminist Reconstructions of Being and Knowing.* New Brunswick, N.J.: Rutgers University Press, 1989.

Keller, Evelyn Fox. "Feminism and Science." *Signs: Journal of Women in Culture and Society* 7 (Spring 1982): 589–602.

Keller, Evelyn Fox, and Christine R. Grontkowski. "The Mind's Eye." In *Discovering Reality: Feminist Perspectives on Epistemology, Metaphysics, Methodology, and Philosophy of Science,* edited by Sandra Harding and Merrill B. Hintikka, 207–24. Boston: D. Reidel, 1983.

Kerr, Elizabeth M. "The World of Eudora Welty's Women." In *Eudora Welty: Critical Essays,* edited by Peggy Whitman Prenshaw, 132–48. Jackson: University Press of Mississippi, 1979.

Knight, G. Wilson. *The Starlit Dome: Studies in the Poetry of Vision.* New York: Oxford University Press, 1971.

Kreyling, Michael. *Author and Agent: Eudora Welty and Diarmuid Russell.* New York: Farrar, Straus, Giroux, 1991.

———. *Eudora Welty's Achievement of Order.* Baton Rouge: Louisiana State University Press, 1980.

———. "Modernism in Welty's *A Curtain of Green and Other Stories.*" *Southern Quarterly* 20 (Summer 1982): 40–53. Reprinted in *Critical Essays on Eudora Welty,* edited by W. Craig Turner and Lee Emling Harding, 18–30. Boston: G. K. Hall, 1989.

Kristeva, Julia. "Women's Time." Translated by Alice Jardine and Harry Blake. *Signs: Journal of Women in Culture and Society* 7 (Autumn 1981): 13–35.

Lawrence, D. H. *Lady Chatterley's Lover.* 1928. Reprint. New York: New American Library, Signet, 1962.

Lee, Hermione. Interview with Eudora Welty. In *Writing Lives: Conversations between Women Writers,* edited by Mary Chamberlain, 250–59. London: Virago Press, 1988.

McGuffey's Fifth Eclectic Reader. Rev. ed. New York: Van Nostrand Reinhold, 1920.

McHaney, Pearl Amelia. "Historical Perspectives in 'A Still Moment'." In *Critical Essays on Eudora Welty,* edited by W. Craig Turner and Lee Emling Harding, 52–69. Boston: G. K. Hall, 1989.

McHaney, Thomas L. "Eudora Welty and the Multitudinous Golden Apples." In *Critical Essays on Eudora Welty,* edited by W. Craig Turner and Lee Emling Harding, 113–41. Boston: G. K. Hall, 1989.

Mahler, Margaret S. *On Human Symbiosis and the Vicissitudes of Individuation.* New York: International Universities Press, 1968.

Manning, Carol S. "Welty, Tyler, and Traveling Salesmen: The Wandering Hero Unhorsed." In *The Fiction of Anne Tyler*, edited by C. Ralph Stephens, 110–18. Jackson: University Press of Mississippi, 1990.

———. *With Ears Opening Like Morning Glories: Eudora Welty and the Love of Storytelling*. Westport, Conn.: Greenwood, 1985.

Mark, Rebecca. *The Dragon's Blood: Feminist Intertextuality in Eudora Welty's "The Golden Apples."* Jackson: University Press of Mississippi, 1994.

Marrs, Suzanne. *The Welty Collection: A Guide to the Eudora Welty Manuscripts and Documents at the Mississippi Department of Archives and History*. Jackson: University Press of Mississippi, 1988.

Matthews, John T. *The Play of Faulkner's Language*. Ithaca: Cornell University Press, 1982.

Miller, J. Hillis. "Yeats: The Linguistic Moment." In *William Butler Yeats*, edited by Harold Bloom, 189–210. New York: Chelsea House, 1986.

Miller, Nancy K. "Emphasis Added: Plots and Plausibilities in Women's Fiction." *PMLA* 96 (January 1981): 36–48.

———, ed. *The Poetics of Gender*. New York: Columbia University Press, 1986.

Minter, David. *William Faulkner: His Life and Work*. Baltimore: Johns Hopkins University Press, 1980.

Mortimer, Gail L. *Faulkner's Rhetoric of Loss: A Study in Perception and Meaning*. Austin: University of Texas Press, 1983.

———. " 'The Way to Get There': Journeys and Destinations in the Stories of Eudora Welty." *Southern Literary Journal* 19 (Spring 1987): 61–69.

Mudd, Roger. Interview with Eudora Welty. "MacNeil/Lehrer Newshour." PBS. WNET, New York. Show no. 3613. 29 November 1989.

Nietzsche, Friedrich. *The Birth of Tragedy Out of the Spirit of Music*. In *Basic Writings of Nietzsche*, translated and edited by Walter Kaufmann, 31–144. New York: Random House, Modern Library, 1968.

Our Wonder World: A Library of Knowledge. 11 vols. Chicago: George L. Shuman, 1930.

Pei, Lowry. "Dreaming the Other in *The Golden Apples*." *Modern Fiction Studies* 28 (Autumn 1982): 415–33.

Phillips, Robert L. "Patterns of Vision in Welty's *The Optimist's Daughter*." *Southern Literary Journal* 14 (Fall 1981): 10–23.

Pitavy-Souques, Danièle. "A Blazing Butterfly: The Modernity of Eudora Welty." In *Welty: A Life in Literature*, edited by Albert J. Devlin, 113–38. Jackson: University Press of Mississippi, 1987.

———. "Technique as Myth: The Structure of *The Golden Apples*." In *Eudora Welty: Critical Essays*, edited by Peggy Whitman Prenshaw, 258–68. Jackson: University Press of Mississippi, 1979.

———. "Watchers and Watching: Point of View in Eudora Welty's 'June Recital'." Translated by Margaret Tomarchio. *Southern Review* 19 (1983): 483–509.

Polk, Noel. "Water, Wanderings, and Weddings: Love in Eudora Welty." In

Eudora Welty: A Form of Thanks, edited by Louis Dollarhide and Ann J. Abadie, 95–122. Jackson: University Press of Mississippi, 1979.

Prenshaw, Peggy W. "Woman's World, Man's Place: The Fiction of Eudora Welty." In *Eudora Welty: A Form of Thanks,* edited by Louis Dollarhide and Ann J. Abadie, 46–77. Jackson: University Press of Mississippi, 1979.

———, ed. *Conversations with Eudora Welty.* Jackson: University Press of Mississippi, 1984.

———, ed. *Eudora Welty: Critical Essays.* Jackson: University Press of Mississippi, 1979.

Price, Reynolds. "The Onlooker, Smiling: An Early Reading of *The Optimist's Daughter.*" *Shenandoah* 20 (Spring 1969): 58–73. Reprinted in *Eudora Welty,* edited by Harold Bloom, 75–88. New York: Chelsea House, 1986.

Randisi, Jennifer Lynn. *A Tissue of Lies: Eudora Welty and the Southern Romance.* Washington, D.C.: University Press of America, 1982.

Rhode, Deborah L., ed. *Theoretical Perspectives on Sexual Difference.* New Haven: Yale University Press, 1990.

Romines, Ann. *The Home Plot: Women, Writing, and Domestic Ritual.* Amherst: University of Massachusetts Press, 1992.

Rorty, Richard. *Contingency, Irony, and Solidarity.* New York: Cambridge University Press, 1989.

Rubin, Lillian B. *Intimate Strangers: Men and Women Together.* New York: Harper Colophon, 1984.

Schmidt, Peter. *The Heart of the Story: Eudora Welty's Short Fiction.* Jackson: University Press of Mississippi, 1991.

Showalter, Elaine. *Sister's Choice: Tradition and Change in American Women's Writing.* New York: Oxford University Press, 1991.

Smith, William Jay. "Precision and Reticence: Eudora Welty's Poetic Vision." In *Eudora Welty: A Form of Thanks,* edited by Louis Dollarhide and Ann J. Abadie, 78–94. Jackson: University Press of Mississippi, 1979.

Smith-Rosenberg, Carroll. "The Female World of Love and Ritual: Relations between Women in Nineteenth-Century America." *Signs: Journal of Women in Culture and Society* 1 (Autumn 1975): 1–29. Reprinted in *Disorderly Conduct: Visions of Gender in Victorian America,* 53–76. New York: Oxford University Press, 1986.

Sophocles. *Oedipus the King.* Translated by David Grene. In vol. 1 of *Greek Tragedies,* edited by David Grene and Richmond Lattimore, 107–76. Chicago: University of Chicago Press, Phoenix Books, 1960.

Spacks, Patricia Meyer. *Gossip.* New York: Alfred A. Knopf, 1985.

Sprengnether, Madelon. "*Delta Wedding* and the Kore Complex." *Southern Quarterly* 25 (Winter 1987): 120–30.

Sword, Helen. "Leda and the Modernists." *PMLA* 107 (March 1992): 305–18.

Tennyson, Alfred. *The Poems and Plays of Alfred, Lord Tennyson.* New York: Random House, Modern Library, 1938.

Thompson, D'Arcy Wentworth. *A Glossary of Greek Birds*. London: Oxford University Press, 1936.

Tiegreen, Helen Hurt. "Mothers, Daughters, and One Writer's Revisions." In *Welty: A Life in Literature,* edited by Albert J. Devlin, 188–211. Jackson: University Press of Mississippi, 1987.

Tillyard, E. M. W. *The Elizabethan World Picture*. New York: Random House, Vintage, n.d.

Trouard, Dawn, ed. *Eudora Welty: Eye of the Storyteller*. Kent, Ohio: Kent State University Press, 1989.

Turner, Victor. *Dramas, Fields, and Metaphors: Symbolic Action in Human Society*. Ithaca: Cornell University Press, 1974.

———. *The Ritual Process: Structure and Anti-structure*. Ithaca: Cornell University Press, 1977.

Turner, W. Craig, and Lee Emling Harding, eds. *Critical Essays on Eudora Welty*. Boston: G. K. Hall, 1989.

Vande Kieft, Ruth M. *Eudora Welty*. Rev. ed. Boston: Twayne, 1987.

Vendler, Helen Hennessy. *Yeats's Vision and the Later Plays*. Cambridge: Harvard University Press, 1963.

Wall, Carey. "Eudora Welty's *Delta Wedding* and Victor Turner's 'Liminality'." *Southern Studies* 25 (Fall 1986): 220–34.

Warren, Robert Penn. "The Love and the Separateness in Miss Welty." *Kenyon Review* 6 (1944): 246–59. Revised and reprinted as "Love and Separateness in Eudora Welty" in Robert Penn Warren, *Selected Essays,* 156–69. New York: Random House, 1958.

Waugh, Patricia. *Feminine Fictions: Revisiting the Postmodern*. London: Routledge, 1989.

Welty, Eudora. *The Bride of the Innisfallen and Other Stories*. 1955. Reprinted in *Collected Stories,* 1980.

———. *The Collected Stories of Eudora Welty*. New York: Harcourt Brace Jovanovich, Harvest, 1980.

———. *A Curtain of Green and Other Stories*. 1941. Reprinted in *Collected Stories,* 1980.

———. *Delta Wedding*. 1946. New York: Harcourt Brace Jovanovich, Harvest, 1979.

———. *The Eye of the Story: Selected Essays and Reviews*. 1978. New York: Random House, Vintage, 1979.

———. *The Golden Apples*. 1949. Reprinted in *Collected Stories,* 1980.

———. Interview. "MacNeil/Lehrer Newshour." By Roger Mudd. PBS. WNET, New York. Show no. 3613. 29 November 1989.

———. *Losing Battles*. 1970. New York: Random House, Vintage, 1978.

———. *One Writer's Beginnings*. Cambridge: Harvard University Press, 1984.

———. *The Optimist's Daughter*. New York: Random House, 1972.

———. *Photographs*. Jackson: University Press of Mississippi, 1989.

———. *The Ponder Heart.* 1954. New York: Harcourt Brace Jovanovich, Harvest, 1978.

———. *The Robber Bridegroom.* 1942. New York: Harcourt Brace Jovanovich, Harvest, 1978.

———. *Short Stories.* New York: Harcourt, Brace, 1950.

———. "A Sketching Trip." *Atlantic* (June 1945): 62–70.

———. *The Wide Net and Other Stories.* 1943. Reprinted in *Collected Stories,* 1980.

Westling, Louise. *Eudora Welty.* Totowa, N.J.: Barnes and Noble, 1989.

———. *Sacred Groves and Ravaged Gardens: The Fiction of Eudora Welty, Carson McCullers, and Flannery O'Connor.* Athens: University of Georgia Press, 1985.

Weston, Ruth D. "The Feminine and Feminist Texts of Eudora Welty's *The Optimist's Daughter.*" *South Central Review* 4 (Winter 1987): 74–91.

Wilde, Meta Carpenter, and Orin Borsten. *A Loving Gentleman: The Love Story of William Faulkner and Meta Carpenter.* New York: Simon and Schuster, 1976.

Winnicott, D. W. *The Maturational Processes and the Facilitating Environment.* New York: International Universities Press, 1965.

———. *Playing and Reality.* New York: Basic Books, 1971.

Woolf, Virginia. *Mrs. Dalloway.* New York: Harcourt, Brace and World, Harvest, 1925.

Yaeger, Patricia S. "'Because a Fire Was in My Head': Eudora Welty and the Dialogic Imagination." *PMLA* 99 (1984): 955–73.

———. *Honey-Mad Women: Emancipatory Strategies in Women's Writing.* New York: Columbia University Press, 1988.

Yates, Gayle Graham. "An Interview with Eudora Welty." *Frontiers* 9 (1987): 100–104.

Yeats, William Butler. *The Collected Poems of W. B. Yeats.* London: Macmillan, 1950.